J. S. Mill

J. S. Mill

Moral, Social and Political Thought

Dale E. Miller

polity

First published in 2010 by Polity Press

Polity Press
65 Bridge Street
Cambridge CB2 1UR, UK

Polity Press
350 Main Street
Malden, MA 02148, USA

ISBN-13: 978-0-7456-2583-6
ISBN-13: 978-0-7456-2584-3(pb)

A catalogue record for this book is available from the British Library.

Typeset in 10.5 on 12 pt Palatino
by Toppan Best-set Premedia Limited
Printed and bound in Great Britain by MPG Books Group Limited, Bodmin, Cornwall

For further information on Polity, visit our website: www.politybooks.com

Contents

Preface

This volume is a general survey of John Stuart Mill's contributions to moral philosophy, including social and political philosophy. While this is a wide ambit for a comparatively slender volume, if one not so slender as its publisher would have preferred, it still means that little or nothing will be said about the important work that Mill did in other fields of inquiry, such as logic, epistemology, the philosophy of science, metaphysics and the scientific elements of political economy. In order to keep the length within some bounds, I have been forced to limit my engagement with Mill's other interpreters. When offering readings of particular texts, I have often had to ignore divergent readings that have been defended by other commentators. Suffice it to say that my failure to discuss another scholar's work should by no means be construed as reflecting a judgement that it is unworthy of discussion.

D. E. M.
Norfolk, Virginia, November 2009

Acknowledgements

This book has been a long time in the making. I am deeply indebted to Polity Press for their patience. I owe a particular debt to Polity's Emma Hutchinson, who has been in charge of this project for the last several years, for her tolerance and support. I would also like to thank her predecessors, including Elizabeth Molinari and Rachel Kerr. And thanks as well to my able and agreeable copyeditor, Gail Ferguson.

Because I have been at work on the book for so long, the prospect of trying to remember everyone who offered help on a portion of it so that I can acknowledge them by name is daunting. I apologize in advance to anyone whom I should inadvertently omit. I owe a special debt of gratitude to Ben Eggleston, who read drafts of nearly every chapter and offered pages of comments and some much-needed encouragement. Roger Crisp and an anonymous reviewer also read a draft of the entire book, and I am grateful for their feedback. A number of other people offered assistance on one or more chapters, including Donald Bruckner, Jacob Busch, Dale Dorsey, Ashley Kennedy, Beth McHose, Stephen Medvic and John Skorupski. Students in my Mill seminars at Old Dominion University also read certain chapters.

Several people also offered help with earlier works on which portions of the book are based. There are too many of these to name all of them individually, but chapter 8 is based on an article that appeared in *Politics, Philosophy and Economics*, and I owe thanks for the help that I received on it from Jonathan Riley and Nicholas Capaldi. This article was in turn based on a master's thesis written under the direction of the late Mark Perlman (for the University of Pittsburgh's economics department). Chapter 9 makes heavy use of an article that was published in *History of Political Thought* and of my doctoral dissertation (written for Pittsburgh's philosophy department). I would like to express my gratitude to my director David Gauthier and the other members of my dissertation committee: the late Tamara Horowitz, Nicholas Rescher and Frederick Whelan. Andrew Valls and I spent much time discussing both the thesis and the dissertation.

Some early work on the book was supported by a summer research fellowship from Old Dominion University's Research Foundation. Additional work was done while I was a visiting fellow in the Centre for Ethics, Philosophy and Public Affairs at St Andrews University, and I would like to thank the Centre for this opportunity and Old Dominion University for the research leave that allowed me to take advantage of it. ODU's College of Arts and Letters generously provided funds to help subsidize the cost of having the book indexed, and Robert Vinten produced said index.

Final words of thanks go to two people who served as mentors to me at formative stages in my career. The first is Kurt Baier, who initially ignited my interest in Mill. He was also my original dissertation supervisor, although he retired before I was prepared to defend. (That project was a long time in the making, too.) The other is Brad Hooker, whose enthusiasm for philosophy rekindled my own when he and his colleagues at the University of Reading welcomed me as an unofficial visiting graduate student. Special thanks go to Brad for having recommended me to Polity for this project.

The book is dedicated to my wife, Cindy.

Part I

*Foundations of Mill's Moral,
Social and Political Thought*

1

A Singular Life

The story of Mill's life is not only engaging in its own right but throws considerable light on his work. It helps us to understand both the influences that shaped him as a thinker and the milieu to which he is responding.

Early years

Mill was born in London on 20 May 1806. He was the first child of James and Harriet Mill. James was a Scot who had been trained for the Presbyterian ministry but chose to pursue a career as a writer instead. Harriet was the daughter of a widow who kept a mental asylum.[1]

Young John Mill was a prodigy. He was educated at home by James, who expected John from an early age to apply himself to learning with the same intensity and seriousness with which an industrious adult might apply himself to earning a living. While James wrote, John studied next to him, and when James broke off from writing John demonstrated to him what he had learned. The method produced its intended results, at least initially: at age three, John began to read Greek; at age eight, he was reading Herodotus and Xenophon in Greek and beginning to learn Latin; by age twelve, he had learned 'elementary geometry and algebra thoroughly, the differential calculus and other portions of the higher mathematics far from thoroughly'.[2]

Mill never experienced what most people would regard as a real childhood. While he had a number of younger siblings, to some of whom he was made a teacher himself, he was never given the opportunity to play with children of his own age. He may never have kicked or thrown a ball in his life. While he was not literally working constantly, he chose to spend his leisure time with more books. For fun, he wrote digests of histories, including a history of Rome, one of Holland and then a 'history of the Roman government, compiled from Livy and Dionysius '.[3]

Philosophical radicalism

James Mill had a specific ambition for his eldest son. This was for John to become the champion of a reformist political view that James Mill shared with his friend the philosopher Jeremy Bentham. This view came to be known as 'philosophical radicalism'.

The philosophical component of philosophical radicalism is the theory known as 'utilitarianism'. Utilitarianism will be discussed in detail in later chapters, but in a sentence it might be crudely described as the view that what it is right for us to do depends upon how we can most effectively promote happiness, and not just the happiness of the person who is to act or of some limited group but everyone's happiness. By itself, utilitarianism gives no specific guidance about what should or should not be done in a given set of circumstances. It gives this sort of guidance only when it is combined with factual propositions about how happiness or well-being can best be promoted.

Philosophical radicalism, of which James Mill and Bentham were the intellectual leaders, combines the abstract utilitarian philosophy with a particular set of 'radical' beliefs about what social and political arrangements are most conducive to happiness. Victorian society was divided into three rather distinct social classes: an 'aristocracy' that owned much of the country's agricultural land and that included both the true aristocrats – peers of the realm who owned the largest landed estates and who sat in the House of Lords – and the 'squires' and 'gentlemen' of the lesser gentry; a commercial middle class that included everyone from wealthy capitalists to shopkeepers to civil servants; and the vast working or labouring class, whose members ranged from skilled workers to manual labourers to unemployed paupers.[4] Oversimplifying greatly, one might say that in the late eighteenth and early nineteenth centuries the interests of the aristocracy were generally represented in Parliament by the Tory party and those of the commercial class by the Whigs. The workers could not vote – indeed, the existence of property qualifications on voting disenfranchised even much of the middle class – and so their interests were unrepresented except where they overlapped with the interests of another class. What the philosophical radicals aimed to do was to minimize the influence of special interests – or 'sinister interests', in Bentham's memorable phrase – on the government and establish a greater harmony between the interests of the rulers and those of the general public. This involved giving the working class the vote, via secret ballot. It involved eliminating artificial restrictions on trade that were imposed in order to benefit particular classes, such as the hated 'Corn Laws', in effect from 1815–46, which inhibited the importation of grain and thus enriched domestic landowners. And it also entailed rationalizing the legal system.

Mental crisis

James Mill intended for John Stuart Mill to become the leader of the next generation of radicals. Given this, John's first encounter with Bentham's utilitarianism came surprisingly late in life, by his precocious standards. He was already fifteen before his father put a copy of the *Traité de Législation* in his hands, a volume of Bentham's work in French edited by Pierre Dumont. The experience was transformative: 'When I laid down the last volume of the *Traité*, I had become a different being. . . . I now had opinions; a creed, a doctrine, a philosophy; in one among the best senses of the word, a religion. . . .'[5]

James Mill's project seemed to be proceeding on schedule, but something was soon to happen that would, if not derail it entirely, at least prevent it from reaching fruition in quite the way that he intended. In 1826, the year of his twentieth birthday, John Mill's life bore many of the outward marks of happiness. He had, for nearly the first time in his life, friends his own age. He had fora in which he could advance his Benthamite views: his articles and reviews were appearing in opinion journals, especially the Radical organ *The Westminster Review*, and he was acquiring a reputation as a speaker in the London Debating Society that he had helped to found. He even had the prospect of a promising career. In 1818, James Mill had published a three-volume work on the history of

British rule in India. A year after this work's appearance, he was hired in the Examiner's Office of the East India Company, which was charged with drafting the instructions sent to company officials in India. As he was promoted to increasingly higher positions within the company, he was able to secure John a clerk's position in the same office. First father and then son would eventually rise to the position of Chief Examiner.[6]

Happiness, however, had begun to elude John. In a chapter in his *Autobiography* titled 'A Crisis in My Mental History', he relates how, in the fall of 1826, he found himself sinking into a state of (what we would now call) depression. When already suffering from a 'dull state of nerves, . . . unsusceptible to enjoyment or pleasurable excitement', he asked himself one day if it would give him any happiness if the Radical political programme that he had been working to advance was adopted in its entirety: 'And an irrepressible self-consciousness distinctly answered, "No!" At this my heart sank within me: the whole foundation on which my life was constructed fell down. . . . I seemed to have nothing left to live for. . . .'[7]

At the root of Mill's depression was the belief that his hyperintellectualized upbringing might have permanently destroyed his capacity for feeling. Fortunately, his darkest despair lasted no more than six months. When reading an account of a young boy's promising his family that he would take the place of his recently deceased father, Mill found himself in tears and realized that his emotions had not entirely deserted him. This encouraged him to turn to poetry for relief, and he found the tonic he was seeking in Wordsworth.[8]

While Mill's 'crisis' is sometimes described as a 'mental breakdown', this is too strong. He continued with all of his usual activities, he writes, albeit without affect, like an automaton.[9] The episode did have a considerable influence on his thinking, though. First, it led him to appreciate what is sometimes called the 'paradox of hedonism', the notion that the direct pursuit of pleasure or happiness is self-defeating: 'Ask yourself whether you are happy, and you cease to be so. The only chance is to treat, not happiness, but some end external to it, as the purpose of life. Let your self-consciousness, your scrutiny, your self-interrogation, exhaust themselves on that; and if otherwise fortunately circumstanced you will inhale happiness with the air you breathe.'[10] (Somewhat curiously, Mill implies that later in life he became convinced that this advice may not apply to people with a superior 'sensibility and . . . capacity for enjoyment', although he still takes it to hold 'for the great majority of mankind'.)

Second, and perhaps even more momentously, Mill began to believe that education needs to be concerned at least as much with fostering the growth of the feelings as with that of the intellect:

> I never turned recreant to intellectual culture, or ceased to consider the power and practice of analysis as an essential condition both of individual and of social improvement. But I thought that it had consequences which required to be corrected, by joining other kinds of cultivation with it. . . . The cultivation of the feelings became one of the cardinal points in my ethical and philosophical creed.[11]

These are the two changes of view that Mill explicitly describes as products of his crisis in the published version of his *Autobiography*. While both involve changes in his conception of how happiness can best be promoted, neither indicates any slackening of his commitment to utilitarianism, and indeed he says explicitly that 'I never, indeed, wavered in the conviction that happiness is the test of all rules of conduct, and the end of life.'[12] In an unpublished early draft of the *Autobiography*, he mentions another respect in which his thinking altered in this period that, if not directly a result of having experienced depression, is clearly a consequence of his having realized that his father and Bentham had overlooked some important truths. It does not pertain to the promotion of happiness, at least not directly, but to his self-understanding and ambitions as a thinker. In describing the beginning of the end of the period of his closest friendship with the future MP John Arthur Roebuck, Mill delineates an emerging difference in their mental dispositions:

> When any proposition came before him as that of an opponent, he rushed eagerly to demonstrate its falsity, without taking any pains to discover and appropriate the portion of truth which there might be in it. . . . I had now taken a most decided bent in the opposite direction, that of eclecticism; looking out for the truth which is generally to be found in errors when they are anything more than mere paralogisms, or logical blunders.[13]

The contrast that Mill draws between Roebuck and himself is similar to the one that he draws between Bentham and the conservative poet Samuel Coleridge in an essay on the latter:

> Bentham judged a proposition true or false as it accorded or not
> with the result of his own inquiries. . . . With Coleridge, on the con-
> trary, the . . . long duration of a belief . . . is at least proof of an adap-
> tation in it to some portion or other of the human mind; and if, on
> digging down to the root, we do not find, as is generally the case,
> some truth, we shall find some natural want or requirement of
> human nature which the doctrine in question is fitted to satisfy. . . .[14]

Mill's aspiration as a thinker is to emulate Coleridge's openness
to the fragments of truth that can be discovered in views that are
partly – maybe even almost entirely – false. But he intends to avoid
the 'too rigid adherence' to this method that even he can detect in
Coleridge and to retain Bentham's (and Roebuck's) willingness to
repudiate views that lacked adequate justification, whatever their
tradition or pedigree. In his essay 'Bentham', a companion piece to
that on Coleridge, he writes in qualified defence of 'one-eyed men',
who see deeply into what they see at all but overlook much: 'Almost
all rich veins of original and striking speculation have been opened
by systematic half-thinkers.'[15] Mill, though, intends to be a 'complete thinker', one who synthesizes the partial truths discovered by
minds more innovative than his own.

During this period Mill travelled in realms of thought very
different from that of his father and Bentham, although always
with the attitude of a tourist looking for souvenirs to bring home
rather than that of someone looking for a new place to live. That is
to say, he was looking for new fragments of the truth that could not
be found in his native utilitarian school of thought, but he was not
looking to become part of a new school. He acquainted himself with
both German Romanticism, whose celebration of the feelings was
obviously congenial to his mental state at the time, and the French
utopianism of Henri de Saint-Simon. Yet he fended off all attempts
to recruit him as a disciple of these or other views.[16]

Mrs Harriet Taylor

John Mill met Mrs Harriet Taylor, the wife of wholesale druggist
John Taylor, at a dinner party at the Taylors' home in the summer
of 1830. Harriet's Unitarian minister, the Reverend W. J. Fox, apparently arranged their meeting after Harriet confessed to having intellectual needs that her husband was not able to satisfy.[17] Soon the
pair was deeply immersed in mutual admiration.

There is no overstating what Harriet meant to John. It is frankly difficult to imagine that any human being could live up to the praise that he lavishes on her. In his autobiography, he calls her 'the most admirable person I had ever known', possessed of 'the qualities which in all other persons whom I had known I had been only too happy to find singly'.[18] She combined the 'general spiritual characteristics' and 'temperament and organisation' of Shelley, but in intellect Shelley 'was but a child compared with what she ultimately became'. Better still, 'Her intellectual gifts did but minister to a moral character at once the noblest and the best balanced which I have ever met with in life.'[19] Where practical philosophy is concerned, she was a master of the 'two main regions of thought', both 'the region of ultimate aims; the constituent elements of the highest realizable ideal of human life' and that of 'the immediately useful and practically attainable'. In contrast, his own 'own strength lay wholly in the uncertain and slippery intermediate region, that of theory, or moral and political science'.

Before long, John was spending most evenings at the Taylor home while Mr Taylor repaired to his club. By 1833, even the tolerant Mr Taylor was fed up with this arrangement and he sent Harriet to Paris for six months. John Mill, though, joined her there for six weeks. In 1834, Harriet effectively began to live apart from her husband. Behaviour that would be considered scandalous even today was obviously so by Victorian standards. The relationship even became a point of contention between John Stuart and James Mill, although the latter died in 1836.[20] (Bentham died in 1832.) John and Harriet insisted, however, that their relationship during this period was strictly platonic.

The 1830s and 1840s were an intellectually fertile part of Mill's life. His first book, the two-volume *A System of Logic*, appeared in 1843; it would go through eight editions. 1848 saw the publication of the *Principles of Political Economy*, of which seven editions would eventually appear. These works became standard textbooks in their respective fields.

Blackheath Park

John Taylor died of cancer in 1849. Harriet tended to him during his illness and even upbraided John Mill when he suggested that she write to him during an 'odd time' when she might find a 'change of subject of thought a relief': 'Good God, sh[oul]d you think it a relief to think of something else some acquaintance or what not while I was dying?'[21] The way being cleared, however, the two of them were married in 1851, and they settled just outside of London in Blackheath Park.

During the 1850s, John largely kept apart from the society he used to keep. He became, in fact, exceedingly prickly. Some former friends were dropped because they were suspected of having gossiped about his relationship with Harriet or, in the case of Roebuck, because they told him directly that they considered the relationship a mistake. He became estranged from many of his siblings and even his mother, on the grounds of their failing to accord Harriet what he considered to be the proper respect and civility. He made little time even for those associates with whom he remained on good terms.[22]

The Mills, as they now were, spent much time travelling in this period, separately or together, a necessity because of their health. They both suffered from 'consumption', that is, tuberculosis. It is quite possible that Harriet caught the disease from him, just as it is quite possible that he caught it from his father. The weather of southern Europe suited them better than cold, damp and smoky England. Neither could count on living much longer. He published relatively little new work on philosophy during much of the 1850s, although he and Harriet were making plans and composing drafts. They discussed various combinations of essays that might serve to convey what they considered to be the most important of their views 'in the state of concentrated thought – a sort of mental pemican, which thinkers, when there are any after us, may nourish themselves with & then dilute for other people'.[23]

They worked on one of these essays in particular, on the subject of liberty. The essay would be published in 1859, but Harriet would not live to see its appearance. In 1858, John retired from the East India Company, which was being nationalized by the British government. He and Harriet headed south again, in pursuit of a healthier climate. They had intended to go to Montpellier, but made it only so far as Avignon when Harriet's respiratory problems worsened severely. She died on 3 November.

It has been argued that Harriet is in fact the unacknowledged co-author of *On Liberty*, and even of the *Principles of Political Economy*.[24] These questions about possible joint authorship shade into the larger question of Harriet's influence on John's thought over the course of their relationship, which some regard as negligible and others as substantial – with those in the latter group differing over whether this influence was beneficial or detrimental. The question about the extent of Harriet's influence can probably never be answered with a high degree of certainty. Too much of their interaction took place behind closed doors, either in the Taylor home or at Blackheath, and too little of the correspondence from the periods when they were apart survives. We cannot even feel confident in any assessment of Harriet's abilities. Mill's testimony has already been recorded, but the other available accounts from her contemporaries register rather different opinions of Harriet, with the least charitable describing her as little more than a parrot of Mill and others judging her abilities to be admirable but entirely on a human scale.[25] That the ensuing discussion treats John as the sole author of all works that were published in his name alone is not meant to prejudice Harriet's claim to be the co-author of some of them. This study is ultimately concerned with the content of a body of work, not with its production or with John Stuart Mill the man, so entering speculation about the authorship of *On Liberty* or the *Principles* would be a digression. For the same reason, the larger question of Harriet's influence will not be broached.

Remaining years

The years immediately after his wife's death saw the publication of some of Mill's best-known works. *On Liberty* has already been mentioned. 1861 marked both the initial appearance of the articles that would be collected together with the title *Utilitarianism* and the publication of *Considerations on Representative Government*. In 1865, Mill published book-length critiques of the work of two other thinkers, Auguste Comte and Sir William Hamilton. While Mill is writing as a respondent in these volumes, they contain important statements of his own views.

Mill bought a small house next to the cemetery where Harriet was buried, and for the rest of his life he would spend half of the year in Avignon. When in London, he renewed many of the social ties that he had earlier severed. He also derived companionship from Helen Taylor, the youngest of Harriet's three children with her first husband, who gave up what seems to have been a career of some small promise on the stage in order to serve as Mill's amanuensis cum collaborator. One issue that heavily engaged the attention of both during this period was women's rights. Helen was an active campaigner in this movement. Mill's *The Subjection of*

Women, published in 1869, elaborates on themes first broached in 'The Enfranchisement of Women', which was published without attribution in the *Westminster* in 1851 but is today generally (although not universally) believed to have been written by Harriet. The absence of a chapter on women's rights may seem like a major lacuna in this study of Mill's thought. This is a deliberate choice, however, made on the grounds that Mill himself does not see the issue of women's rights as *sui generis*. He believed that women ought to have the same rights as men for the same reasons that men ought to have them. From his perspective, therefore, the questions of women's liberty to pursue the careers of their choice or of their right to the ballot do not demand separate treatment. (The real lacuna is a chapter on Mill's views on the family.)

Mill also found another venue in which he could seek to advance women's rights and otherwise put theory into practice. In 1865, he accepted an invitation to stand for Parliament for Westminster, and despite his making only a token effort to campaign he was returned. He served three years in Parliament, in which he was generally considered a successful speaker (after a rough start), although he was defeated in his bid for re-election.[26] One of his most notable actions in Parliament was to propose, albeit unsuccessfully, an amendment to the Reform Bill of 1867 that would have given women the vote on equal terms with men.

Mill spearheaded another cause during this period, both in and out of Parliament. The British Governor of the colony of Jamaica, Edward James Eyre, had brutally suppressed a rebellion of former slaves. Mill headed the 'Jamaica Committee' that sought unsuccessfully to see Eyre prosecuted for murder – or, when that effort failed, for anything.[27]

Mill's last years were spent in relative quiet. He worked on writings that were to be published posthumously. This included, in addition to his *Autobiography*, a work titled *Three Essays on Religion*. Mill is not a Christian, nor does he subscribe to any other recognized religion. In his *Autobiography*, he remarks that he 'was brought up from the first without any religious belief, in the ordinary acceptation of the term'. In the essay 'Theism', included in the *Three Essays*, Mill claims that the design (or 'teleological') argument succeeds in supplying some evidence in favour of the claim that the 'present order' of the universe was created by an 'Intelligent Mind', although this evidence is 'insufficient for proof' and amounts 'only to one of the lower degrees of personality'.[28] This suggests that he might accept some sort of deism; he might believe, in other words, in a God who created the universe but then left it (including us) to its own devices. But he adds that if the then-nascent theory of the 'survival of the fittest' should be borne out by empirical investigation, then this would 'greatly attenuate the evidence for' creation.[29] As Alan Millar claims, the evidence for evolutionary theory that has 'accumulated since fatally weakens the argument from design in the form in which Mill considers it'.[30]

In 1873, John Stuart Mill died quickly of fever in Avignon. He was just short of his 67th birthday; the date is usually given as 7 May. He was, of course, buried next to Harriet. His last words, spoken to Helen, were 'You know that I have done my work.'[31]

2

Mill's Understanding of Human Nature

One theme that will emerge very clearly over the course of this book is the strength of Mill's conviction that only a few exceptional people realize anything approaching their full potential as human beings. He is dismayed by the selfishness, intellectual laxity and general lack of vigour in the pursuit of anything besides money that prevail in every part of even the most advanced societies. Mill believes that through better education these shortcomings could be overcome, although 'education' is being used here in what he calls 'its largest acceptation', in which 'Whatever helps to shape the human being; to make the individual what he is, or hinder him from being what he is not – is part of his education.'[1]

But while Mill believes that people could be much improved, he also believes that there are some unalterable facts about human nature. These fixed elements are the raw materials with which any method of education has to work, and they limit what it is capable of accomplishing. This chapter will be a survey of some of the fixed elements that Mill believes can be found in our nature.

What can we know and how can we know it?

A discussion of Mill's views on epistemology, or the theory of knowledge, might seem out of place in a chapter on his understanding of human nature. Many epistemological questions, though, can be framed as questions about us, most importantly that of what in our nature, if anything, enables us to acquire knowledge.

The history of epistemology in the modern period is standardly taught as an ebbing and flowing war between the doctrines of rationalism and empiricism.[2] According to classical empiricism, the mind begins as a tabula rasa, 'a blank slate'. This slate is 'written on' by experience. Against the rationalists, who maintain a belief in the existence of innate ideas, the empiricists contend that all of our ideas come from experience. The classical empiricists take our ideas to be nothing more than less 'lively' copies of what David Hume calls our 'impressions', a heading under which he includes not just sensations but also passions and emotions.[3] Ideas can be simple or complex. John Locke, author of the first great statement of empiricism, defines simple ideas as 'nothing but *one uniform appearance* or conception in the mind'.[4] Complex ideas are composed of multiple simple ideas. To borrow an example from Mill, our idea of an orange is a complex idea that '*consists* of the simple ideas of a certain colour, a certain form, a certain taste and smell, etc . . .'.[5] Empiricists can allow that some of our knowledge, in particular knowledge of the relations between our ideas, is a priori, that is, not derived from experience. Empiricists, though, characteristically maintain that our knowledge of the external world is derived from experience or, in other words, that it is a posteriori.

Mill is an empiricist, and in many ways he is a more thoroughgoing empiricist than any of the other major figures in the tradition. He contends that even mathematical knowledge is a posteriori.[6] He is willing to follow empiricist reasoning even when its implications strike many people as counter-intuitive. For example, he embraces 'phenomenalism', the view that we are not justified in believing in the existence of anything that exists independently of being perceived. The belief in matter is justified, he tells us, only if 'matter' is defined as nothing more than 'a Permanent Possibility of Sensation'.[7]

A number of philosophers, including some of the classical British empiricists themselves, have maintained that empiricism entails that many of the beliefs that the average person would feel most confident about are unjustified. Empiricism threatens to lead us into scepticism, a denial of the possibility of knowledge. Hume, for one, is a forthright sceptic. His famous challenge to induction begins with the observation that inductive reasoning, which in this context means reasoning from particular observations to more general claims, depends on the assumption that nature is 'uniform' in the sense that the same fundamental regularities in nature that obtain when and where we make our observations will still obtain in all of the places, and at all of the times, to which our generalizations apply. Yet if we have made no observations in particular places and times, we have no way to know what if any regularities obtain there. This means that we have no justification for believing that the regularities that we have observed in the past will continue to obtain in the future, even for another moment, since by definition we have made no observations of the future. We cannot know that unsuspended objects will continue to fall towards the Earth, that the sun will continue to rise in the East and so on. Hume does not intend to convince us that we should not believe that the laws of physics will continue to operate in the future; indeed, he says that we cannot help but believe that they will. His point is that beliefs like this one are unjustified, however inescapable they are, so they cannot be counted among the things we know.[8]

As thoroughgoing as Mill's empiricism is, though, he is no sceptic. His treatment of induction, as John Skorupski notes, anticipates the 'naturalized epistemology' that is today associated most closely with W. V. O. Quine. Quine argues that epistemology should be reconceptualized as a branch of empirical psychology that studies how people do in fact acquire beliefs and develop theories.[9] Quine simply refuses to engage with wholesale scepticism of the Humean variety, and insofar as he offers a justification of induction at all, his answers presuppose scientific results arrived at via induction: '*That* there are or have been regularities [in nature] . . . is an established fact of science; and we cannot ask better than that.'[10] From the standpoint of traditional epistemology, according to which refuting the sceptic is a central preoccupation, this is a viciously circular argument. It is this very conception of epistemology, though, that Quine rejects. Mill handles the problem of induction in a very similar manner. His view is that we can infer that nature is uniform by way of a 'meta-induction'. The fact that so many inductions have been successful entitles us to infer inductively that 'the course of nature is uniform', an 'induction by no means of the most obvious kind'.[11] His treatment of induction in his *System of Logic* is intended to refine our understanding of what separates good inductive generalizations from bad ones, and to help us to make better use of inductive reasoning, and that is all.

On other points, though, Mill offers a more direct reply to the sceptic. The clearest instance of his doing this is his explanation of why we can regard the faculty of memory as generally reliable, which entails that the past is real, that is, that we were not all created this instant with a set of apparent memories. The explanation refers to the possibility of 'intuitive knowledge':

> Dr Ward . . . challenges me to explain 'where the distinction lies between acts of memory and other alleged intuitions' which I do not admit as such. The distinction is, that as all the explanations of mental phenomena presuppose Memory, Memory itself cannot admit of being explained. Whenever this is shown to be true of any other part of our knowledge, I shall admit that part to be intuitive.[12]

Mill's willingness to admit that we know intuitively that the memory is reliable may be a sign that he is willing to go a certain distance with another epistemological tradition, one that is usually seen as a competitor to empiricism. This is the so-called 'Scottish common sense' school. Thomas Reid is its best-known representative; others include Dugald Stewart and Sir William Hamilton. The common-sense view, like empiricism, says that experience is the primary source of our knowledge. It differs from empiricism, however, in being much freer in its claims about how much knowledge we can glean from this source. Roughly stated, the common-sense theorists assert that people share, not innate beliefs, but rather certain innate dispositions to form beliefs on the basis of experience. They maintain that 'doxastic' or belief-forming dispositions can be regarded as innate if – and only if – they satisfy certain conditions, such as being irresistible (that is, we feel such certainty about the beliefs to which they give rise that we cannot seriously doubt them), universally shared, and incapable of being explained as products of experience.[13] Empiricists might say this much, but the common-sense theorists make a further assertion as well, which is that the beliefs generated by our innate doxastic dispositions are genuine items of intuitive knowledge. Keith Lehrer summarizes Reid's defence of this outlook in terms of a series of claims: Without some reliance on our innate faculties, philosophical thought is impossible. Sceptics trust our faculty of reason, but they doubt our other innate faculties. There is no justification for supposing this one innate faculty to be any more trustworthy than the rest, though; if we trust one, we must trust all. So when we reason, we must take the deliverances of our other innate faculties as givens that cannot be called into question. They must serve as reason's starting points.[14] For instance, we do not know innately that matter exists independently of our own minds, according to common-sense philosophy. Nevertheless, those who hold this view maintain, given experiences that we all have, we cannot help but believe that it does. The disposition to believe this is irresistible, universally shared and the disposition itself is not one that could be acquired via experience. It is therefore an 'original principle' of our mind, and hence we must regard the belief to which it gives rise as a piece of intuitive knowledge.

In the passage in which he responds to Ward on the reliability of the memory, Mill implicitly concedes the converse of his final statement: Whenever anything is shown to be an intuition, he will admit that it is an item of knowledge.[15] This suggests that he has one foot in the camp of common-sense philosophy, or at least a few toes. Skorupski emphasizes this affinity when he writes that '. . . Mill stands loosely in the tradition of Reid.'[16] Yet on the whole Mill must still be regarded as a critic of the 'intuitionists', for he believes that most of those who assert that we have intuitive knowledge vastly overstate how much of it we have. The next section explains this point in more detail.

The fundamental laws of the mind

The classical British empiricists, Mill included, all accept some version of a psychological theory known as 'associationism'. Empiricism and associationism developed together, inasmuch as both have historical roots that go back at least as far as Aristotle and both came into their own as theories in Britain during the modern period.[17]

Mill says that there are four basic categories of mental states: 'Thoughts, Emotions, Volitions, and Sensations'.[18] Thoughts are simply ideas, including beliefs. Volitions are 'willings', or in other words, choices about how to act. Because sensations are caused by 'states of body', the 'laws of body' that govern them 'manifestly belong to the province of Physiology'. Psychology is concerned with the laws of mind that govern the production of the other three states of consciousness. In the *System of Logic*, Mill states what he takes to be two of the most fundamental and general principles of psychology (using Hume's term 'impression'). One, that 'every mental *impression* has its *idea*', is the converse of the empiricist contention that all of our ideas come from experience. The other is that

these ideas, or secondary mental states, are excited by our impressions, or by other ideas, according to certain laws. . . . Of these laws the first is, that similar ideas tend to excite one another. The second is, that when two impressions have been frequently experienced (or even thought of) either simultaneously or in immediate succession, then whenever one of these impressions, or the idea of it, recurs, it tends to excite the idea of the other. The third law is, that greater intensity in either or both of the impressions, is equivalent . . . to a greater frequency of conjunction.[19]

These laws of mental association purport to explain why ideas enter an individual's consciousness or 'come to mind' when they do. The classical empiricists make subtle uses of association to explain how experience can give rise to all of our ideas, including the ideas that rationalists maintain must be innate. Ideas that are not obviously products of experience, at first glance, are shown to be complex ideas made up of simple ideas acquired by experience and compounded together by association. Mill's approach is especially subtle because he believes that it is possible for a complex idea to be formed from simple ones in such a way that the constituent simple ideas are no longer recognizable within it. He contrasts the complex idea of an orange, in which 'the original elements may still, by an ordinary effort of consciousness, be distinguished in the compound,' with cases in which 'mental phenomena, joined together by association, may form a still more intimate, and as it were chemical union – may merge into a compound, in which the separate elements are no more distinguishable as such, than hydrogen and oxygen in water. . . .'[20]

Now we can say more about where Mill agrees and disagrees with the intuitionists. He agrees that if people universally share a disposition to form a particular belief after having ordinary human experiences, a disposition that is irresistible and that cannot be accounted for as a product of experience, then that belief can be counted among the things that we know. If there is a psychological explanation for why we are disposed to form beliefs of a certain kind that reveals that the disposition in question is acquired via experience, though, then the belief is not known intuitively to be true. In Mill's opinion, the sorts of thinkers who are usually called intuitionists, including the devotees of common sense, are far too quick to assume that no psychological explanation can be given for the belief-forming dispositions that they treat as founts of intuitive knowledge. Mill believes that the existence of these dispositions can nearly always be accounted for in terms of the association of ideas, and hence he believes that there are at most a very few fundamental truths that can be known via intuition. (That the memory is reliable is the only item of intuitive knowledge that he explicitly acknowledges that we possess.) This explains why, for example, he disagrees with the common-sense philosophers when they say that we have intuitive knowledge of the existence of matter, where matter is conceived of as a substance that exists independently of minds. Association, he maintains, can account for why we are disposed to form this belief.[21]

The laws of association apply to more than ideas. In the *Logic*, Mill states that 'A desire, an emotion, an idea of the higher order of abstraction, even our judgements and volitions when they have become habitual, are called up by association, according to precisely the same laws as our simple ideas.'[22] This aspect of human nature plays a pivotal role in Mill's moral philosophy. It means that by way of association we can come to have new desires, and chapter 3 will demonstrate that this is very important in the context of Mill's conception of happiness. It also means that ways of thinking, feeling and acting can become habitual for us; we will return to this point later in this chapter.

Mill does not claim that association entirely explains human feelings and actions, however, for he accepts that there are some 'primitive' or pre-associational factors at work as well, factors that have their roots in physiology. This makes him more willing than his father to recognize inherent individual differences between people in terms of their abilities and their susceptibilities to different pleasures and pains. Mill's biographer Michael St. John Packe reminds us that 'According to James Mill's theory, all minds started as much alike as all stomachs or all hands or any other physical organs. . . . Thus, minds differed only in so far as they recorded different chains of experiences, and from them formed different habits of association.'[23]

This is why James Mill did not seek any evidence of John's superior ability before commencing with his demanding scheme of education; he assumed that *any* child could be made into a genius if the right instruction were supplied at an early age. John Mill, in contrast, is willing to recognize that there are organic (today we would say genetic) differences between people that may produce individual peculiarities in their mental make-ups. For example, he allows that differences in people's nervous systems may affect how strongly they experience various sensations, and this in turn may affect what associations they form. Differences in the relative intensities with which people experience distinct physical pleasures may have significant effects on what they desire and how strongly they desire it.[24] Furthermore, 'mere differences in the intensity of the sensations generally' may even produce 'different *qualities* of mind, different types of mental character'.[25]

Mill recognizes too that at the level of the species as a whole there is a shared 'animal' element in human psychology and an 'instinctive' element in human behaviour. He hastens to add, though, that this claim 'in no way conflicts with the indisputable fact that these instincts may be modified to any extent . . . by other mental influences, and by education'.[26] Mill identifies the growth of civilization, in large part, with the overcoming of the instinctive behaviours that are characteristic of humans in a 'savage' condition.[27]

Sympathy and attention

Mill attaches tremendous importance to the human capacity for sympathy, for reasons that will emerge over the course of this study.[28] His understanding of sympathy is generally similar to that of Hume, who takes it to be 'a disposition we have to feel what others are feeling'.[29] If it differs at all, Mill's conception of sympathy is perhaps a bit broader; he refers approvingly to his friend and biographer Alexander Bain's description of it as the disposition or capacity 'of taking on the emotions, or mental states generally, of others'.[30] The simplest form of sympathy is the one Mill describes when he writes that 'The idea of the pain of another is naturally painful; the idea of the pleasure of another is naturally pleasurable.'[31] Here is a motive for helping others: pleasing someone with whom you sympathize also pleases you.

Mill sees sympathy as a part of our 'natural constitution'; even children possess it. Yet there is still a sense in which sympathy is acquired. In order for sympathy to operate we must make someone else's feelings an object of our attention. This is why 'There is no selfishness equal to that of children. . . . The pains of others, though naturally painful to us, are not so until we have realised them by an act of imagination, implying voluntary attention; and that no young child ever pays, while under the impulse of a present desire.'[32] What children lack is the *habit* of paying attention to others' feelings. Unless and until we develop the habit of focusing our attention on someone else's feelings, it will be rare that we sympathize strongly with him or her.

What habits we form governing the bestowal of our attention on the sentiments of other people will depend on the extent to which our daily life *forces* us to do so. We all have a few people whose feelings we must pay attention to, because we cannot get what we need from them otherwise. As Mill recognizes, though, it is perfectly possible for someone's sympathy and benevolence to be limited to a very tight circle of intimates: '[S]ympathetic characters, left uncultivated, and given up to their sympathetic instincts, are as selfish as others. . . . [T]hey may be very amiable and delightful to those with whom they sympathize, and grossly unjust and unfeeling to the rest of the world.'[33]

Whether you need to pay much attention to the feelings of any wider group of people will depend on how your society operates and your place in it. The question is whether there are people to whose feelings you are forced to pay attention. Mill thinks that one concomitant of increasing civilization is a widening of people's sympathies: 'Not only does all strengthening of social ties, and all healthy growth of society, give to each individual a stronger personal interest in practically consulting the welfare of others; it also leads him to identify his feelings more and more with their good, or at least with an even greater degree of practical consideration for it. . . .'[34] While Mill believes that civilization is 'increasing' in the West, in this sense and others, he does not believe that there is anything inevitable about this process continuing.

The moral feelings

We have seen that Mill is generally hostile to intuitionism, not because he denies that anything is known by intuition but because he believes that the so-called intuitionists tend to exaggerate wildly how much is known in this way.[35] He reserves his deepest scorn for 'moral intuitionism', the doctrine that we can have intuitive knowledge of moral rules. Defenders of moral intuitionism like Adam Sedgwick, William Whewell and William Hamilton maintain that the moral feelings, the feelings of moral approval or disapproval that we experience towards our own actions and those of others, are a reliable source of moral knowledge.[36] They typically depict these feelings as having been given to us by God for this purpose, making them an innate element of human nature. Mill's critique of moral intuitionism comprises four claims:

1   Associationism better explains the existence of the moral feelings.

2   Moral intuitionism impedes moral progress by teaching that there is no need to call into question whatever moral views happen to be prevalent.

3   Moral intuitionism is pluralistic to the point of being indeterminate because it teaches that there are a number of general moral rules but gives us no guidance about how to act when these rules conflict (an oversight that you would hardly expect if humans came pre-equipped with a moral sense courtesy of an omniscient God).

4   Moral intuitionism by itself has no power to explain why the rules of morality are what they are and, on those few occasions when intuitionist philosophers have sought to provide such explanations, they have inevitably fallen back on utilitarian reasoning.

Discussion of the last three parts of this critique will need to wait until chapter 6. Mill's dispute with the intuitionists over the nature and origin of the moral feelings, however, is a question about human nature. He employs the name 'feeling of duty' for the 'mass of feeling which must be broken through in order to do what violates our standard of right, and which, if we do nevertheless violate that standard, will probably have to be encountered afterwards in the form of remorse.'[37] The feeling of duty's source is the conscience, which Mill describes as the 'internal sanction of duty'.[38] When experienced after the fact, this feeling also bears the more common names of guilt and self-reproach. The emotion of guilt occupies a central place in Mill's distinctive moral theory, as will become clear in chapter 6. However, it is worth emphasizing that the conscience does more than make us feel guilty after we have acted. As the passage just quoted suggests, it can also act while a person is deliberating about what to do, with the result that 'the idea of placing himself in such a situation is so painful, that he cannot dwell upon it long enough to have even the physical power of perpetrating the crime.'[39]

In opposition to the intuitionists, Mill holds that the feeling of duty is 'implanted', that is, acquired through experience, rather than innate.[40] (Mill's term is not felicitous, since intuitionists might also say that the feeling is implanted in us – by God.) A person acquires this feeling when the idea of violating a certain rule of conduct becomes associated in his or her mind with feelings of pain. Because the disposition to experience this feeling can be explained in terms of associationist psychology, it has no claim to be regarded as innate or to be viewed as a source of intuitive knowledge of right and wrong. The ordinary childhood experience of being threatened with punishment can generate this association.[41] Indeed, people can be made to 'internalize' nearly any set of rules – to feel guilty about violating them – if they are 'educated' in the right way, 'so that there is hardly anything so absurd or so mischievous that it may not . . . be made to act on the human mind with all the authority of conscience.'[42]

The association between violations of particular rules and punishment can come to appear 'artificial and casual' to a person with analytical habits of thought who recognizes how this association is formed, Mill notes. This may result in the association's dissolution.[43] Mill takes this point to hold true of the feelings more generally, in fact; recognizing them for the products of association they are tends to make a person cease to experience them. He blames the depression he experienced when he was twenty years old specifically on the fact that his early education had made 'precocious and premature analysis the inveterate habit' of his mind, while not enough had been done to cultivate his feelings and maintain 'a due balance among the faculties'.[44] It was his powerful analytical disposition that he feared had altogether dissolved his shallowly rooted feelings. In the case of the moral feelings specifically, his concern is that if a person reflects on the mental associations that lead one to experience the feeling of duty and sees them as nothing more than unnatural products of one's upbringing, then these associations might be dissolved: 'moral associations which are wholly of artificial creation, when intellectual culture goes on, yield by degrees to the dissolving force of analysis.'[45]

Fortunately, Mill believes, the development of every society's popular morality has been implicitly influenced by utilitarian considerations; this is fortunate because it means that the rules that most people have internalized have some connection with protection and promotion of the happiness of others. To the extent that the rules that an individual feels bound by the internal sanction to obey are conducive to 'the general happiness', sympathy with the resentment that other people will feel upon violations of those rules (and recognition of the naturalness of their feeling it) can prevent the feeling of duty from being experienced as something artificial.[46] This works to buffer the corrosive power of analytic habits of thought, habits whose cultivation Mill absolutely wishes to encourage.

Habits and character

Associations between thoughts, emotions, volitions and sensations are mental habits. Your character, at least in Mill's view, comprises the sum total of your mental habits. There is a growing awareness among Mill scholars of just how central the idea of character is to Mill's moral philosophy. His test of a matter's practical significance is the difference that it makes to the enjoyment of happiness, and he firmly believes that no factor is more important in determining how much happiness a society will enjoy than the characters of its members.

Mill distinguishes between the different types of habits that constitute a person's character when he refers to our having 'dispositions, and habits of mind and heart'.[47] 'Dispositions' denotes volitional habits; these are habits of the will or faculty of choice. According to Mill's account of motivational psychology, when we choose what to do on the basis of deliberation, choice (between the options that we consider) will be determined by our desires (and aversions, but an aversion to something is really only a desire to avoid it). Mill sometimes refers to desires as 'motives', and he observes that it is part of their nature to provide 'a positive stimulation to action'; desire is the 'initiatory stage of the will'.[48] If a sufficiently strong association is formed between some idea and the choice of a certain kind of action, however, as might happen if the choice is repeatedly made after the idea has been excited, then the idea may be capable of summoning up the volition all by itself. This is what it means to have a habit of the will; habits of this sort can render whatever deliberation precedes choice irrelevant or cause a choice to be made before deliberation ever begins. Even if the desires that originally led the agent to 'get into the habit' of making this choice have faded, the action may still be chosen: 'This, however, is but an instance of that familiar fact, the power of habit. . . . Many indifferent things, which men originally did from a motive of some sort, they continue to do from habit.'[49]

While Mill is not a proponent of the sort of view that is today described as 'virtue ethics', which is generally conceived of as an alternative to an ethics of morality and obligation, he is a firm believer in the importance of cultivating moral virtue. The conscience is not an entirely reliable source of motivation, he admits, and so we cannot really count on someone to do what morality requires until he or she does so out of habit.[50] Having a character that facilitates your doing your duty is what it means to be morally virtuous, from a Millian perspective.

Although Mill believes that our characters are products of our circumstances, he does not take this to show that we are not morally responsible for our actions. On the contrary, he holds that 'we are under a moral obligation to seek the improvement of our moral character.'[51] If a person's character is shaped by circumstances, then 'his own desire to mould it in a particular way is one of those circumstances, and by no means one of the least influential. . . . We are exactly as capable of making our own character, *if we will*, as others are of making it for us.'[52] This claim, that people can alter their own characters, is a point on which Mill places great emphasis and a very central part of his thinking; it will come up again in later chapters, especially in the context of discussing *On Liberty*.

While he criticizes Bentham for lacking an adequate 'knowledge of the formation of character', Mill is painfully aware of the limitations of his own knowledge in this domain. In the *Logic*, he proposes a new science of human character that he calls 'ethology'.[53] Ethology would be concerned with the 'middle principles' of the mental sciences, in between the most general laws of psychology and the most specific and narrow observed regularities. 'Ethology', Mill tells us, 'is the science which corresponds to the art of education, in the widest sense of the term, including the formation of national or collective character as well as individual.'[54] It is, as Wendy Donner writes, 'the source of the scientific knowledge that enables educators to promote the ends of their moral art, namely, the production of desirable features of human character formed out of the interaction of the laws of mind and the social and physical environment.'[55]

Mill acknowledges that ethology 'is still to be created'.[56] In the early 1840s, when he is writing the *Logic*, he intends to undertake the first systematic investigation of the laws of ethology himself. In 1859, he remarks, perhaps with some frustration, that he has never yet felt prepared to write on this subject, although he indicates that he still plans to do so in the future, 'at least in the form of some Essays'.[57] Unfortunately, however, he never does feel prepared, and the essays remain unwritten.[58]

Race and gender

Mill never provides us with an extended discussion of the subject of race, as we understand this concept today, although references to it are scattered through his corpus. As Georgios Varouxakis documents, in a definitive study of Mill's views on race and 'national character', starting in the late 1840s Mill 'went out of his way to stress how little importance race had'.[59]

To take a case in point, Mill states in the clearest possible terms that we cannot draw any inference about the inferiority of people of African descent from the fact that Europeans were able to enslave them. He makes this assertion most adamantly in his response to Thomas Carlyle's notorious essay 'Occasional Discourse on the Negro Question', which was originally published in *Fraser's Magazine* in 1849.[60] 'Black Quashee' was born to a servant, Carlyle insisted, and if he would not serve voluntarily then he should be compelled.[61]

The next issue of *Fraser's* contained Mill's 'The Negro Question', a point-by-point demolition of Carlyle's argument. Mill writes that '[S]pontaneous improvement, beyond a very low grade – improvement by internal development, without aid from other individuals or peoples – is one of the rarest phenomena in history. . . . No argument against the capacity of negroes for improvement could be drawn from their not being one of these rare exceptions.'[62]

Mill also notes that the 'Greeks learnt their first lessons in civilization' from the 'original Egyptians', who are 'inferred, from the evidence of their sculptures, to have been a negro race'. His view, in sum, is that while European culture is vastly superior to African this is not due to any inherent differences between Europeans and Africans. The situation was reversed in the past, and Mill offers no reason for doubting that in the future Europeans and Africans will attain parity in their moral and intellectual development (at a higher level than either has reached so far). Admittedly, he thinks that the most direct route to this end will require that Africans submit to a kind of tutelage from the West, although in a form – colonialism – that he considers quite different from slavery. He thinks the same of other non-European races, including those of the Subcontinent. David Theo Goldberg calls this a 'contingent' or 'polite' form of racism, preferable to Carlyle's 'negrophobia' but racism none the less.[63] This criticism, however, is patently unfair to Mill. How can a view be racist if it assigns no explanatory role to race? He may well be too sanguine about colonialism, but this is a separate issue.[64] (Mill's vigorous efforts to have Eyre prosecuted bear remembering here as well.)

Part II

Mill's Moral Philosophy

3

The 'Proof' of the Principle of Utility

The main task of this chapter is that of examining Mill's much-maligned argument for the proposition that only happiness has intrinsic value. Understanding the proof requires having a certain amount of background knowledge, however, so it will be necessary to begin with some preliminary remarks on the notions of well-being and happiness.

Theories of well-being

Utilitarians believe that something has intrinsic value – that is, that it is valuable for its own sake – only if including it in your life is enough, in and of itself, to make your life go better in the sense of being more worth living from your own perspective.[1] This is the utilitarian 'theory of the good' or 'axiology', and it can be labelled 'welfarism'. We can therefore say that utilitarians believe that only the well-being of sentient beings has intrinsic value. We might also say that utilitarians believe that only *happiness* has intrinsic value. This is convenient, although – for reasons that will be described below – it is true of all utilitarians only if 'happiness' is used in an unusually broad sense. Utilitarians may find other things desirable as means to obtaining that which makes for a good life, but their value will merely be 'instrumental'. If something neither improves someone's life itself nor can be used to obtain something else that can, then according to the utilitarian it is of no value whatsoever.

There is no limit to the number of ways in which you might specify what human well-being consists in, but a distinction can be drawn between two general approaches. 'Desire-satisfaction' accounts of well-being say that your level of well-being depends upon the extent to which your desires or preferences are satisfied, or at least on the extent to which whatever you desire for its own sake (and not merely as a means of satisfying some further desire) happens. 'Objective' accounts of well-being say that your level of well-being depends upon the extent to which your life includes certain elements whose value is independent of your 'subjective' desires. Aristotle's account of *eudaimonia* illustrates what an objective conception of well-being might look like. To have *eudaimonia* is to possess and display some combination of the virtues. A person who is *eudaimon* will enjoy pleasure, Aristotle tells us, but this is not what makes *eudaimonia* valuable.[2] Note that these are only general categories of views and they would need to be filled in with further details before we could really say what the elements of human well-being are. A specific desire-satisfaction view may include claims about what people desire for its own sake (and it may allow for the possibility that this varies between individuals). A particular objective view would need to say what things are objectively good for us.

It may look like a third option is missing from the list above, namely that of accounts that say that how well off you are depends upon the extent to which you have certain mental states and, perhaps, do not have others. The best known 'mental state' view is hedonism, which equates well-being with pleasure and the absence of pain. While much is going to be said about hedonism in what follows, though, we do not need to see it or the larger category of mental state theories of well-being as a third category sitting alongside the two described above. We can say instead that there are two different versions of hedonism (or of mental state views generally). The desire-satisfaction version says that our level of well-being depends entirely upon our experiences of pleasure and pain because pleasure and freedom from pain are the only things that any of us desire for their own sakes. The objective version says that how well off we are depends upon how much pleasure and pain we experience because only pleasure and freedom from pain are objectively valuable. So these two versions of hedonism agree on what the elements of human well-being are, but they disagree about what gives them this status. Notice that the desire-satisfaction version of hedonism depends on a controversial factual claim that we desire pleasure for its own sake. In contrast, an objective hedonist could admit that we desire things other than pleasure for their own sakes or even deny that we desire pleasure for its own sake. But the objective hedonist owes us an explanation of how we can know that pleasure and freedom from pain are valuable irrespective of any desire that we have for them.[3]

How comfortable one is using 'happiness' and 'well-being' as synonyms may depend on precisely what one takes the elements of human well-being to be. We normally talk about happiness as something that we feel, so the more elements of well-being that one recognizes that are not feelings, the less appropriate it may seem to use 'happiness' to mean 'well-being'. This is not a problem for a hedonist, though. And in a philosophical context, the meaning of 'happiness' can be stretched far enough to cover nearly any account of well-being, which is why *eudaimonia* is often translated as 'happiness'.

'Utility' can also serve as a synonym for 'well-being'. Philosophers like Hume originally used this term as a name for the ability to enhance well-being, that is, the property of being instrumentally useful, which is more or less its ordinary non-technical meaning. At some point, however, the word acquired an additional meaning when economists and philosophers began to employ it as a name for well-being itself. This new meaning became firmly established during the twentieth century. (It is not always clear how Mill employs the term, but he does appear to use it in the newer sense at least some of the time, especially when he seems to identify utility with happiness.[4])

Objections have been raised to both desire-satisfaction and objective accounts as general approaches to thinking about well-being but it is not necessary for us to grapple with these here. We do, though, need to get an objection that has been raised against hedonism, one that has force against either its desire-satisfaction or objective variants, onto the table. Hedonism says that all pleasure is valuable, regardless of where it comes from. Critics have pointed to two kinds of cases in particular to suggest that this is implausible. First, there are cases in which pleasure stems from 'evil' sources; think of the pleasure that a terrorist might get from a successful attack. Second, there are cases in which a person enjoys pleasure as a result of false beliefs. As an extreme example of this, consider the pleasure of someone who believes that she is enjoying a perfectly 'normal' life, but who is actually on life support and receiving simulated experiences via virtual reality technology, as in *The Matrix*.

Since the person's pleasure would be real, even though it was the product of false beliefs, the hedonist must regard it as being just as valuable as any other pleasure. Long before *The Matrix*, the philosopher Robert Nozick raised the possibility of an 'experience machine' as an objection to hedonism.[5]

Mill's account of happiness: A first look

The one thing that can be said about how Mill understands well-being without generating any controversy whatsoever is that he identifies well-being with happiness. And happiness, he maintains, is the only thing that has intrinsic value. Or, in his terminology, it is the only thing 'desirable as an end'. However, as we have already seen, happiness can be conceived of in many ways.

A single passage from *Utilitarianism* might seem to put any question about how Mill understands happiness to rest. At the beginning of chapter 2, he explains that

> By happiness is intended pleasure, and the absence of pain; by unhappiness, pain, and the privation of pleasure. . . . [P]leasure, and freedom from pain, are the only things desirable as ends; and . . . all desirable things (which are as numerous in the utilitarian as in any other scheme) are desirable either for the pleasure inherent in themselves, or as means to the promotion of pleasure and the prevention of pain.[6]

This passage looks like an unequivocal endorsement of hedonism and of a hedonistic account of happiness. Nevertheless, some interpreters deny that this is Mill's view.[7] Critics of the hedonistic reading offer two primary kinds of evidence against it. First, they contend that an alternative account of happiness fits better with some parts of Mill's social and political philosophies. Second, they contend that Mill makes other explicit statements about happiness that contradict the hedonistic reading. They claim that he does this in two places in particular: chapter 4 of *Utilitarianism*, where he presents his 'proof' of utilitarianism, and the stretch of chapter 2 immediately following the passage quoted above, in which he states that pleasures can be separated into different qualitative grades. This contention enjoys somewhat more support than the first. While Mill's social and political philosophies are entirely consistent with hedonism, or so Part III of this book will argue, he does say a few things about happiness in *Utilitarianism* that do not fit perfectly with a hedonistic conception. Still, on balance, we are warranted in reading Mill as a hedonist, albeit one who does not always spell his position out as perspicuously as he might. Those interpreters who take him to have a non-hedonistic conception of happiness are well meaning. Typically they see hedonism as so obviously flawed that they try to find an alternative reading of Mill that avoids saddling him with it. They may not be wrong about the problems with hedonism. Well intentioned though they may be, however, these commentators value charity too much and fidelity to Mill's words too little. The evidence for the hedonistic reading is just too strong for us to accept any alternative.

There is a distinction to be drawn between two varieties of hedonism, however, which raises the question of which Mill holds. This question will turn out to be quite important in what follows. The distinction at issue is really one between two different ways of defining 'pleasure'. The first view, which L. W. Sumner calls 'internalism', takes pleasure to be one specific and distinctive feeling which is present in all pleasurable experiences. The second, 'externalism', says that any subjective experience can be a pleasure for a given person at a given time (where 'subjective experience' just refers to what it feels like to do, to have or to undergo something).[8] All that matters is that we have the right kind of favourable attitude ('pro-attitude') towards the experience. The externalist theory of pleasure might be formulated in terms of desire, for instance, by saying that a given feeling is a pleasure for a particular person at a particular time if and only if we desire that feeling, for its own sake, at that time. This could mean that we either desire to experience the feeling in question, if we aren't experiencing it already, or desire to continue experiencing it if we are. James Mill appears to endorse a view of pleasure similar to this in *An Analysis of the Phenomena of the Human Mind*:

> I have one sensation, and then another, and then another. The first is of such a kind that I care not whether it is long or short; the second is of such a kind that I would put an end instantly to it if I could; the third is of such a kind that I like it prolonged. To distinguish these feelings I give them names. I call the first Indifferent; the second, Painful; the third, Pleasurable; very often, for shortness, I call the second, Pain, the third, Pleasure.[9]

Notice that James Mill is here using 'pleasure' as a countable noun: the third sensation is '*a* pleasure'. The externalist can also use 'pleasure' as a non-countable noun to refer collectively to pleasures in general. Notice too that, as James Mill illustrates, an externalist account of pain can be given as easily as one of pleasure.

There is much to be said for this externalist view of pleasure. It seems to fit the phenomenology of pleasure, the way that pleasurable experiences feel to us, more closely than internalism. What do pleasurable physical experiences, like back rubs, and pleasurable intellectual experiences, like working out a favourite type of puzzle, have in common? Nothing, it seems, except that we want both. Externalism might seem to have trouble explaining the phenomenon of masochism, since masochists by definition want to feel pain, but this turns out not to be a problem. The externalist can allow that the words 'pleasure' and 'pain' have another sense in which they refer to the sensations caused via particular nerves. For the masochist, the lash of the crop is painful in the sense of stimulating the pain nerves, but it is pleasurable in the sense of being a sensation towards which he or she has a pro-attitude.

The question of which view of pleasure J. S. Mill holds turns out not to have an obvious answer because the relevant texts offer up some conflicting evidence. One piece of evidence supporting an externalist reading is his declaration in *Utilitarianism* that 'Neither pains nor pleasures are homogeneous.'[10] Another bit of evidence, albeit a negative one, is that he does not add a note dissenting from his father's account of pleasure in the edition of the *Analysis* that he edited. On the other hand, he does add a note shortly thereafter in which he tries to explain how it is that we can find a sensation pleasurable at one time and not at another in terms of the pleasure's being conveyed by different nerves from the sensation itself.[11] This sounds like an internalist's way of explaining the phenomenon; an externalist's explanation would characteristically refer to a change in the person's attitude towards the sensation, such as a loss of the desire for it. On balance, though, for reasons that will be spelled out later, the externalist reading is more compelling.

An overview of Mill's proof

Chapter 4 of *Utilitarianism* is titled 'Of What Sort of Proof the Principle of Utility is Susceptible'. This title immediately raises the question of what Mill means by the 'principle of utility'. It may come as a surprise that there could be any uncertainty over his use of this phrase, yet he never offers us a sentence of the form 'The principle of utility is the principle that ___.' The assumption that 'the utility principle' must name a moral principle of some sort is perfectly natural, especially given the fact that Bentham did employ the phrase in this way, or at least as a name for an action-evaluating principle of some variety: 'By the principle of utility is meant that principle which approves or disapproves of every action whatso-ever, according to the tendency it appears to have to augment or diminish the happiness of the party whose interest is in question: or, what is the same thing in other words, to promote or to oppose that happiness.'[12]

Mill's assertion that the utilitarian creed 'holds that actions are right in proportion as they tend to promote happiness, wrong as they tend to produce the reverse of happiness' resembles Bentham's definition, and many have taken it for his official statement of the utility principle.[13] D. G. Brown, however, makes a compelling case for a different reading.[14] The 'utilitarian creed' passage tells us not only that utilitarians hold a particular view about the morality of actions (the details of which are not made at all clear) but also that this view is grounded on the proposition that 'happiness is the only thing desirable as an end'. Brown argues forcefully that it is this axiological proposition that Mill has in mind when he refers to the 'principle of utility' or 'greatest happiness principle'.

The caveat offered earlier about the difficulties that we face in interpreting *Utilitarianism* applies with particular force to chapter 4 of the essay. From very early on, Mill's critics have alleged that his reasoning in this chapter involves a series of obvious logical mis-steps. There is a surface plausibility to this allegation; on a superfi-cial reading, it does look as if he moves from one bad inference to the next. Indeed, the very title of the chapter, 'Of What Sort of Proof . . .', appears to be designed to lower our expectations for the rigour of his argument, suggesting as it does that he thinks that it is only possible to argue for the principle of utility in some special and seemingly inferior sort of way. The impression that he is not even going to attempt to give us a sound argument for the principle of utility is only reinforced by his statement in the chapter's first paragraph that the principle is 'incapable of proof by reason'. To some of Mill's critics, this smacks of an admission of defeat right at the outset.

Happily, one aspect of the more general renaissance in Mill studies has been a whole series of charitable re-readings of the 'proof', and the treatment of it presented here will be in this spirit. Its aim will be to show that Mill's presentation of the proof is highly elliptical, and that far more is going on in his argument than immediately meets the eye. It will not claim that the argument is entirely successful, for it is not. It will, though, attempt to show that it does not fail in the clumsy ways that his more vociferous detractors maintain.

The notion that Mill never intends to make a rigorous argument for the utility principle is a good place to begin. On the contrary, there is little question that he takes chapter 4 of *Utilitarianism* to discharge the obligation that he accepted when he wrote in an earlier essay that 'Those who maintain that human happiness is the end and test of morality are bound to prove that the principle is true. . . .'[15] He is working with a specific understanding of what counts as a proof in *Utilitarianism*, though, and he believes no argument that something is desirable as an end can be a proof in this narrow sense. He explains this in chapter 1: 'Questions of ultimate ends are not amenable to direct proof. Whatever can be proved to be good, must be so by being shown to be a means to something admitted to be good without proof. . . .'[16] This does not preclude the possibility that an intellectually satisfying case can be made for the principle, however: 'We are not, however, to infer that [the utility principle's] acceptance or rejection must depend on blind impulse, or arbitrary choice. . . . Considerations may be presented capable of determining the intellect either to give or withhold its assent to the doctrine; and this is equivalent to proof.'[17]

What definition of 'proof' could Mill be operating with here, according to which a set of 'considerations . . . capable of determining the intellect . . . to give . . . its assent' to the utility principle would not count as a proof? In the absence of a reason to think otherwise, we should assume that he is applying his 'official' definition of 'proof' here, which he states in his *System of Logic* when he writes that 'We say of a fact or statement, that it is proved, when we believe its truth by reason of some other fact or statement from which it is said to *follow*.'[18] A proof, in short, is simply a successful inference. Thus Mill is telling us that this 'argument that is not a proof' incorporates a move that provides intellectual support for some proposition and yet that is not an inference. Since the argument of chapter 4 of *Utilitarianism* is commonly described as 'Mill's proof', we will use this label for it here despite the fact that Mill would consider it an utter misnomer. (While 'proof' really ought to be placed in scare quotes every time that it is used, that would quickly grow tedious.)

We can now turn our attention to the proof itself. The usual way to approach it is to decompose the larger argument into three steps, with each step constituting an argument for a particular claim:

1 Happiness is desirable as an end.
2 The 'general happiness' is desirable as an end.
3 Nothing except happiness is desirable as an end.

The arguments for the first two of these claims are both very brief, and both appear in the chapter's third paragraph:

> The only proof capable of being given that an object is visible, is that people actually see it. The only proof that a sound is audible, is that people hear it: and so of the other sources of our experience. In like manner, I apprehend, the sole evidence it is possible to produce that anything is desirable, is that people do actually desire it. . . . No reason can be given why the general happiness is desirable, except that each person, so far as he believes it to be attainable, desires his own happiness. This, however, being a fact, we have not only all the proof which the case admits of, but all which it is possible to require, that happiness is a good: that each person's happiness is a good to that person, and the general happiness, therefore, a good to the aggregate of all persons.[19]

The remainder of chapter 4 is devoted to arguing for the proposition that nothing except happiness is desirable as an end. Having said that the fact that something's being desired as an end is evidence of its desirability, Mill has put himself in the position of needing to show that nothing except happiness is desired as an end. This is a difficult position to be in, for, as he acknowledges, it certainly looks as if many people desire things as ends that are entirely distinct from happiness: misers desire money for its own sake, good people desire virtue as an end and so on. Mill must do one of two things: either he must show that no one really desires things like money or virtue as ends or he must show that all of these other objects of desire can actually be parts of happiness. Ostensibly, he chooses the latter course: 'Virtue, according to the utilitarian doctrine, is not naturally and originally part of the end, but it is capable of becoming so; and in those who love it disinterestedly it has become so, and is desired and cherished, not as a means to happiness, but as a part of their happiness.'[20]

Some criticisms of the proof

Much has been written about each step in Mill's argument, and until fairly recently most of it has been quite mordant. The stock objection to the first step is that Mill moves illegitimately from the descriptive claim that happiness is desired as an end to the normative claim that it is desirable, seeking to obscure this in the reader's mind by playing on the homophonicity between 'visible' and 'desirable'. G. E. Moore advances a version of this objection in his *Principia Ethica*: 'Well, the fallacy in this step is so obvious, that it is quite wonderful how Mill failed to see it. The fact is that "desirable" does not mean "able to be desired" as "visible" means "able to be seen". The desirable means simply what *ought* to be desired or *deserves* to be desired.'[21]

The complaint most often voiced with respect to the argument's second step is that Mill commits a logical blunder known as the fallacy of composition. This is the mistake of reasoning that something must be true of a collection of items because it is true of each item individually. This is a mistake, because collections will not necessarily share all the properties of their constituents; individual feathers are very light, for example, but a sufficiently large pile of them could be very heavy. Critics allege that Mill commits this fallacy when he moves from saying that each individual's happiness is a good to that individual, which presumably means that increasing a person's net happiness benefits him or her, to saying that 'the general happiness' is 'a good to the aggregate of all persons', which the critics take to mean that increasing the sum-total of net happiness that is enjoyed benefits people collectively. Even if individuals have the property of being benefited by additions to the total amount of net happiness they experience, the objection runs, it would be a mistake to conclude from this that the same must be true of groups.

The chief criticism of the third step of Mill's argument is that his suggestion that things like money or virtue could be part of a person's happiness is inconsistent with his hedonistic definition of happiness with pleasure and the absence of pain. Moore again:

> Does Mill mean to say that money, these actual coins, which he admits to be desired in and for themselves, are a part either of pleasure or of the absence of pain? . . . If this is to be said, all words are useless: nothing can possibly be distinguished from anything else; if these two things are not distinct, what on earth is?[22]

Reconstructing the proof

After this fusillade, it may be hard to believe that anything can be salvaged of the proof. Passing it over in silence may seem to be the kindest course. Yet perhaps the situation is not so grim as this; a reading of the proof that depicts it as a serious piece of philosophical argumentation may not be out of reach. The place to begin a reconstruction of the proof is with the final step. Recall that at this stage of the proof Mill is trying to establish that happiness is the only thing that humans desire as an end. His strategy appears to be that of agreeing that people can desire money, virtue or anything else as an end, while saying that whatever a person desires for its own sake is part of that person's happiness. This view, though, is inconsistent with his hedonistic conception of happiness, as Moore gleefully points out.

In looking for a way to make sense of all of this, we must give up the hope of finding a reading according to which all of Mill's statements, taken literally, turn out to be consistent. We must suppose either that he holds an inconsistent position or that his view is internally consistent but imperfectly expressed. If neither supposition is entirely flattering to Mill, the latter is still the more charitable. The challenge, therefore, becomes that of saying precisely what Mill's actual position is and explaining why he fails to convey it properly. If it is not possible to do a convincing job of this, then we may have to conclude that he is guilty of self-contradiction in thought and not just in expression.

One way to maintain that Mill's position is internally consistent is to suggest that he 'does not really mean it' when he defines happiness as pleasure and the absence of pain. If this were true, though, then it would be somewhat mysterious why he devotes so much attention to pleasure in chapter 2 of *Utilitarianism* and even in the course of presenting the proof itself, not to mention the rest of his body of work. More likely is that he does not really mean it when he says that we can desire things other than pleasure as ends.

Mill's response to those who insist that we can desire things other than pleasure for their own sakes is based upon an account of how we come to desire new things as ends. There are only a few things that we 'naturally' desire as ends, he believes, and the objects of these 'primitive desires' are all pleasurable feelings. If we begin to desire anything else as an end, then this must be something we learn to do. And insofar as this is something we can learn to do,

Mill believes, associationism can account for how we learn it. It is possible for such a strong mental association to develop between pleasurable experiences and something else that this something else becomes a source of pleasure in its own right. This something else will often, if not invariably, be something that originally served only as a means to attaining pleasure. It could be doing a particular type of action.[23] It could also be something that a person might possess – either something material or a personal quality – in which case the person derives pleasure from reflecting on the belief that he or she possesses it. For instance, someone who has tried to act virtuously in order to be treated well by others can begin to associate the pleasurable experiences enjoyed as a result of this good treatment with the thought of him- or herself as virtuous. In this case, the belief that he or she is a virtuous person will itself be a source of pleasure, over and above the pleasure of any external rewards – in the form of better treatment from others – that being virtuous might allow him or her to enjoy. (This is not meant as a complete account of the pleasure that a person might take in the thought of himself or herself as virtuous; more will be said about this in the following chapter.)

This may look like an explanation of how individuals acquire new sources of pleasure, not how they come to desire new things as ends. The point, however, is that for Mill these two processes are really one and the same. What Mill is implicitly doing in this part of chapter 4 of *Utilitarianism* is providing an analysis of what is *really* going on in situations in which it might ordinarily be said that a person has come to desire something other than pleasure as an end. On the surface, he seems to be entirely satisfied with our ordinary way of speaking, in which we might say that a person desires something like virtue as an end; indeed, he appears to embrace this claim without reservation. But it is a mistake to overlook how Mill analyses the love of virtue for its own sake in terms of pleasure and pain:

> Those who desire virtue for its own sake, desire it either because the consciousness of it is a pleasure, or because the consciousness of being without it is a pain, or for both reasons united; as in truth the pleasure and pain seldom exist separately, but almost always together, the same person feeling pleasure in the degree of virtue attained, and pain in not having attained more.[24]

This opens up a way of understanding this step of the proof that does not require us to suppose that Mill is anything other than a thoroughgoing hedonist. Those people who love virtue do not literally desire a virtuous character for its own sake, as Mill sees it; instead, what they really desire for its own sake is the pleasure that they have learned to take in the belief that their character is good (along with freedom from the pain that accompanies the thought that some of their habits are vicious). Thus the apparent counterexample to the proposition that we desire something distinct from pleasure for its own sake is neutralized, leaving us with no reason to suppose that anything other than pleasure has intrinsic value.

Why would Mill say that it is possible for people to desire something like virtue for its own sake, if he does not really believe this? This is likely because he takes himself to agree with the main point of those who do take this to be literally true, namely that we can desire to be virtuous for a reason other than virtue's external rewards. He is presumably looking for a way to express that fundamental agreement without getting too bogged down in subtleties. When the reason that one wants something is that one gets pleasure from the mere knowledge that one has it, then describing the object of desire as a means to pleasure is somewhat misleading. Mill wisely wants to avoid that way of speaking but he lacks a convenient way to express the idea that desiring something as a means and desiring it for its own sake – in the strictest, most literal sense – may not be the only possibilities.

At first glance, the first step of the proof might seem to be less controversial than the final one. Mill's critics may accuse him of offering a mere verbal sleight of hand in place of an argument, but they seldom deny that pleasure and the absence of pain are in fact desirable as ends. Even Moore admits that pleasure might be intrinsically valuable, if only just a little, and he regards pain as a great intrinsic evil.[25] If the third step of the proof turns out to be successful, then this claim may be even harder to contest. It would border on nihilism to deny that the one and only thing that humans are capable of desiring as an end is worth desiring for its own sake, and nihilists are a rare breed. So Mill might easily have got away with it if he had not offered any reasoning at all in support of the claim that happiness is desirable as an end. Since his reputation has been so damaged by what he says here, though, it is worth looking at the reasoning that he does offer to see if it is really as facile as his critics maintain.

The closest analogue in Mill's 'epistemology of fact' to the move that he is making in this step of the proof is his defence of the claim that the memory is generally reliable. In defending this claim,

Mill meets the sceptic with the 'common-sense' response that we know intuitively that the memory is generally reliable, on the basis of a shared doxastic or belief-forming disposition. Likewise, here he seems to be suggesting that our innate disposition to desire pleasure justifies us in claiming to know intuitively that it is desirable. Just as we are justified in 'trusting' that beliefs resulting from an innate belief-forming disposition are true, he apparently reasons, so too are we justified in trusting that innate desires have objects worthy of being desired. Mill does not make any explicit attempt to show that our disposition to desire pleasure is innate, but his reasoning in support of the third step of the proof suffices to show that it meets all three criteria for innateness. The desire for pleasure is universally shared, it is 'primitive' rather than acquired via experience (although we can learn to find pleasure in new things), and the disposition to desire pleasure is irresistible (which is not to say that we cannot resist *acting on* desires for particular pleasant experiences). As Skorupski writes, 'The objectivity of happiness as an end is, and can only be, grounded in reflective agreement . . . of spontaneous *desires*.'[26]

This interpretation lets us make sense of Mill's denial that he is giving a true proof of the principle of utility. To come to know something on the basis of intuition is not to infer it; Mill distinguishes between what we know on the basis of proof or inference and what we know intuitively.[27] At the same time, it is not inconsistent with Mill's assertion that the truth or falsity of an axiological doctrine 'is within the cognisance of the rational faculty; and neither does that faculty deal with it solely in the way of intuition. Considerations may be presented capable of determining the intellect either to give or withhold its assent to the doctrine; and this is equivalent to proof.'[28] While the first step of the proof rests on an appeal to intuition, the other steps do not. So the rational faculty deals with the utility principle partly, yet not 'solely', by intuition.

The fact that Mill believes that we only desire pleasure and freedom from pain as ends does not necessarily mean that his axiological theory is an example of desire-satisfaction hedonism. Mill believes that we only desire pleasure as an end, but this does not mean that he believes that its value is due to our desires. He commits himself to no more than the epistemic claim that we can know it has value because of our innate disposition to desire it. He may well believe that its value is objective; he leaves the question open. The idea that an innate disposition to believe could give rise to knowledge may strike some people as more plausible than the idea that an innate disposition to desire could do so. It is possible, though, that Mill takes an innate doxastic disposition to play a role in his proof as well. Within the space of a single sentence, he moves from speaking of 'desiring a thing' as an end to speaking of thinking 'an object desirable'.[29] To do one is to do the other. This implies that he takes us to share something more than a desire for happiness, namely a belief that happiness is desirable. (More evidence for this will be adduced in the next chapter.) We might describe having this belief as 'affirming' our desire for happiness, inasmuch as the belief in question amounts to a belief that the object of that desire really is worth desiring. If he takes this belief to spring from an innate disposition, then he might also take it to do at least part of the work of justifying our claim to know that happiness is desirable for its own sake.

This leaves us with the so-called second step of the proof to consider, in which Mill moves from the desirability of each individual's happiness or pleasure being desirable for him or her to the desirability of the 'general happiness'. Recall that we have glossed this claim to mean that it is desirable for the sum-total of net happiness to be as great as possible. Strictly speaking, it may be a mistake to consider this move part of the proof itself – hence the qualifier 'so-called'. After all, if the conclusion of the proof is meant to be that happiness is desirable and the only thing desirable as an end, then what we have been calling the first and third steps are really all that Mill needs. That the general happiness is desirable as an end is probably better thought of as a consequence or corollary of the utility principle than as part of its proof. Still, the common label for it is convenient, and we may as well continue to use it. To understand the argumentative move Mill makes in this step, we need to examine more closely the belief about the desirability of happiness that Mill takes us all to share. Does someone who desires happiness and believes that this desire is 'accurate', that is, that happiness really is valuable or worth having, believe that:

1 Happiness is valuable when experienced by me; or that
2 Happiness is valuable *simpliciter*, regardless of who gets to enjoy it?

Mill takes it that the latter is the case. The reason that we affirm our desire for happiness is that we believe that happiness has value regardless of who enjoys it. It is because happiness is valuable *tout court*, in this absolute sense, that whoever gets to enjoy some of it for him- or herself thereby benefits; this is why an experience of happiness is a good to an individual.[30]

Part of what Mill takes us to know when we know that happiness is valuable, then, is that it is valuable regardless of who enjoys it. In fact, he takes us to know that equal amounts of it are equally valuable, regardless of who gets to experience them. In a footnote in *Utilitarianism's* final chapter, he replies to Herbert Spencer's assertion that the principle of utility presupposes the prior principle that everyone has an equal right to happiness: 'It may be more correctly described as supposing that equal amounts of happiness are equally desirable, whether felt by the same or by different persons. This, however, is not a presupposition; not a premise needful to support the principle of utility, but the very principle itself. . . .'[31]

So how, then, does Mill move from the idea that equal amounts of happiness are always equally valuable to the claim that the general happiness is desirable? If happiness is always valuable, then a state of affairs that contains more of it is better than one that contains less, other things being equal. And, for Mill, other things always *are* equal. A common criticism of utilitarianism is that a state of affairs that contains less total net happiness might be better than one that contains more, if the distribution of happiness in the former is more equal. Compare two worlds with the same number of people. In one, everyone is positively happy on balance, and equally so. In the other, everyone enjoys slightly less net happiness than the people in the first world. Except for one person, that is, who enjoys so much more that the total amount of net happiness in the second world is greater than that in the first. A critic of utilitarianism might say that the first world is better than the second. Mill can answer this critic, however, by drawing on the third step of the proof. This objection assumes that equality, or at least equality in the distribution of happiness, is of value in its own right. Mill, though, takes himself to have shown that only happiness itself has intrinsic value. The first world may contain more 'equality of happiness' than the second, but in and of itself this adds nothing to the total amount of good that it contains. Nor is there anything else that a state of affairs could contain – fairness, proportion between happiness and desert, knowledge or what have you – that would make it better than a state of affairs that contains more happiness than it does, according to Mill, since nothing besides how much happiness a state of affairs contains has any bearing on how good or bad it is.

What of Mill's claim that the general happiness is 'a good to the aggregate of all persons'? It was this claim that gave rise to the objection that he commits the fallacy of composition. Given the discussion of sympathy in chapter 2, it might be tempting to think that because sympathy enables one person to derive pleasure from the pleasure of others, Mill believes that everyone would benefit if the general happiness were to be greater rather than less. If people 'share' in one another's pleasure and pain, very loosely speaking, then maximizing the aggregate level of happiness maximizes each individual's level as well.

Yet Mill explicitly repudiates this interpretation in a letter that he writes to Henry Jones in 1868:

> As to the sentence you quote from my 'Utilitarianism'; when I said that the general happiness is a good to the aggregate of all persons I did not mean that every human's happiness is a good to every other human being; though, I think, in a good state of society and education it would be so. I merely meant in this particular sentence to argue that since A's happiness is a good, B's a good, C's a good, &c., the sum of these goods must be a good.[32]

So while Mill believes that people's capacity for sympathy could develop to the point where each individual would derive happiness from the happiness of every other, his argument does not depend on the assumption that it has or will. That much is clear. Yet although the last sentence just quoted is meant to clarify what is going on in *Utilitarianism*, it is little clearer than the passage that it is intended to elucidate. It can, though, be read as an elliptical way of saying that (1) the happiness experienced by any arbitrarily selected person is good *simpliciter*, and hence makes a positive contribution to the goodness of a state of affairs in which that person is included; (2) the magnitude of the contribution is determined by the amount of happiness; and so (3) the aggregate happiness enjoyed by everyone in a state of affairs can be viewed as making a contribution to the goodness of the state, with the amount of the sum determining the contribution's magnitude. The contribution made by the aggregate happiness is an alternative way of viewing the contribution made by the happiness enjoyed by each individual; the former contribution is not made on top of or in addition to the latter. (Strictly speaking, (1) would need to be reworded to take account of the possibility than an individual might on balance be unhappy, making his or her happiness a 'bad' or an 'evil' rather than a good.) Mill's claim in *Utilitarianism* that the general happiness is a good to the 'aggregate of all persons' may simply have to be written off as a misleading way of making the point that the aggregate happiness is good *simpliciter*, from an impersonal point of view that is not that of any particular individual.

An externalist reading of the proof

This treatment of the proof is complicated enough as it stands, perhaps, but it is about to get more complicated still. The extra complexity arises from the distinction between internalist and externalist ways of thinking about pleasure. Mill's exposition of the proof lends itself most easily to an internalist reading, and the reconstruction worked out above implicitly assumed that he is an internalist. However, the claim has been made that on balance the evidence supports interpreting Mill as an externalist about pleasure. (The decisive evidence for this claim will come in the next chapter.) We must therefore consider whether the proof can be reworked in a way that makes it consistent with externalism. For simplicity, we will assume in what follows (both the rest of this section and everything thereafter) that if Mill is an externalist then he is one of roughly the same variety as his father, namely one who identifies a person's pleasures with subjective experiences that he or she desires. There are other possibilities. For instance, one could always read Mill as taking an experience to be a pleasure for an individual just if the individual believes it to be desirable. Sidgwick's account of pleasure is something like this.[33] The precise nature of Mill's externalism is too esoteric a question to explore in detail here, though, and the different candidates for being his view are similar enough that nothing crucial for our purposes will turn on the differences between them.

The first step of the proof is the most difficult to rework in externalist terms. If Mill is an externalist, it is no longer possible to say that the reasoning behind this step begins with the empirical observation that everyone desires pleasure. If we define a pleasure as a subjective experience desired for its own sake, then the proposition that pleasure is desired is true by definition; it is not an empirical observation. The empirical claim with which the reasoning behind this step of the proof begins would instead have to be that everyone *has* pleasures, or in other words, that each and every person desires some experiences or others as ends. But what if everyone's pleasures turn out to be different? From an externalist perspective, there is not necessarily any one particular experience that we all desire. The reasoning behind this step of the proof is supposed to turn on the idea that we have an innate disposition to desire pleasure (and, perhaps, the further idea that we have an innate disposition to believe that pleasure is desirable). But if which experiences are desired varies from person to person, this would complicate Mill's appeal to intuition. Only innate dispositions can give rise to intuitive knowledge, and one of the hallmarks of an innate disposition is that it is universally shared. If there are no specific experiences that we are all disposed to desire (and, perhaps, all believe to be desirable), then we cannot know intuitively that anything is intrinsically valuable.

If we read Mill as an externalist about pleasure, then his proof can succeed only if people do desire the same experiences for their own sakes. Unless this happens to be true as a contingent matter of fact, then there may just be no way to square the proof with this view about pleasure. At first glance, the idea that we all desire the same experiences for their own sakes might appear to be not just false but absurd. It may seem obvious that different people want different experiences – some like roller-coasters and some do not, for instance. Perhaps, though, this idea can be refined in a way that makes it harder to reject out of hand. To see how this might be done, we must first recognize that if riding on a roller-coaster counts as a single experience, then it is a complex one. It involves many physical sensations: the rush of the air past one's face, the peculiar feeling of one's stomach rising as the car plunges, the excitement as adrenalin begins to flow and so on. The feeling of fear is also involved – mild fear for some people, intense terror for others. Some people might have strong mental associations with roller-coasters, like fond memories of having ridden them with a parent as a child, which will also figure into their experience. One could say that we have many experiences at once while riding on a roller-coaster, but it may be more convenient to say that we have a single experience with numerous components or elements. There is nothing special about roller-coasters, in this regard; most of our experiences will be similarly complex. With the recognition that one experience might have many different elements, and that a person's attitudes towards these different elements could vary, we can revise the version of externalism that we are supposing Mill might hold to say that an *element of* a subjective experience is a pleasure for a person if he or she desires it. This lets us say, for example, that one and the same experience might include several distinct pleasures, and that an experience can be simultaneously pleasurable and painful.

We can also now say that two people engaged in the same activity, or having the same thing done to them, might not be having identical subjective experiences. Some of the elements of their experience might be the same, but others might be entirely different. There might be physical disparities between them that account for this difference, at least in part. Someone prone to motion sickness will experience different sensations on a roller-coaster than someone with a cast-iron stomach. Some people just cannot detect certain tastes in their food unless these are very strong, if even then, and for them the experience of, say, drinking a particular wine may be very different from that of a preternaturally sensitive 'supertaster'.[34] We saw in chapter 2 that Mill is cognizant of the fact that differences in people's physiology can make a difference to how susceptible they are to various kinds of sensations. Also, there will clearly be significant differences in terms of what associations they have formed between different ideas and how strong these associations are, and this can lead to their having very different experiences while they are ostensibly doing the same thing. For one person the taste of a certain food is linked with the sensation of nausea, due to an earlier case of food poisoning, while for another it is not. Watching football may be an intellectual experience for a person who understands the strategy behind the sport, while for someone who does not even know the rules it may just be exciting to watch the athletes run around and hear the crowd roar. (Mill would add here that how susceptible our physiology makes us to different kinds of experiences will also affect what kinds of associations we form, as was noted in chapter 2.)

Thus two people can be engaged in the same activity and yet have quite different subjective experiences. Conversely, two people might be engaged in very different activities, and yet some of the same elements might be present in each of their experiences. These two points together suggest that it might not be entirely absurd to think that there could be considerable convergence between us regarding what elements of subjective experience we desire (and, perhaps, believe that we are right to desire). The major differences between us might instead have to do with what kinds of activities we have to engage in if we are to have experiences that include those elements. Perhaps it could turn out to be true, of some group of elements or aspects of experiences, that everyone who has experienced them has a disposition to desire them as ends. And perhaps this latter disposition could meet the other requirements, beyond being universally shared, for being innate. In that case, Mill could claim that we know intuitively that these particular pleasures are intrinsically desirable, and that equal amounts of a particular pleasure are equally valuable regardless of who experiences them. (This claim would only be strengthened if we also possess an innate doxastic disposition to affirm the desires in question.) Of course, showing that this idea is not obviously false is a very different thing from showing that it is true. Perhaps it could never really be proven beyond all question. Still, we might be able to find some empirical evidence that counts for it or against it. Scans that show what parts of different people's brains are engaged when they are doing different things might be illuminating, for example.

Once the necessary assumptions are made to recast the first step of the proof in a manner that is consistent with externalism, reworking the last two steps is a comparatively easy matter. The second step in particular goes through more or less as it stands. The third step does require a slight restatement. What it will need to say is that the components of subjective experiences that we desire as ends can, through association, become parts of experiences to which they previously did not belong, and that it is when this happens that we can loosely say that whatever it is that produces that experience – participating in some activity, having something done to us, possessing something – has become part of our happiness.

Evaluation of Mill's argument

With our reconstruction of Mill's proof complete, we can now turn to appraisal. Hopefully the argument has been vindicated against the charge that it is a clumsy piece of work, riddled with obvious errors. As we stated from the outset, though, we can hardly claim to have shown that it is a smashing success. The proof rests on assumptions about human psychology that are far from self-evident. If we did read the proof along the lines of the internalist conception of pleasure that its language suggests, then we would have to take it to presuppose that there is one feeling of pleasure, which is not very plausible at all. On the other hand, if we read the proof in externalist terms, then it depends on the assumption that we all desire the same elements of subjective experiences as ends, and it is far from obvious that this is true.

Whichever reading we favour, moreover, the proof assumes that no one desires anything but elements of subjective experiences for their own sakes. This is a highly dubious contention, although it has to be admitted that it is difficult to refute it decisively. Its defenders can always find *something* to say in answer to the standard objections to it.

One of these objections can be traced back to Bishop Joseph Butler's *Sermons on Human Nature*. According to Butler, we feel pleasure as a response to getting something that we really wanted for its own sake:

> That all particular appetites and passions are towards *external things themselves*, distinct from the *pleasure arising from them*, is manifested from hence – that there could not be this pleasure, were it not for that prior suitableness between the object and the passion: There could be no enjoyment or delight for one thing more than another, from eating food more than from swallowing a stone, if there were not an affection or appetite to one thing more than another.[35]

The Butlerian challenge to Mill's view would be to ask why lovers of virtue would take any pleasure in the belief that they have a good character, unless they desire a good character for its own sake in the most literal sense. Mill's associationism, though, provides an answer to this question, which is that loving virtue simply means having the idea of virtue so firmly linked in your mind with pleasure that the thought of yourself as virtuous is followed by pleasant feelings. The belief pulls the pleasure along after it.

The other standard objection to the claim that we desire nothing but pleasure (or mental states more generally) is that there are counterexamples that clearly show it to be false. Nozick's 'experience machine', which might be interpreted to mean that we have a desire for 'authenticity', has already been mentioned. Another familiar case involves soldiers who throw themselves on grenades to save their comrades, knowing that they will almost certainly die and will suffer horribly if they do not. Yet someone thoroughly wedded to the idea that all we desire for its own sake is pleasure can always find something to say in reply to examples like these. Maybe people who are contemplating the experience machine have a hard time convincing themselves that their artificial experiences would truly be indistinguishable from real ones or that the artificial life the machine offered them would really suit their individual tastes. Perhaps the soldiers expect to be dogged for the rest of their lives by a sense of shame if they let their comrades die. Or perhaps their action is so impulsive or instinctual that it is not caused by their desires.

That Mill could make answers to these sorts of objections is clear enough. Whether we ought to be satisfied with the answers he could make is a very different question, however. The answer that it was suggested that he might give to Butler depends upon the details of his mechanistic associationist psychology, a view that strikes many people today as excessively crude. As far as the possible replies that were proposed to the putative counterexamples are concerned, one must question whether these reinterpretations of the scenarios are remotely plausible. For instance, is it not possible to appreciate fully just how pleasurable the experience machine would be, and yet still prefer – for its own sake – an authentic life? The answer is almost certainly that this is more than possible. Lots of people would probably have this preference, in fact. And if Mill is wrong as a matter of fact about what things we desire as ends, then this is a devastating blow to his defence of hedonism.

Some hard questions must also be raised about Mill's defence of impartiality in the second step of the proof. There may be reason to worry about what kind of answer, if any, he can make to the egoist who acknowledges that happiness is valuable regardless of whom enjoys it, but who concludes from this it is only rational for each individual to get as much of it as possible for themselves. Sidgwick was famously forced to conclude that there is a 'duality' in practical reason, inasmuch as it is no less rational to promote one's own happiness than to promote the general happiness, or vice versa.[36]

4

The Higher Pleasures

The last chapter mentioned in passing that Mill believes that pleasures can be sorted into different qualitative grades, that is, that some are better than others. This chapter analyses this distinctive feature of his hedonism in detail.

An overview of the higher pleasures doctrine

In chapter 2 of *Utilitarianism,* Mill contends that the value of particular experiences of pleasure depends not just on the *quantity* of pleasure 'contained' in the experience, but also on the pleasure's *quality*. Some 'kinds' of pleasure make greater contributions to our happiness, he maintains, and are thereby of a correspondingly higher value: 'It is quite compatible with the principle of utility to recognize the fact, that some kinds of pleasure are more desirable and more valuable than others. It would be absurd that while, in estimating all other things, quality is considered as well as quantity, the estimation of pleasures should be supposed to depend on quantity alone.'[1]

There are three parts to Mill's 'higher pleasures' doctrine: the definition of what it is for one pleasure to be of relatively higher quality than another, the test for determining the relative qualities of two pleasures, and the answer to the question of which pleasures this test picks out as being of higher quality. We will consider each of these in turn.

Mill's definition of 'higher quality pleasure' comes directly from the passage just quoted. The statement that one pleasure is of higher quality than another means that a given quantity of the former is 'more desirable and more valuable' than the same quantity of the latter. There is an ambiguity in the meaning of 'quality' to which we need to be alert here. 'Quality' can be used in a generic sense that makes it synonymous with 'property' or 'characteristic'. 'The quality' of a thing can also refer to something like its degree of fineness or excellence when judged by a particular standard. We might use the qualifiers 'descriptive' and 'evaluative' to distinguish these two senses of 'quality'. For Mill, the evaluative quality of a pleasure depends upon the contribution that it makes to happiness, that is, on its desirability or value. Talk about the qualities of pleasures in what follows should all be understood in terms of their evaluative qualities, except where otherwise noted.

Mill's belief that a particular quantity of a higher quality pleasure contributes more to a person's happiness than the same quantity of a lower quality pleasure raises the question of what it means to speak of a given quantity of a pleasure. To answer this question, we must go back to Bentham's 'felicific calculus'. There are seven factors that must be taken into account when judging a pleasure's value, Bentham maintained: its intensity, duration, degree of certainty, how soon it is to be experienced (propinquity), its likelihood of being followed by other pleasures (fecundity), its likelihood of being followed by pain (purity) and the number of people who will share it.[2] To describe these all as factors affecting the value of a particular experience of pleasure, though, is misleading, because only the first two are really this. That an experience of pleasure is likely to be followed by pain does not diminish the value of the experience itself, for example. The 'calculus' is best described as a framework for thinking about the probable pay-off from pursuing a particular pleasurable experience, one that takes into account the desirability of the pleasure itself, the probability of the pursuit's success, the costs and additional benefits that the pursuit would entail, etc. In any event, when Mill refers to the quantity of pleasure in an experience, we should understand this to be a reference to the product of the intensity (in the ordinary sense of forcefulness) and duration of the pleasurable aspect of the experience. The more intense the pleasurable part of an experience is, and the longer it lasts, the greater the quantity of pleasure enjoyed. Mill sometimes shortens this formula to 'intensity' and uses this as a synonym for 'quantity'.

Now we have come to the dispositive reason not to read Mill as an internalist about pleasure. If we think of pleasure as one specific feeling, then it is impossible to make sense of the idea that some kinds of pleasure are *better* than others. All an internalist could say is that one pleasurable experience is better than another if it contains *more* pleasure. Some of Mill's critics assume that he is an internalist about pleasure and deny that he can account for qualitative differences between pleasures without reducing them to quantitative ones. Sidgwick, for example, writes that:

> It seems to me that in order to work out consistently the method that takes pleasure as the sole ultimate end of rational conduct, ... all qualitative comparison of pleasures must really resolve itself into quantitative. For all pleasures are understood to be so called because they have a common property of pleasantness, and may therefore be compared in respect of this common property.[3]

It is only when an internalist account of pleasure is presumed that this problem exists, however. From an externalist perspective, there need be no property of pleasantness that is common to all pleasurable experiences, at least not one that admits of degrees. The version of externalism that we have concentrated on here says that whatever elements of a subjective experience that a person desires are pleasures for her. How 'strong and absorbing' (Sidgwick's phrase for describing intensity) some desired element of the experience is and how long it lasts together determine the quantity of that pleasure in the experience.[4] Its evaluative quality depends on its phenomenal descriptive quality; what it feels like to experience it. As an externalist, Mill can believe without inconsistency that some kinds of pleasures are more worth having than others, that is, they are more desirable. This is not because they have more of something than pleasures that are less desirable; pleasures need have no intrinsic properties in common at all, beyond being elements of subjective experiences. Some are just better than others.

It is important to emphasize that Mill's qualitative hedonism is still genuinely hedonistic because pleasures are the only 'bearers of value'. Speaking very loosely, we might say that the total value of a particular experience of a pleasure can be thought of as the product of the pleasure's evaluative quality and quantity (which is to say the product of its quality, intensity and duration). An analogy might help here: suppose that precious gems were the only objects of economic value. (It may help to think of a game with tokens that represent gems.) If the gems were all the same type of stone, then how wealthy you were would depend only on quantitative factors – how many gems you had and their sizes. If there are instead a variety of stones with different intrinsic values, however – rubies, diamonds and so on – then you might be wealthy in spite of having only a few small jewels, if they were of the best sort. Mill's qualitative hedonism is no barrier to speaking in terms of the quantities or amounts of happiness that people enjoy, by the way. It implies only that while the amount of happiness that people enjoy is a function of the pleasures that they enjoy, the amount of happiness does not depend purely on the *amount* of pleasure.

Given the impossibility of reconciling the higher pleasures doctrine with an internalist view of pleasure, and the strength of Mill's apparent commitment to this view, the sensible course is to conclude that he is an externalist and seek to 'explain away' any passages in which he sounds more like an internalist.

The second part of the higher pleasures doctrine, the test that Mill proposes for determining the relative qualities of different pleasures, is the so-called 'informed' or 'decided' preference test:

> Of two pleasures, if there be one to which all or almost all who have experience of both give a decided preference, irrespective of any feeling of moral obligation to prefer it, that is the more desirable pleasure. If one of the two is, by those who are competently acquainted with both, placed so far above the other that they prefer it, even though knowing it to be attended with a greater amount of discontent, and would not resign it for any quantity of the other pleasure which their nature is capable of, we are justified in ascribing to the preferred enjoyment a superiority in quality, so far outweighing quantity as to render it, in comparison, of small account.[5]

For Mill, then, determining which pleasures are most desirable requires us to begin by observing which pleasures are most strongly desired by those individuals who have had a wide range of experiences. The first sentence of this passage states the 'official version' of the decided preference test. People who have experienced two different pleasures are to be asked which they would prefer to experience again. The quantities of pleasure in these two experiences should be assumed to be equal. (When Mill discusses the notions of quantity and quality in the *System of Logic*, he illustrates the first with a comparison between one gallon and ten gallons of water and the second with a comparison between one gallon of water and one of wine. He recognizes, in other words, that the

most effective initial presentation of the idea of qualitative difference is one in which quantities are equal.[6]) If there is a consensus
that experiencing one pleasure would be preferable to experiencing
the same amount of the other, then we should judge the former
to be of higher quality. This is the real decided preference test,
in the sense that its satisfaction is all that is required for us to conclude that one pleasure is of higher quality than another. The
passage's final sentence points out that if the competent judges not
only prefer a given quantity of one pleasure to the same quantity
of another, but in addition decidedly prefer any quantity of the
first to any quantity of the second 'which their nature is capable of',
then we can conclude not only that the first is of higher quality but
that it is of vastly higher quality, and hence that it is many times
more valuable.

This passage is sometimes misread, with the result that Mill is
taken to hold the view that the smallest amount of a pleasure is
always more valuable than the greatest amount of any other pleasure of a lower quality. This view is open to obvious counterexamples. Suppose, for instance, that you somehow had it in your power
to bring it about that the world would contain one more brief experience of any higher quality pleasure than it otherwise would. This
experience, though, would come at a price: for the next billion years,
no human would ever experience any physical sexual pleasure.
Everything else about the world would remain unchanged; in particular, people would still engage in the same sexual activities (so
reproduction would not be affected), and they would continue to
experience any emotional pleasures that might arise out of lovemaking. The characteristic physical pleasure associated with sexual
stimulation and orgasm would be lost, though, until it returned one
billion years later (if humanity still existed to enjoy it). Surely that
would be far too high a price to pay for one transitory experience
of any pleasure, however lofty in character, and surely paying it
would leave the world a less happy place.

Fortunately, we need not impute this view to Mill.[7] Those commentators who do so make two mistakes. The first is to fail to notice
that the second sentence of the passage states a criterion that is
distinct from the one stated in the first sentence, a stronger criterion
that will not necessarily be satisfied by any pair of pleasures that
differ in quality. The second is to ignore the phrase 'of which their
nature is capable' in the last sentence, reading it as if Mill offers his
competent judges a choice between a finite quantity of one pleasure
and an infinite quantity of the other. At most, the sentence implies

that a single experience of one pleasure can exceed in value the greatest amount of another pleasure that could be experienced within a single human life. Strictly speaking, Mill does not even commit himself to the existence of pairs of pleasures such that one is this much more valuable than the other; he only leaves the possibility open. We are entitled to take him to be committed to the existence of very significant differences between the values of different types of pleasure, certainly, but that is all.

The third part of Mill's higher pleasures doctrine is his answer to the question of which pleasures are of higher quality.[8] This answer is of course well known: 'the pleasures of the intellect, of the feelings and imagination, and of the moral sentiments'.[9] In order to enjoy these pleasures at all, a being must have what Mill calls the 'knowing', aesthetic and moral faculties, and those faculties must have been developed to at least a certain minimal degree.[10] As only humans are capable of developing these faculties to the requisite extent, as far as we know, the capacities and the pleasures that they yield can both be described as 'distinctly human'. More highly developed faculties make it possible to enjoy greater quantities of these pleasures. Nearly any person, even one who is more or less an 'idiot', can experience these pleasures in at least very small quantities, and so is capable of more happiness than a pig. An individual with highly-developed capacities – Socrates is Mill's example – can enjoy vastly more happiness than a person of more ordinary abilities.

Further thoughts on the higher pleasures

With this initial survey of Mill's qualitative hedonism behind us, we can now examine a few aspects of the higher pleasures doctrine in more detail. We will start with a closer look at the different types of pleasures that he describes as having an elevated quality. Then, after we consider how the higher pleasures fit into Mill's epistemology of value, we will consider some possible objections to the doctrine and how he might meet them.

Mill says surprisingly little about the nature of the intellectual pleasures, despite the fact that these are often taken to be paradigmatic of the higher quality pleasures. He says a bit more about the moral pleasures. The chief source of pleasure that Mill might call a 'moral faculty' is our capacity for sympathy. The quality of pleasure that we derive purely via sympathy is not always of a higher quality, but this is sometimes the case, especially when sympathy assumes one of its more 'complex' forms: 'the love of *loving*, the need of a sympathizing support, or of objects of admiration and reverence'.[11] Mill also assigns sympathy a role in explaining how we come to have a conscience, as we saw in chapter 2, and he believes that a person with a conscience will take pleasure in the knowledge that a wrongdoer has been punished. This is a moral pleasure in a stricter sense of 'moral'.[12]

Mill offers the most detail concerning the pleasures of the imagination, the aesthetic pleasures, and it is worth spending some time on his account of them because they turn out to play a larger role in his conception of a good human life than is apparent at first. His starting point is the art critic John Ruskin's account of the feelings that we experience in response to beauty:

> Mr. Ruskin . . . undertakes . . . to investigate the conditions of beauty. The result he brings out is, that everything which gives us the emotion of the Beautiful, is expressive and emblematic of one or other of certain lofty or lovely ideas, which are, in his apprehension, embodied in the universe, and correspond to the various perfections of its Creator. He holds these ideas to be, Infinity, Unity, Repose, Symmetry, Purity, Moderation, and Adaption to Ends. . . .[13]

Ruskin believes that it is a brute fact of human nature that the things that inspire us to feel aesthetic pleasure happen to be things that embody these ideas; Mill characterizes Ruskin's views in terms of a 'pre-established harmony'. In contrast, Mill maintains that the feeling of beauty or sublimity is a result of the powerful associations which we have formed with these ideas. We experience aesthetic pleasure just when something 'suggests vividly' one of these ideas. People may vary both in what ideas they associate with aesthetic pleasure and in what kinds of things make a 'lively suggestion' of one or more of these ideas to them.

Among the objects of appreciation which can give rise to the aesthetic pleasures, according to Mill, are human characters. This point will turn out to be important in our examination of his views on liberty and individuality in chapter 7, so we will say more about it then. There are two points that ought to be made in this connection now, though.

The first is that Mill assumes that one element of a beautiful human personality is moral virtue. While possessing moral virtue is not a sufficient condition for having an attractive character, it is a necessary one.[14] It is in this sense that Mill agrees with Goethe that 'the Beautiful is greater than the Good, for it includes the Good, and adds something to it: it is the Good made perfect, and fitted with all the collateral perfections which make it a finished and completed thing.'[15] In the last chapter, we saw that Mill believes that someone can come to take pleasure in the belief that he or she has a virtuous character. The account that was given there of what makes this possible focused on the associations that can form between virtue and the external rewards that are frequently conferred on virtuous people (at least when they are recognized as such). We can see now that this account was incomplete, though. For a person who has a sense of beauty, the love of virtue also incorporates an element of aesthetic pleasure, which comes from an appreciation of the contribution that virtue makes to a character's beauty.

Second, Mill's belief that the mere possession of developed faculties can be a source of aesthetic pleasure is also worth mentioning at this point. This emerges when he invokes the notion of a sense of dignity to explain why individuals with developed faculties would not willingly surrender those faculties for any quantity of the lower pleasures:

> We may give what explanation we please of this unwillingness . . . but its most appropriate appellation is a sense of dignity, which all human beings possess in one form or other, and in some, though by no means in exact, proportion to their higher faculties, and which is so essential a part of the happiness of those in whom it is strong, that nothing which conflicts with it could be, otherwise than momentarily, an object of desire to them.[16]

Mill's claim here is analogous to his contention that a person can come to take pleasure in the thought of being virtuous and to find the thought of being vicious painful.[17] To possess a sense of dignity is to take pleasure in the thought of your having reached whatever level of development that you have and to find the thought of regressing in your internal culture painful. This higher quality pleasure results from the operation of the imaginative faculty; it comes from an individual's aesthetic appreciation of the degree of perfection that he or she has attained. There will not necessarily be a strict proportionality between the level of development attained and the amount of happiness enjoyed. Perhaps some of the most advanced individuals will still be most conscious of and troubled by their own remaining limitations.

Although it means venturing back into difficult terrain, it is necessary to take a look at the epistemology that underlies the higher pleasures doctrine. The interpretation of Mill's epistemology of value presented in the last chapter can be extended to account for this doctrine. He takes people who have experienced the distinctly human pleasures to be disposed to desire them more strongly than other pleasures. It is quite plausible that he would take this disposition to meet the criteria for innateness, so that we could claim to know intuitively that the higher pleasures are more valuable. He makes no suggestion that the disposition to prefer the higher quality pleasures is one that we acquire via experience; while we cannot enjoy these pleasures until we have undergone some mental development, Mill's account of them is at least consistent with and may even imply that we prefer them from the first instant that we experience them. It seems even clearer that he considers the disposition to prefer them irresistible; we may be able to resist *pursuing* higher pleasures, but not *preferring* them.

Admittedly, Mill allows at one point that people who have experienced each of a pair of pleasures might disagree in their preferences, and that in this case whether the pleasures differ in quality must be decided by 'a majority among them'.[18] This might be taken to imply doubt about whether the disposition to prefer higher quality pleasures is universally shared. Yet Mill does not seem to anticipate any real disagreement between competent judges in cases in which there is a qualitative difference between pleasures. After all, he also writes that 'It may be questioned whether any one who has remained equally susceptible to both classes of pleasures, ever knowingly and calmly preferred the lower. . . .'[19] In fact, the 'majority among them' line is an obvious slip on Mill's part. If the two pleasures being compared were of *equal* quality, then we would expect that somewhat more of the judges might prefer one to the other simply in virtue of their different personal tastes. It would be a real coincidence if it were a perfect tie (and what if an odd number of competent judges were consulted?). Nor do Mill's competent judges have only their desires in common. He says that they also make the same 'judgements' about which pleasures are most desirable; they share, in other words, the same axiological beliefs.[20] (The textual evidence here that Mill believes that there is a spontaneous agreement of our beliefs about desirability, in addition to our desires themselves, is even stronger here than in chapter 4 of *Utilitarianism*.)

Mill acknowledges that people with weak characters often choose to pursue lower pleasures in preference to higher ones, when the lower pleasure is easier to get or can be had more quickly. 'But this', he notes, 'is quite compatible with a full appreciation of the intrinsic superiority of the higher.'[21] Moreover, some people who keenly pursue the higher pleasures early in life may spend all of their time and energy on bodily indulgences late in life. This does not mean that they think of these pleasures as more worth having, however, Mill maintains. Instead, it only shows that they have lost the ability to enjoy the higher pleasures: 'Capacity for the nobler feelings is in most natures a very tender plant, easily killed, not only by hostile influences, but by mere want of sustenance. . . .'[22]

Some people find the higher pleasures doctrine off-putting because they imagine that it entails that the best life for all of us would involve spending our days in the library and our nights at the opera, or some such, seven days a week, and this is not a life that attracts them very much at all. It is important not to have a mistaken impression about the doctrine's practical implications, though. The higher pleasures doctrine does not necessarily entail that the ideal world would be one in which opera and similar sedate and esoteric activities completely took the place of activities like sports. A wide variety of activities could offer people rich opportunities to exercise their higher faculties. Indeed, if it is undertaken in the right way, then almost any activity might make it possible for a person to enjoy a significant quantity of the pleasures of the intellect, the imagination or the moral sentiments. To revert to an earlier example, watching football might generate a considerable amount of intellectual pleasure for someone who has a deep understanding of the sport's underlying strategy and who sees the competition as, in part, a game of chess unfolding on the field. Similarly, although physical sexual pleasure may be the paradigm of lower quality pleasure, deeply emotional lovemaking can simultaneously yield a great deal of higher quality pleasure. Perhaps no one gets as much higher-quality pleasure out of football as aria aficionados do out of opera. Nevertheless, even Mill recognizes that we have a natural need for occasional periods of excitement, alternating with those of tranquillity.[23] There is nothing inconsistent with the higher pleasures doctrine in the idea that we will be happiest if we combine a mix of very different activities in our lives, activities that give rise to the distinctly human pleasures in their own ways and stimulate adrenalin flow to varying degrees.

Yet there may still be something to a related worry, which is that none of the pleasures that Mill describes as being of higher quality would really be shown by the decided preference test to be of higher quality than the 'base' pleasures of eating, sex and so on. The decided preference test seems to say that one of a pair of pleasures is of higher quality than the other if and only if people who have experienced both would *always* rather have an experience of the first than an experience of the second. This rings false, though, even of pairs of pleasures that Mill takes to be paradigmatic of the higher and lower varieties respectively. There are probably very few philosophers who would prefer a life in which they spend lots of time doing philosophy and are celibate to one in which they spend slightly less time doing philosophy and have a healthy sex life.[24] We cannot say that this is only because of the profounder emotions to which lovemaking can give rise, either, because sometimes people just want to copulate, and – if the rumours that one sometimes hears at professional conferences are to be believed – this is no less true of accomplished philosophers than of anyone else. Nor is it merely the case that they are sometimes too intellectually exhausted for philosophy and need a break; how many philosophers would really exchange a healthy sex life that includes moments of purely physical enjoyment for increased intellectual stamina? Or, for that matter, would accept increased intellectual stamina as compensation for forgoing all of the other activities that we occasionally like to indulge in that involve nothing but 'animal' pleasures – 'pigging out' on comfort food that makes no demands on the discriminating palate, say?

Well, you might be tempted to say, Mill would. That is quite possibly true. He did not indulge much in the sensual pleasures in general, and sexual intercourse in particular appears to have held little appeal for either him or Harriet. Bain writes that 'in the so-called sensual feelings', Mill 'was below average' and 'was not a good representative specimen of humanity in respect of these'.[25] Bain adds that although Mill 'was not an ascetic in any sense' and 'desired that every genuine susceptibility to pleasure should be turned to account, so far as it did not interfere with better pleasures', he 'was exceedingly temperate as regarded the table' and 'made light of the difficulty of controlling the sexual appetite'. If the gossip in Mill's own day was that he and Harriet were cuckolding her first husband, today Mill scholars speculate about whether their own marriage was ever consummated.[26] His decidedly negative attitude towards sex is apparent in his characterization of rape as 'the lowest degradation of a human being, that of being made the instrument of an animal function contrary to her inclinations'.[27] His abhorrence of rape comes not just from the fact that it involves having something invasive done to you without your consent, but also that what is being done is of an abjective nature under the best of circumstances. Harriet, for her part, denies that the 'non-exercise of the [sexual functions] is necessarily a deprivation'.[28] But whatever Mill's own opinion, there is no consensus among philosophers that the pleasure of doing philosophy is unconditionally preferable to purely sexual pleasure. If Mill thinks otherwise, then we might have to question whether his limited experience of the bodily pleasures disqualifies *him* as a competent judge. The usual assumption would be that everyone is well acquainted with the bodily pleasures, so that anyone whose faculties are sufficiently well developed to be well acquainted with the distinctly higher ones as well is a competent judge of the difference between them. Yet Mill's rather unusual life might make him a rare exception to this rule.

As it stands, then, Mill's 'official' decided preference test may fail to yield the results that he expects. An interesting and seldom remarked-upon shift in Mill's terms of discussion in chapter 2, though, suggests that he himself might have had some awareness of this problem. At any rate, it points us in the direction of a possible solution. When Mill first introduces the decided preference test, he formulates it in terms of the choices that competent judges would make when they are faced with choices between different pleasures. Shortly thereafter, though, he begins to speak of the choice they face as one between different 'manners' or 'modes' of existence, that is, different types of lives, for example, 'Now it is an unquestionable fact that those who are equally acquainted with, and equally capable of appreciating and enjoying, both do give a most marked preference to the manner of existence which employs their higher faculties.'[29]

When Mill claims that people who have experienced a wide range of pleasures would always rather experience a distinctly human pleasure as opposed to one that we share with the other animals, he is on relatively weak ground. When he claims that such individuals would much rather have a life that is rich in the distinctly human pleasures than a life that is highly pleasurable but that contains only sensual pleasures, though, he puts himself in a stronger position. The latter claim is consistent with the recognition that the competent judges might still prefer a life that contained occasional episodes of purely sensual pleasure over one that involved nothing but distinctly human pleasures. A 'revised' decided preference test that asks competent judges what kind of life they would prefer therefore might get around the problem with Mill's original version of the test. This revised test would still be consistent with his hedonism, so long as the judges' choice is construed as one between different combinations or series of pleasures; this still allows us to say that pleasures are the only bearers of value. It might seem that this revised test would preclude describing particular pleasures, as opposed to modes of existence, as 'higher' or 'lower', but that would not need to be the case. If we presume that people who have experienced a wide range of pleasures would want the distinctly human pleasures to 'set the tone' for their lives, inasmuch as they would only rarely go in for experiences that involved purely sensual pleasure when the distinctly human pleasures might be had instead, then it still makes sense to describe these pleasures as being of an elevated quality.[30]

Genuinely happy lives for all

The 'unofficial' version of the decided preference test towards which Mill gravitates in *Utilitarianism* meshes closely with some things that he says in the *System of Logic*. There he briefly engages with the question of what it means for a person's life to be a happy one. There are two standards by which a person's life could be said to be happy, he suggests. The lower of these is the 'comparatively humble' standard of containing more pleasure than pain. A life could be happy in this sense, Mill writes, and yet still be 'puerile and insignificant'. The higher standard is that of a life's being one 'such as human beings with highly developed faculties can care to have', which could clearly only be true of a life that involves a considerable amount of higher quality pleasure.[31] Although the phrase is not Mill's, we could describe lives that are happy in this higher sense as being 'genuinely happy'. Here things are not so cut and dried, for how close a life comes to the ideal is a matter of degree. A significant amount of grey area will be ineliminable. Nonetheless, some lives will clearly deserve to be called happy in this sense, and many more clearly will not.

Indeed, Mill relates that the lives of his contemporaries are 'almost universally' unhappy when judged by this higher standard, and this is a result of the fact that the vast majority of people in every socio-economic class have failed to develop any of their distinctly human faculties to any significant degree. It is hardly surprising that this would be true of the working class, whose members often did not enjoy much even in the way of lower pleasures. Many of the labourers would have not even have had the equivalent of a primary school education before plunging into a working life that was a regime of drudgery and poverty. (The Factory Act of 1833 dictated that children working in English factories must receive two hours of schooling per day. An attempt in 1843 to limit the working hours of children so that they would have half of each day free for schooling failed.[32]) Mill does not consider the bulk of the supposedly well-educated members of the middle and upper classes to be models of development either, however. This is largely due to an over-reliance on rote memorization in their schooling, which contributes little to the cultivation of the intellectual faculty and nothing to that of the aesthetic or moral faculties.[33] Genuine happiness requires that all of the faculties be developed to some non-trivial degree. Mill could hardly think otherwise, given that his own life was so miserably unhappy during his mental crisis despite his prodigally developed intellect.

Mill might very easily have claimed that the existence of roughly the state of affairs that he observes in Victorian Britain, one in which the distinctly human faculties of the vast majority of people are insufficiently developed for them to enjoy genuinely happy lives, is a permanent fact of human society. In this case, given his qualitative hedonism, we might well expect him to propose that societies ought to be organized around the small number of elites in every generation whose faculties could be developed highly enough for them to enjoy significant amounts of the best and most valuable sorts of happiness. Under this scheme, our most important task would be to ensure that those precious few with the ability to enjoy lives rich in the higher quality pleasures did in fact do so. Even if this imposed considerable hardship on everyone else, or at least denied them many opportunities for enjoyment, it would be the optimific course of action. This is hardly an appealing state of affairs. In fact, some critics of utilitarianism object to the theory precisely because there might always be a few individuals capable of far more happiness than everyone else, with the consequence that happiness could best be promoted through institutions and practices that conflict with our intuitions about fairness. The critics' vivid name for these individuals is 'utility monsters'.[34]

Mill might have offered such a view, but he does not. What he says, instead, is that what can and should be done is to make it possible for virtually everyone to lead a genuinely happy life. He does this in the stretch of *Utilitarianism*'s second chapter that immediately follows his account of the higher quality pleasures. Mill begins by adding substance to the idea that lack of development is the main reason that people fail to lead satisfying lives. He points first to the failure to cultivate the moral faculty – the capacity for sympathy – and then to the failure to develop the intellectual and aesthetic faculties:

> When people who are tolerably fortunate in their outward lot do not find in life sufficient enjoyment to make it valuable to them, the cause generally is, caring for nobody but themselves.... Next to selfishness, the principal cause which makes life unsatisfactory is want of mental cultivation. A cultivated mind ... finds sources of inexhaustible interest in all that surrounds it; in the objects of nature, the achievements of art, the imaginations of poetry, the incidents of history, the ways of mankind, past and present, and their prospects in the future.

He then asserts that this situation is remediable:

> Now there is absolutely no reason in the nature of things why an amount of mental culture sufficient to give an intelligent interest in these objects of contemplation, should not be the inheritance of every one born in a civilised country. As little is there an inherent necessity that any human being should be a selfish egotist. .... Genuine private affections and a sincere interest in the public good are possible, though in unequal degrees, to every rightly brought up human being. In a world in which there is so much to interest, so much to enjoy, and so much also to correct and improve, every one who has this moderate amount of moral and intellectual requisites is capable of an existence which may be called enviable. . . .[35]

There are two things that we should take away from this second passage. The first is that Mill believes that even someone whose faculties cannot be cultivated to the levels that might be attained by those individuals with the greatest natural gifts could still reach a level of development sufficient for a genuinely happy life. You do not need to be Socrates, or even to have been born with the potential to become Socrates, in order to have 'an existence which may be called enviable', an expression that it seems fair to gloss as equivalent to what we have been calling a genuinely happy life. The second is that it should be more than possible to bring nearly everyone to at least this level of development.

One of the primary aims of Mill's programme of social and political reform, the subject of Part III of this study, is the widest possible extension of the opportunity to develop the distinctly human faculties. Another aim, about which more will be said in chapter 6, is to ensure that every member of society enjoys 'security', a term that he uses in a rather broad sense. The cultivation of your faculties and a sense of security are, as Mill sees it, the two main requisites of a genuinely happy life. An individual whose intellectual, aesthetic and moral faculties have all been well developed and who enjoys a sense of security should have excellent prospects for leading a genuinely happy life. Even if there are points in an individual's life when opportunities to employ these faculties are hard to come by, so that the quantity of the higher pleasures that he or she is able to enjoy is quite low, there will still be the aesthetic pleasure derived from the sense of dignity and (presumably) from the consciousness of that individual's own virtue. Mill believes that it ought to be possible for a society to provide all of its members endowed with normal human abilities and capacities a very good chance of enjoying genuine happiness. One caveat that needs to be inserted here is that he does not suppose that the extension of opportunities for development that this would entail can be achieved quickly. He expects that it would take many generations, for 'the future generation is educated by the present, and the imperfections of the teachers set an invincible limit to the degree in which they can train their pupils to be better than themselves.'[36] There would necessarily be a long, slow, reciprocating process, in which social and political reforms are made, people's attitudes change a little as a result, these changes facilitate further reforms and so on. Skorupski aptly describes this process as 'a virtuous spiral of interactions between improving states of society and improving states of characters'.[37]

The only thing that might prevent a person who possesses highly developed faculties and security from enjoying genuine happiness would be purely personal misfortune that causes crushing amounts of pain. Mill is not such a pie-in-the-sky optimist that he believes real suffering can ever entirely be eliminated from human life. Some people will always have to endure it, as a result of bad luck. Yet he is certain that if the moral and intellectual progress that he believes that he observes taking place continues, it should eventually prove possible to reduce 'the positive evils of life, the great sources of physical and mental suffering – such as indigence, disease, and the unkindness, worthlessness, or premature loss of objects of affection'.[38] (Mill's reference to the premature loss of loved ones here is poignant, given that he was writing shortly after the death of Harriet.) The distinction that Mill draws in *Utilitarianism* between happiness and contentment is useful here. Contentment is at least roughly a function of how much happiness you enjoy relative to your capacity for it. It takes far more, therefore, to render highly developed beings content, and Mill is not necessarily committing himself to the idea that a society full of highly developed people who are entirely content with life is possible. He is only saying that they ought to be able to enjoy ample happiness, measured in absolute terms.[39]

Making it possible for every member of a society to develop their human capabilities sufficiently to enjoy a genuinely happy life is going to require making it possible for them to have a thoroughgoing, lifelong educational experience. Later chapters will have much to say about what this involves for adults, but to avoid calling to mind the spectre of Maoist re-education camps, maybe it is worth saying now that this will largely be a matter of providing them with opportunities for self-education that they can be encouraged but not required to take.

Education begins in childhood, however, and Mill – the product of a unique educational experiment – has things to say about the form it should take. To his credit, he does not engage in false modesty by saying that James Mill's methods would have succeeded with anyone as well as they did with him, but he takes his case to prove a general point 'about how much more than is commonly supposed may be taught, and well taught, in those early years which, in the common modes of what is called instruction, are little better than wasted'.[40] He would require all parents to see to it that their children are educated, boys and girls alike. Public funding must be available to subsidize this expense for poorer families, but preferably this will be done without the state itself operating many (if any) schools.[41] (The state's role in education will be discussed briefly in chapter 8 on Mill's political economy.) Qualitative changes in formal education are needed as well, Mill contends. Emphasis needs to shift instead towards methods that require students to exercise faculties other than the memory: 'As the memory is trained by remembering, so is the reasoning power by reasoning; the imaginative by imagining; the analytic by analysing; the inventive by finding out. Let the education of the mind consist in calling out and exercising these faculties. . . . Let *cram* be ruthlessly discarded.'[42]

5

Utilitarianism: The 'Happiness Morality'

This chapter offers an overview of utilitarianism, which Mill well describes as the 'happiness morality'.[1] It pays special attention to the differences between two specific versions of utilitarianism, act utilitarianism and rule utilitarianism. These two forms of utilitarianism will figure importantly in the next chapter.

What is utilitarianism?

In his own excellent Mill book, Roger Crisp defines a moral theory as 'a systematic account of what makes actions right or wrong'.[2] Utilitarianism is often described as a moral theory, but because there are many versions of utilitarianism it might be more accurate to call it a family of moral theories or a general approach to moral theorizing. But what is this approach? William H. Shaw observes that 'Two fundamental ideas underlie utilitarianism: first, that the results of our actions are the key to moral evaluation, and second, that one should assess and compare those results in terms of the happiness they cause (or, more broadly, in terms of their impact on people's well-being).'[3]

The first of these two tenets, the proposition that the moral standing of actions depends on their consequences or results, is known as consequentialism. Thus utilitarian theories belong to the broader family of consequentialist moral theories. For the consequentialist, assessing the results of people's actions involves judging the extent to which these actions 'promote the good'. Something is said to have intrinsic value or be intrinsically good if it is desirable or valuable for its own sake, and not only because of what it leads to or can be used to get or do. How well an action promotes the good depends upon how much of whatever has intrinsic value would exist were that action to be performed. It also depends upon how much the world would contain of those intrinsically bad things that are *undesirable* for their own sakes. How these things with intrinsic value and disvalue are distributed may also be a factor.

While consequentialists agree about this, they disagree about what things have intrinsic value. Shaw's second tenet gives the utilitarian answer to this question which, as we have already seen, is that only well-being or happiness has intrinsic value.

There is a third fundamental tenet underlying utilitarianism. This is the idea that everyone's happiness must always be taken into account when assessing the consequences of actions and that this must be done impartially, with equal importance being attached to the interests of each individual. This is what separates utilitarianism from 'ethical egoism'. The idea of 'equal importance' can be interpreted in different ways, but most utilitarians construe it in a relatively strong sense, according to which equal amounts of well-being or happiness are equally valuable regardless of who enjoys them. Usually, if not invariably, they evaluate the results of actions based on the total or aggregate amount of happiness that will be enjoyed if they are performed, or rather the total amount of what Shaw calls 'net happiness' – total happiness minus total unhappiness.[4] The more net happiness that would be enjoyed if a particular action were to be performed, the better the results of that action are. So if you imagine a list of all of the different things that a given person might do at a given time, in descending order of how much net happiness they will yield in the long run (with all of the different people that each action would affect being taken into account), then according to most utilitarians the action with the best result would be the one at the very top of the list.[5] Notice that this might not be the action that makes the most people happy. People sometimes take utilitarianism to say that the best thing to do is whatever would yield happiness for the maximum number of people, but this is a misinterpretation. The potential for confusion on this point is heightened by some early utilitarians' use of the slogan 'the greatest happiness of the greatest number', as when Bentham referred to the 'fundamental axiom' that 'it is the greatest happiness of the greatest number that is the measure of right and wrong.'[6] This motto made sense in a historical context in which utilitarianism was important primarily as the intellectual underpinning of philosophical radical-ism, aimed as it was at removing the special privileges of the upper classes and thereby benefiting the much larger working class. Nevertheless, it is more accurate to say that what matters for utili-tarians is the 'greatest happiness, which will often but not always be the happiness of the greatest number'.

A more general point can be made here. Utilitarians who contend that only the total amount of net happiness that is enjoyed is rele-vant to the evaluation of states of affairs do not attach any signifi-cance to how happiness or unhappiness is distributed. They do not, for example, consider a world in which everyone enjoys an equal but moderate level of positive happiness superior to one in which some people are very happy and a few are miserable, if the total amounts of net happiness in the two worlds are the same. So utili-tarians will generally maintain that, of all the things a person can do at a given point in time, the action with the best outcome is the one that will maximize total net happiness.

Act utilitarianism

Some utilitarians will also say something more, which is that it would be morally right for the person to perform this action and that to do anything else would be morally wrong. This moral theory, known as act utilitarianism, is the most straightforward version of utilitarianism. It holds, in other words, that an action is morally right if and only if there is no other action that the agent could perform instead that would yield more total net hap-piness, and otherwise it is wrong. ('Agent' here means moral agent, someone whose acts can be morally evaluated.) Whether an action is right therefore depends not only on its own consequences but also on those of all of the other actions available to the agent, that is, everything else that he or she could do instead. J. J. C. Smart and R. M. Hare are among act utilitarianism's best-known recent defenders.[7]

One of several standard criticisms of act utilitarianism is the 'epistemic objection', which says that mere humans could seldom, if ever, know which of the actions that they could do at a given time would maximize happiness. For the act utilitarian, everything that will happen in the future if an action is performed – the entire future of the universe from that point in time forward – is counted among its consequences. Neither how far in the future the event is nor whether the agent could predict it matters. Whether the action would have had a different upshot if some other agents had acted differently does not matter either. Taking these points together, it follows, for example, that all of Hitler's ancestors performed acts whose consequences include the Holocaust. Since act utilitarianism says that we are obligated to produce the best outcomes possible, events that will happen no matter what the agent does – events that the agent cannot prevent – have no bearing on what it would be right or wrong for him or her to do. But any experience of happiness or unhappiness that will ever result if the agent does one thing rather than another could make a difference to which action it is right for the agent to perform.

A standard act-utilitarian reply to this objection is that it does not follow from the fact that the right action is one that maximizes happiness that agents should always decide what to do by trying to calculate how much happiness would result from each of the different courses of action open to them. Sophisticated act utilitarians say that agents should usually follow a very different 'decision procedure'. These alternative decision procedures normally involve a set of 'summary rules' or 'rules of thumb' that direct agents to perform types of actions that usually have good consequences and avoid types of actions that usually have bad ones. Whatever rules it is proposed that agents should follow must be simple and few enough in number for ordinary people to learn, and they must be rules that can be properly applied with the amount of information that people usually have available to them when they must act. The better formulated these rules, the better the behaviour of the people who follow them will be when judged from the act-utilitarian perspective, although no set of usable rules of thumb could do more than to keep us from producing outcomes that are too sub-optimal too often. Act utilitarians simply have to accept that we will often be unable to know what it would be right to do, according to their theory, or even whether actions performed in the past were right. Admittedly, though, it may be fair for them to ask why we should take for granted that we should always or even usually be able to know this.[8]

Another move that some act utilitarians make in order to meet the epistemic objection is to 'subjectivize' the theory. Typically there will be multiple different sets of consequences that *might* issue from an action, as far as the agent could know at the time – different ways in which the future might unfold. How the future will turn out may depend on how other people will act, which the agent cannot predict with certainty, or on other facts that the agent cannot know. Think of taking the amount of total net happiness that would be enjoyed in one of these possible outcomes and multiplying this by the probability – relative to the information available to the agent at the time – that this outcome will occur. Now think of doing the same for all of the other possible outcomes the action might have and adding up the results. The result would be the 'expected value' (or 'expected utility') of the action. 'Subjective' or 'expected consequence' act utilitarianism says that at every opportunity we have to act we are required to perform the action with the highest expected value.[9] By following an appropriate set of summary rules, people might be able to comply with subjective act utilitarianism in most situations.

Critics of act utilitarianism also frequently point out that its implications can be sharply at odds with our 'considered moral judgements', that is, the convictions that we have about what it would be right for people to do in particular situations after we have reflected on all of the relevant information. Sometimes this objection takes the form of the claim that the theory can require actions that we can see to be wrong. Illustrations of this claim often involve cases in which the happiness-maximizing or optimific action would violate widely recognized human rights, such as killing innocent people so that their organs can be used to keep 'more valuable' individuals – ones who produce, or at least enjoy, more happiness – alive. Act utilitarianism seems to be inherently incompatible with the existence of rights, because rights that must be overridden whenever doing so would result in an outcome that is even slightly better are no rights at all, a notion that Ronald Dworkin captures with his description of rights as 'trumps' over the pursuit of collective goals.[10] A sophisticated act utilitarian can recommend that we act 'as if' people have rights, as part of our decision procedure but, when so acting results in our failing to maximize net happiness, then an act utilitarian will still have to say that we acted wrongly. The objection that act utilitarianism conflicts with our considered moral judgements can also take the form of the claim that act utilitarianism demands extreme personal sacrifice from individuals in the name of humanitarian causes such as famine relief.[11]

Act utilitarians have various ways of responding to this objection. One is to point out that many of the scenarios in which their theory has implications that are at odds with widely shared considered moral judgements are so unrealistic that it is highly unlikely they would ever actually arise. Realistically speaking, for example, it is hard to imagine that killing people to harvest their organs would be happiness maximizing. How could a medical team manage this without its becoming public and causing a panic? Another response, which is applicable even if there are more realistic cases in which the theory entails that we are obligated to do something contrary to our convictions, is to question why we should ever trust our pre-theoretical considered moral judgements more than a theory for which a compelling intellectual case can be made. As Smart writes, if the results of act utilitarianism 'conflict with common-sense ethics', then '[s]o much the worse for common-sense ethics!'[12]

Rule utilitarianism

Whereas act utilitarianism applies the criterion of happiness maximization directly to individual actions, rule utilitarianism applies it to moral codes, that is, sets of moral rules. Whether actions are right or wrong depends upon whether they are permitted or forbidden by the moral code that is 'best' from a utilitarian standpoint. As a starting point, at least, rule utilitarianism can be characterized in terms of the following two tenets:

1   Whether an action is right or wrong depends upon whether the 'authoritative' set of moral rules would permit or forbid actions of that general kind; and
2   The authoritative set of moral rules is the one whose general acceptance would yield more total net happiness than the general acceptance of any other set.

These two tenets define what is sometimes called 'ideal-code' rule utilitarianism. As it is usually understood, it says that one moral code is binding on everyone, or at least upon all members of a specified group (like the members of a particular society). This is the code that it would be optimific for them to accept, with all other facts about them – or at least all facts that do not depend upon what moral code they accept – being assumed to remain the same. Crucially, the rule utilitarian's authoritative moral rules are 'true' moral rules in a sense in which the act utilitarian's summary rules are not: that an action violates the authoritative rules is a necessary and sufficient condition for its being wrong.

The notion of the general acceptance of a set of moral rules is vague, and there are different ways of sharpening it. One obvious possibility is to say that rules are generally accepted if and only if everyone obeys them, but David Lyons has famously demonstrated that if rule utilitarians go this route then their theory will agree perfectly with act utilitarianism about which actions are right and which wrong.[13] Lyons argues that the moral code that would produce the best results for people to comply with is one with a specific moral rule for every possible situation that agents might face, a rule that says to do the utility-maximizing action. This would mean that the theories reached the same answer about the moral standing of every action. The same does not hold true, however, if the notion of acceptance is cashed out in terms of 'internalization', where internalizing a set of rules means having a psychological disposition to try to obey them or to feel guilty about violating them. Since human psychology puts some limits on the size and complexity of the moral codes that we can internalize, this way of understanding the theory entails that the authoritative set of rules cannot include specific rules for every conceivable situation that a person might ever encounter. If rule utilitarianism is not 'extensionally equivalent' to act utilitarianism, then there must be some cases in which rule utilitarianism holds that we are not obligated to maximize happiness. In fact, most rule utilitarians would probably agree that their theory sometimes entails that an optimific action would be morally wrong. This leaves the question of what the 'general' in 'general acceptance' means. It may make a difference, for instance, whether we define the authoritative code as the one that it would be optimal for everyone to internalize or the one that it would be optimal for, say, 90 per cent of the people to internalize.[14]

The leading objections to act utilitarianism appear to have much less force against rule utilitarianism, if they apply at all. Figuring out what rule utilitarianism requires from us should not prove as difficult. We might never be able to determine the precise content of the authoritative rules, which may in any case change over time as the world changes, but making a good approximation should not be beyond us. Working out the different outcomes that actions of a given kind will produce, and with what probabilities, may be difficult, but it is a much more tractable problem than working out the consequences of particular actions. It is akin to, albeit not precisely the same as, the problem the act utilitarian faces in formulating act-utilitarian summary rules. Also, rule utilitarianism can be subjectivized; the rule utilitarian could say that the authoritative moral rules are the ones whose general acceptance a reasonable and well-informed person would take to have the best consequences.

Second, the content of rule utilitarianism's authoritative rules would likely be much closer to our ordinary morality than is act utilitarianism's simple requirement to maximize happiness. There is no fundamental tension between rule utilitarianism and moral rights. Take for instance so-called 'negative rights', rights not to be treated in particular ways. The claim that people have a right not to be Φed (killed, censored and so on) in particular circumstances can be 'reduced' to the claim that we are bound by one or more moral rules – at minimum, a rule that forbids Φing in the circumstances in question. To the extent that the authoritative set of rules contains rules like these, people could be said to have negative rights. The presence of certain other sorts of rules in the authoritative code would justify the ascription of other species of rights. In fact, a strong case can probably be made for the claim that rule utilitarianism's authoritative moral code will contain the rules that correspond to most widely recognized human rights. Rule utilitarianism is also likely to demand less sacrifice from us in the name of solving large-scale problems like famines. Starvation, after all, could likely be eliminated if everyone able to makes a modest contribution towards this goal without doing real harm to themselves or their families. So the best moral rule for everyone to accept might be one that required some modest donation by everyone able to make one.

A different objection is often raised against rule utilitarianism, however, especially by act utilitarians. This is that rule utilitarianism is 'incoherent', since no one whose fundamental commitment is to utilitarianism ought to believe that it could ever be wrong to do something that maximizes happiness. More succinctly, the objection is that rule utilitarians are guilty of 'rule worship'. As Smart argues, 'the rule-utilitarian presumably advocates his principle because he cares about human happiness; why then should he advocate abiding by a rule when he knows it will not in the present case be most beneficial to abide by it?'[15] This objection does not point to a problem with rule utilitarianism's account of right and wrong per se; rather, it says that there is a tension between this account and the kinds of arguments that could be given for the view, all of which (it is supposed) must be premised on the claim that we are rationally required to maximize happiness.

6

Mill's Theory of Right and Wrong

This chapter considers the question of what version of utilitarianism Mill holds. While Mill never addresses the question of precisely what makes actions right or wrong directly, which means that interpreters are relegated to unearthing a moral theory that lies implicit in his writings, and while different passages in *Utilitarianism* and other works seem to lend support to different readings, the chapter argues that on the whole the best interpretation is one that depicts Mill as holding a sophisticated rule-utilitarian view.

The art of life

We are finally ready to examine Mill's own moral theory, although there is one last preliminary matter we must consider before we turn directly to his views on morality proper. This is the 'Art of Life', a notion of which he offers an all-too-brief sketch in the final book of his *System of Logic*. Here he discusses the logic of prescriptive arts, as opposed to that of descriptive sciences. All arts, according to Mill, have an axiological first principle which affirms that the end at which the art aims is valuable. Further first principles, which pertain to how the art's end might be realized, are drawn from science. These first principles jointly serve as a foundation for the main body of the art, a set of 'rules or precepts' that direct us to act in ways that will usually result in the realization of the art's end. The axiological first principle of the art of building, for instance, is that buildings are desirable. Its other first principles might include principles drawn from the material sciences, elementary physics and so on. The main body of the art of building comprises precepts that instruct us to do all of the things that must normally be done in order to produce sound inhabitable structures.[1]

In addition to the various particular arts, Mill tells us, there must be an overarching 'master' art, and this is the Art of Life. This master art serves as Mill's theory of practical reason. Its business is to tell us which of the different particular arts we should be pursuing at a given time. According to Mill, the axiological first principle of the Art of Life is none other than the principle of utility: '[T]he general principle to which all rules of practice ought to conform, and the test by which they should be tried, is conduciveness to the happiness of mankind, or rather, of all sentient beings: in other words, that the promotion of happiness is the ultimate principle of Teleology.'[2]

Happiness is thus the 'justification' and 'controller' of all other ends. But while the promotion of any other end is only desirable insofar as it contributes to the promotion of happiness, this contribution may be an indirect one. The *Logic* makes clear how much importance Mill attaches to the indirect promotion of happiness. He claims there that 'the cultivation of an ideal nobleness of will and conduct should be to individual human beings an end, to which the specific pursuit either of their own happiness or of that of others . . . should . . . give way.' He adds, though, that 'the very question, what constitutes this elevation of character, is itself to be decided by a reference to happiness as the standard.'[3] In directly aiming at developing their characters, therefore, people should still be indirectly aiming at promoting happiness; they should be seeking to develop the traits that it is best for them to have, from the standpoint of the long-term promotion of happiness. (As we saw in chapter 3, Mill has settled on a slightly different formula by the time he comes to write *Utilitarianism*, in which he says not that people should make the perfection of their characters or the acquisition of the virtues *paramount to* their happiness, but that they should make it *part of* their happiness. This reformulation does not alter the substance of his point in the *Logic*, though, which is that the consequences of an action that are mediated by the action's effects on the agent's character can be quite significant from the utilitarian perspective.)

While the Art of Life has a single axiological principle, Mill makes the puzzling and surprising claim that the Art is divided into three 'departments' of 'Morality, Prudence or Policy, and

Aesthetics; the Right, the Expedient, and the Beautiful or Noble, in human conduct and works'.[4] If these departments really are to be distinct, then different sets of rules must correspond to them. Moreover, different categories of reasons must correspond to these rules. That an action is required by the rules of prudence is a prudential reason to do it, for instance, that it is required by the rules of morality is a moral reason and so on. After asserting that practical reason is trifurcated, however, Mill leaves the point almost entirely undeveloped. He essentially says nothing in the *Logic* about what distinguishes the different departments of the Art of Life. What marks a rule as a rule of morality, for instance, as opposed to one of prudence? He does not address the relations between the departments of the Art of Life, either. Is it possible for our prudential reasons to favour one alternative on balance and our moral ones another, for example, and if so, what determines what it is most rational for us to do on balance? He does not say. He does not even tell us specifically what he means by 'prudence', in the *Logic*.[5] The answers to these questions have to be found elsewhere in his body of work.

We are not yet in a position to consider Mill's answer to the question of what makes a rule part of the department of Morality, but we can say something now about his understanding of prudence or expediency. We commonly understand acting prudently to mean acting in your own best interest. The notion of acting prudently or expediently can also be understood impartially, though, so that it means producing the best result *tout court*. Mill's definition of 'prudence', as 'a correct foresight of consequences, a just estimation of their importance to the object in view, and repression of any unreflecting impulse at variance with the deliberate purpose', is neutral between these 'partialist' and 'impartialist' meanings.[6] Although he does sometimes refer to a 'prudential regard to self-interest', in *Utilitarianism*, where his subject matter is very close to that of the final chapter of the *Logic*, Mill says that it is only in the lowest popular sense of 'expediency' that the expedient means nothing more than 'that which is expedient for the particular interest of the agent himself'.[7] On balance, therefore, it is most probable that his uses of 'expediency' and 'prudence' in his account of the Art of Life are intended to be understood in impartialist terms, which would mean that he has something resembling an 'act-utilitarian' theory of prudence.

We can also say something now about the relative priorities that Mill assigns to moral and other sorts of reasons. 'Moral rationalism' is one name for the view that if we have a moral obligation to do something – if it would be wrong for us not to do it, in other words – then we automatically have a reason to do it. 'Strong' moral rationalism, then, might be used as a label for the idea that if we have a moral obligation to do something then we have a reason to do it that outweighs or 'trumps' any other sorts of reasons that we might have not to do it. Mill's emphatic identification of 'the right' with that which we must do 'at whatever cost' is a clear endorsement of strong moral rationalism.[8] Further support for reading Mill as a strong moral rationalist comes from 'Bentham' and *Utilitarianism*; in both works, Mill acknowledges that there are perspectives other than that of morality from which actions can be evaluated but affirms the primacy of the moral perspective.[9] So if an agent has a reason derived from the department of Morality to choose one course of action and a reason derived from that of Prudence (or Aesthetics) to choose another, in Mill's view he or she is on balance rationally required to choose the former.

Interpreters interested in what sort of utilitarian Mill is have looked to his treatment of the Art of Life for clues. And there are clues to be found here, although they do not all point in the same direction. Commentators who read him as an act utilitarian call attention to his claim that the rules of each art must be constructed 'for the most numerous cases, or for those of most ordinary occurrence' in order to keep the art from becoming too cumbersome. This view leads him to give an account of the role of practical rules that seems to suggest that they can never serve as more than 'provisional' rules of thumb or summary rules:

> [Rules of conduct] point out the manner in which it will be least perilous to act, where time or means do not exist for analyzing the actual circumstances of the case, or where we cannot trust our judgment in estimating them. But they do not at all supersede the propriety of going through (when circumstances permit) the scientific process requisite for framing a rule from the data of the particular case before us.[10]

Those who favour the rule-utilitarian reading, on the other hand, can point to the divisions Mill draws within the Art of Life. What support does this offer to the claim that he is a rule utilitarian? First, if Mill is indeed using 'prudence' in its impartialist sense when he describes the Art of Life, and if he understands the department of Morality along act-utilitarian lines, then it seems that he must take the rules of these two departments to be quite similar, if not identical. In that case, though, why would he distinguish them? Second, the very division of practical reason into departments may constitute an obstacle to reading Mill as an act utilitarian. Act utilitarianism tells us that there is typically just one thing that it is right for us to do at any given moment, with exceptions arising only when two or more actions might yield equal amounts of total net happiness and more than any of the agent's other alternatives. If Mill thinks of morality in this way, then – given his strong moral rationalism – the department of Morality would swell to the point where there is hardly any room within the Art of Life for the other two. Prudential or aesthetic reasons would make almost no difference to what we have the most reason to do, all things considered. In contrast, rule utilitarianism will presumably say that in most situations there are multiple actions that are entirely acceptable from the moral standpoint so, even on the assumption of strong moral rationalism, we will normally need to consider types of reasons other than our moral reasons to know what we have the most reason to do.

Some further evidence for the act-utilitarian reading

At last we can turn directly to Mill's writings on morality. While his utility principle is not a moral principle, he takes it to have direct implications for morality because he takes the truth of consequentialism for granted: "That the morality of actions depends on the consequences which they tend to produce, is the doctrine of rational persons of all schools; that the good or evil of those consequences is measured solely by pleasure or pain, is all of the doctrine of the school of utility, which is peculiar to it."[11] Mill's utility principle, understood as he understands it, incorporates both welfarism and impartiality – the latter, recall, because he takes the claim that 'equal amounts of happiness are equally desirable, whether felt by the same or by different persons' to be 'the very principle itself'.[12] Given this, consequentialism and the utility principle together entail the truth of utilitarianism.

One indisputable fact about Mill's utilitarianism is that he recognizes the need for moral rules that are distinct from any general requirement to maximize happiness. These are moral rules that refer to 'ordinary' types of action such as lying, voting, fighting and so on, and tell us that we are required to perform actions of these types in some circumstances and to refrain from them in others. We see this clearly, for instance, in *Utilitarianism*:

> But to consider the rules of morality as improvable, is one thing; to pass over the intermediate generalisations entirely, and endeavour to test each individual action directly by the first principle, is another. . . . The proposition that happiness is the end and aim of morality, does not mean that no road ought to be laid down to that goal, or that persons going thither should not be advised to take one direction rather than another. . . . Whatever we adopt as the fundamental principle of morality, we require subordinate principles to apply it by. . . .[13]

That Mill attaches this sort of significance to 'subordinate' moral rules does not by itself let us brand him a rule utilitarian, though; we have already seen that sophisticated act utilitarians also regard such rules as important – albeit only as aids to choosing morally correct actions rather than as the ultimate criteria by which the moral standing of actions is to be judged. Someone who starts with the assumption that Mill is an act utilitarian could read the passage as an explanation of why act utilitarians should recommend that agents employ sets of subordinate rules to guide their decision making, and a very cogent one at that.

The passage, though, stops well short of an explicit endorsement of act utilitarianism. There are two further passages that, together with the 'data of the particular case' passage from the *Logic* that was quoted in the prior section, are sometimes regarded as offering such an endorsement. The first is his famous assertion, previously quoted in chapter 4, that the utilitarian creed 'holds that actions are right in proportion as they tend to promote happiness, wrong as they tend to produce the reverse of happiness'. The second appears in a letter to the logician John Venn. Here Mill agrees with Venn that 'the right way of testing actions by their consequences, is to test them by the natural consequences of the particular action, and not by those which would follow if every one did the same.'[14] Brown finds this letter to constitute such 'direct and unequivocal' evidence of Mill's act utilitarianism that he considers it reasonable to hope that it will close 'the whole controversy'.[15]

While they are suggestive, there is still room to quibble about whether either of these new passages really amounts to an explicit endorsement of act utilitarianism. The first refers to the results that actions 'tend' to have, and it is not immediately clear what 'tend' means here. The first passage's use of the phrase 'in proportion' is also difficult to make sense of if we assume that Mill is an act utilitarian, since for the act utilitarian, any action that is not right in the fullest sense is wrong – and therefore no action can be 'even more right' than another. Even if we concede that these passages constitute *some* evidence for reading Mill as an act utilitarian, we are still left with the worries raised previously about whether this is consistent with his trifurcation of the Art of Life, so we still have some reason to be dissatisfied with how well the act-utilitarian reading fits the passages that we have considered thus far. And a number of other pertinent passages remain to be introduced. So we should suspend judgement for the moment.

Morality and punishment

This section and the next will make a case for reading Mill as a rule rather than an act utilitarian. Generally speaking, this case follows lines initially laid down by John Gray, David Copp and (especially) David Lyons – the fact that none of these writers describes Mill as a rule utilitarian notwithstanding.[16] Its starting point is the conceptual connection that Mill perceives between morality and the appropriateness of punishment. In a stretch of text in the final chapter of *Utilitarianism*, Mill offers what can be read as an analysis of the concept of morally wrong action, that is, an account of its content that distinguishes it from other related concepts:

> We do not call anything wrong, unless we mean to imply that a person ought to be punished in some way or other for doing it; if not by law, by the opinion of his fellow-creatures; if not by opinion, by the reproaches of his own conscience. This seems the real turning point of the distinction between morality and simple expediency.[17]

If we read this passage as an attempt to explicate the concept of moral wrongness, the most literal way to construe it is to take Mill to say that actions are morally wrong just if it is appropriate or desirable for them to be punished in any way. Yet Lyons takes Mill to mean something more specific, namely that an action is morally wrong just if it is desirable or appropriate for agents who perform actions of that kind to feel guilt. In other words, Lyons thinks that it is the appropriateness of one particular kind of punishment – that meted out by the conscience, the internal sanction – that Mill takes to be constitutive of immorality or moral wrongness: 'Mill seems to be saying that wrong acts are those for which guilt feelings are appropriate. . . . When the stakes are high and additional grounds can accordingly be given, social measures may be justified, such as public condemnation and legal punishments. But these are added on, as the case demands.'[18]

Lyons takes 'Mill to claim that wrongness is conceptually connected with justified guilt feelings, whereas it is only *synthetically* connected with external sanctions.'[19] Lyons acknowledges that in some cases we might think that a person should suffer social punishments, especially legal ones, for something that he or she has done, but yet not believe that it would be appropriate for that person to experience guilt. In these cases, he asserts, Mill would in fact not hold that we should describe the action in question as morally wrong.[20]

Lyons's reading is tempting because there does seem to be a close conceptual connection between moral wrongness and the appropriateness of guilt. The analysis of morally wrong action that he attributes to Mill seems to have great potential, if not as an account of what people are consciously saying when they describe actions as morally wrong, then as a revisionary account that assigns definite meaning to a familiar expression that at present lacks one and that does so in a way that is consistent with ordinary moral discourse. (Think, for example, of how natural it is to meet the suggestion that one has acted wrongly with the protest that one has nothing to feel guilty about.) Still, it is worrisome that while Mill lists the 'reproaches of . . . conscience' as one type of punishment in *Utilitarianism*, he does not single it out there as having any especially close connection to the notion of moral wrongness. Another possible problem for this reading is that in *Utilitarianism* Mill is not as clear as he might be that he means to offer any sort of analysis of wrongness; Alastair Norcross has recently questioned whether this passage is really meant to do any more than to point out 'some features of the ordinary usage of the term "wrong."'[21]

However, a letter of Mill's from 1859 goes a considerable distance towards addressing these concerns:

> Now as to the still more important subject of the meaning of *ought*. . . . I believe that the word has in some respects a different meaning to different people. We must first distinguish between those who have themselves a moral feeling – a feeling of approving & condemning conscience, & those who have not, or in whom what they may have is dormant. I believe that those who have no *feeling* of right & wrong cannot possibly *intue* the rightness or wrongness of anything. They may assent to the proposition that a certain rule of conduct is right; but they really mean nothing except that such is the conduct which other people expect & require at their

hands. . . . This you will probably agree with, & I will therefore pass to the case of those who have a true moral feeling, that is, a feeling of pain in the fact of violating a certain rule, quite independently of any expected consequences to themselves. It appears to me that to them the word *ought* means, that if they act otherwise, they shall be punished by this internal, & perfectly disinterested feeling.[22]

Lyons does not cite this letter, but his interpretation is far more plausible in light of it. Here there can be no question that Mill is trying to give an analysis of a concept or of the meaning of a term. While he speaks of the meaning of 'ought', rather than that of 'morally wrong', in context it is clear that the 'ought' in question is that of moral obligation. The analysis is framed specifically in terms of guilt. It does refer to the circumstances in which the speaker *would* experience guilt rather than those in which she thinks that it *should be* experienced, so in this respect it differs from the analysis that he seems to be gesturing towards in *Utilitarianism*. Since the letter establishes that Mill was thinking about analysing the notion of wrongness in terms of guilt at the time that he was writing *Utilitarianism*, however, it is reasonable for us to read the essay along these lines and to take it to contain a refined version of this type of analysis. Mill is aware that it is possible for us to step back from our actual dispositions to experience the feeling of duty and reflect upon whether we are experiencing it when, and only when, we should. This, after all, is what is at issue between him and the moral intuitionists.[23] His account in *Utilitarianism* of what it means to call an action wrong is what you get when you start with the comparatively simple analysis in the letter to Ward and then add the recognition that it would be queer to call an action wrong if on reflection you did not believe that a person *should* feel guilty for doing it, even if you also believed that you would, or to refuse to call an action that you believe that a person should feel guilty about wrong, even if you do not believe that in fact you would. Notice that once he refines the analysis in this way then Mill no longer needs to say, as he did in the letter to Ward, that a person who lacks a conscience cannot use moral language in the same sense as everyone else.

This letter is also important because of Mill's description of guilt as 'a feeling of pain *in the fact of violating a certain rule*'. That the conscience can be viewed as an 'enforcer of rules' – which means in part that the kinds of actions an individual will typically feel guilty about doing can be characterized in terms of a set of general rules – was implicit in his discussion of the internal sanction, which we examined in chapter 2. Here, though, it is stated clearly. This is a specific sense in which an individual can be said to have internalized a rule: to be disposed to feel guilty upon violating it. Note that while he claims that the operation of each individual's conscience is tied to a set of rules, Mill is not committed to the claim that we can always fully articulate the rules that we have internalized.

For Mill, then, moral rules are rules that the conscience 'enforces'. In a purely descriptive sense, we can say that rules are moral rules for certain agents if they have internalized them. Prescriptively, we can talk about the moral rules that particular people ought to internalize. We can also talk about moral rules at the social level. To the extent that the members of a given society have internalized a common set of rules, those rules can be described variously as that society's moral code, its popular or ordinary morality, or – using a term that Mill commends the legal philosopher John Austin for coining – its 'positive' morality.[24] This makes the rules that the members of a society *should* internalize its positive morality 'as it ought to be'.

Rules and happiness

There is nothing specifically utilitarian about Mill's account of what it is for an action to be morally wrong. The next question for us to ask is which rules people should internalize, though, and this is where his utilitarianism comes into play. His view, somewhat roughly stated, is that the rules that people's consciences should enforce are the ones that it would be optimific for them to internalize. Actions contrary to these rules are wrong. While many moral theorists might be able to accept the notion that actions are wrong if and only if people ought to internalize rules that forbid them, Mill's utilitarian approach is distinctive. Most moralists would begin by offering a moral standard for judging whether actions are wrong that makes no reference to the notion of guilt. Having decided which actions are wrong, they would then say that those are the actions for which guilt is appropriate. Mill comes in from the other direction. He starts with a utilitarian criterion for determining what rules it is desirable for people to internalize, and hence which actions it is appropriate for them to feel guilty about performing. Then he invokes his account of what it means for actions to be wrong in order to derive his moral standard.

Through this approach he arrives at what we would now call a rule-utilitarian view.

At the end of the last section we introduced the descriptive idea of a society's positive morality and the prescriptive idea of its positive morality as it ought to be. A few small caveats and qualifications may need to be made to this claim, but at worst it is not far from the truth to say that Mill is an ideal-code rule utilitarian and that he identifies the moral code that is authoritative for a given individual with her society's positive morality as it ought to be at that time.

The most direct evidence that Mill believes that utilitarian considerations should be used to determine which rules are appropriately enforced by the conscience comes from his discussions of the justification of punishment. Lyons calls attention to Mill's praise for Bentham's theory of legal punishment. According to Bentham, the state should only punish people who violate criminal laws, and we should determine which laws to enact by asking which laws it would maximize happiness for the state to promulgate and enforce, taking into account both the pain caused by the offences which the laws are meant to deter people from committing and the pain caused by the punishments themselves.[25] Mill writes that Bentham left this part of the philosophy of law 'nearly complete'.[26] Although Bentham was thinking only of legal sanctions, Mill classes the reproaches of conscience as punishments as well.

That this reading solves so many interpretative riddles also counts strongly in its favour. To begin with, it at least may let us give an answer to the question of how Mill locates morality within the Art of Life, which is governed by the principle of utility, yet distinguishes it from expediency impartially conceived. What follows is a very brief sketch of how that answer might go, albeit one that leaves many questions unanswered.

Suppose that Mill believes that we experience a given feeling or emotion at the appropriate times when we have the dispositions to experience them that it would optimific or utility-maximizing to cultivate in people generally. Suppose further that he believes that we have reason to do what (if anything) certain feelings or emotion would tend to cause a person in our situation who had the appropriate dispositions to experience them to do.[27] On this (admittedly speculative) way of understanding the Art of Life, utilitarian considerations govern what dispositions to experience the 'moral emotions' are appropriate, and corresponding to the department of Morality are moral reasons in virtue of which we have reason to act in the way that these emotions would tend to cause a person with the appropriate dispositions to experience them to act in our situation. The primary moral emotion is guilt, since it is at the heart of our very understanding of what it is for an action to be morally wrong. Experiencing guilt tends to cause us to make amends for whatever we did that caused us to feel it. Even more to the point, knowing that we would feel guilty about doing something tends to make us avoid doing it. Hence we have a moral reason not to do actions forbidden by rules that it would be happiness-maximizing for people to internalize. This would mean that we have moral reasons not to do actions that the rule-utilitarian theory being ascribed to Mill here says are morally wrong – reasons, apparently, that Mill takes to trump prudential reasons.

A similar account could potentially be given of the aesthetic emotions. One question that the view leaves unanswered, though, is why the Art of Life would have so few departments; why not more departments corresponding to more emotions?[28] In an early essay Mill says that actions can be evaluated in terms of their 'loveableness', for instance, in addition to their morality and beauty, so why not a department of the Loveable?[29] Given that Mill's account of the Art of Life is so brief and cryptic, however, we will likely have to learn to live with unanswered questions no matter how we understand it.

The rule-utilitarian reading of Mill presented here also lets us make sense of the following assertion, which would be very perplexing if we thought of him as an act utilitarian:

> In the case of abstinences indeed – of things which people forbear to do from moral considerations, though the consequences in the particular case might be beneficial – it would be unworthy of an intelligent agent not to be consciously aware that the action is of a class which, if practised generally, would be generally injurious, and that this is the ground of the obligation to abstain from it.[30]

Here Mill states quite explicitly that we can be morally obligated to abstain from all acts that belong to a particular class, even acts with desirable consequences, if the consequences of a general practice of acts of that kind would be bad enough. Elsewhere, he offers lying as an illustration of this general point: 'The duty of truth as a positive duty is also to be considered on the ground of whether more good or harm would follow to mankind in general if it were generally disregarded and not merely whether good or harm would follow in a particular case.'[31] While these passages do not refer to moral rules as such, they fit perfectly with the rule-utilitarian reading. An action is wrong if a general rule prohibiting an entire class of actions to which it belongs would be optimific, which will usually be the case when a general practice of actions of that class would produce sufficiently bad outcomes.

Then there is Mill's embrace of 'supererogation', the notion that it is possible for an action to go above and beyond the call of moral duty. Consider, for example, the following passage from *Auguste Comte and Positivism*:

> There is a standard of altruism to which all should be required to come up, and a degree beyond it which is not obligatory, but meritorious. . . . The object should be to stimulate services to humanity by their natural rewards; not to render the pursuit of our own good in any other manner impossible, by visiting it with the reproaches of other [sic] and of our own conscience. The proper office of those sanctions is to enforce upon every one, the conduct necessary to give all other persons their fair chance: conduct which chiefly consists in not doing them harm, and not impeding them in anything which without harming others does good to themselves. To this must of course be added, that when we either expressly or tacitly undertake to do more, we are bound to keep our promise. And inasmuch as every one, who avails himself of the advantages of society, leads others to expect from him all such positive good offices and disinterested services as the moral improvement attained by mankind has rendered customary, he deserves moral blame if, without just cause, he disappoints that expectation.[32]

Act utilitarianism precludes the possibility of an action's being better than it is morally required to be, since it requires perfection. Mill, though, plainly believes that this is possible. This is little problem, on the rule-utilitarian position being attributed to him here. An action is praiseworthy, he can say, when it is one of several morally permissible things the agent could do – that is, one of several actions that would not be wrong – and it will both yield more aggregate net happiness and be worse for the agent personally than some of the rest. This does depart subtly from the usual understanding of supererogation, insofar as the action's superiority is not moral in nature, strictly speaking. Still, this account of what makes an action especially praiseworthy is at least a utilitarian one. Notice, by the way, that Mill is presupposing that the costs involved in getting people to internalize the moral rules that they would have to accept in order to be driven by their consciences to comply with a high standard of 'altruism' would just be too high to make this worthwhile.

Clearly there is much to be said for the rule-utilitarian reading of Mill. Still, if one of the passages that have been offered in favour of the act-utilitarian reading were sufficiently compelling, or if the combination of them were, then a conscientious interpreter might still have to come down on that side. Frankly, however, none of the putative evidence for the act-utilitarian interpretation cuts much ice.

Consider first the passage from the *Logic* in which Mill suggests that rules of conduct are only for use in cases in which we lack the time to decide what to do based on 'the data of the particular case before us' or cannot trust ourselves to do so. The mistake in treating this passage as evidence for an act-utilitarian interpretation is that of failing to see that Mill considers moral rules to be just one special sort of practical rule. In the passage in question, Mill is talking about the rules of arts very generally, including the myriad particular arts like the art of building. Certainly builders will do well to regard general maxims of construction as provisional and to work out what to do based on the unique features of their materials, site and so on. People will also do well to treat general rules of prudence as rules of thumb that can be readily set aside when there is sufficient reason to do so. Moral rules are different, though, because when your conscience is enforcing a rule you cannot just set the rule aside. This is not to deny that the rules that an individual has internalized can change over the course of his or her life, and it is certainly not to deny that the positive morality of an entire society can change over generations. But Mill's model of the conscience seems to suggest that when a decision must be made – 'in the heat of the moment', so to speak – one's conscience will enforce whatever rules one has internalized to that point. This will not necessarily make it impossible for one to disobey these rules, but doing so will involve breaking through 'a mass of feeling', to recall a line from *Utilitarianism* that was quoted in chapter 2.[33]

It is only fair to acknowledge that late in chapter 2 of *Utilitarianism*, when Mill compares moral rules to advice given to travellers 'to take one direction rather than another', his language probably fits slightly better with sophisticated act-utilitarian thinking than with the rule utilitarianism attributed to him here. There is a vague implication in this passage that maximizing happiness is the target of every individual action and that the rules of morality are no more than 'advice' intended to help agents hit this target. This smacks of act-utilitarian reasoning. The rule utilitarian, in contrast, might be said to think of maximizing happiness as the target not of individual actions but of the practice of inculcating moral rules. The difference is subtle but important. Still, given the weight of the evidence for the rule-utilitarian reading, it seems far more likely that Mill was simply not fastidious with his language than that he was trying to signal his adherence to act utilitarianism. The real point of the passage in question is merely that utilitarians do not suppose that people should be constantly performing calculations, but instead believe that they should guide their decisions based on a set of secondary rules grounded in centuries of human experience. This point is common ground between rule and sophisticated act utilitarians. The chief aspect of this passage that favours an act-utilitarian reading is the fact that Mill's simple analogies, which are meant to illustrate the function of these secondary principles, are a bit more perspicuous when read as descriptions of the act- than of the rule-utilitarian viewpoint. Yet if they do not perfectly convey the rule-utilitarian view of moral rules, neither do they contradict it. And even if Mill recognized that they did not render his view transparent, he probably could not have found a clearer analogy that was not inordinately complicated. The passage is thus a thin reed on which to hang an act-utilitarian interpretation.

This leaves us with the 'right in proportion as they tend to promote happiness' passage from *Utilitarianism* and the letter to Venn to consider. The mistake that interpreters who take these passages to support an act-utilitarian interpretation of Mill are making can be stated simply, although these stretches of text raise deeper issues that can only be discussed cursorily here. The mistake is that of taking Mill to be referring to moral rather than prudential evaluation of actions. When Mill writes to Venn that 'the right way of testing actions by their consequences, is to test them by the natural consequences of the particular action, and not by those which would follow if every one did the same', for instance, he might have added that it is when we make prudential rather than moral evaluations that we test actions in this way. This response may seem to be a reach. The passage in the letter to Venn follows immediately upon Mill's correction of Venn's misreading of Kant's fundamental moral principle, and the one from *Utilitarianism* refers specifically to judgements about the rightness and wrongness of actions. Nevertheless, we can make the best overall sense of all of the passages that we are considering here if we suppose that Mill takes the 'tendency' of an action to promote happiness or its oppo-site to be directly relevant only to its prudence or imprudence. So understood, an action's tendency would still bear indirectly on its moral standing, since an act's being highly imprudent is a good prima facie reason to think that it is wrong, that is, that it would be prudent to bring it about that people internalize a rule that would forbid it. This explains why Mill feels able to speak first from one of these evaluative standpoints and then the other, without always calling attention to the change in perspective. On this reading, the puzzling 'the creed which accepts as the foundation of morals, Utility' passage in *Utilitarianism* concerns the relation between an act's prudence (or imprudence) and its moral standing. The point of the passage is not that actions' rightness or wrongness is proportionate to their tendency to promote happiness or unhappi-ness, but instead that the confidence that utilitarians have that their knowledge of an action's tendency tells them its moral standing is proportionate to the tendency's magnitude, whether positive or negative. 'In proportion' modifies 'hold', in other words, not 'right'.[34]

So on balance the textual evidence argues strongly, if not une-quivocally, in favour of reading Mill as a rule utilitarian. We might also describe him as a 'conscience' or 'internal sanction' utilitarian.[35] On his view, whether an act is wrong depends on whether agents are appropriately punished by the internal sanction for it. The criterion of happiness-maximization governs when the use of the internal sanction is appropriate. Given empirical facts about how the conscience works – namely that it punishes perceived violations of internalized rules – it follows that actions are wrong if they are prohibited by the rules that it would best promote happiness for people to internalize. The principle of utility therefore serves as the controller and justification of the rules of the department of Moral-ity, as Mill says that it must, and we have a moral reason not to perform actions that violate these rules. 'For morality itself is not a science but an art; not truths, but rules.'[36]

Mill's conception of morality can be described as instrumental. He regards the conscience as a tool for controlling human behav-iour. It may be a somewhat crude tool, since we can only internalize rules of limited complexity. Still, it is the best means available at present for addressing various pervasive shortcomings with our motivations – shortcomings that often make us unwilling to do what we think would best promote total net happiness. One is simply that so few people care at all about the general good. Call this the 'Anglo-American' problem, because he takes this sort of selfishness to be especially characteristic of Britain and the United States. Most people in these societies care only about themselves and their families. At best, they might care something for the good of some larger but still particular group to which they belong, like their class. Where insufficient sympathy exists to motivate people to work for the general happiness, the internal sanction can make up for some of the shortfall. It can certainly constrain the things that people will do *to* their neighbours in order to advance their own interests. When it operates with enough force, it can even move people to provide positive assistance to others at substantial personal sacrifice, although the costs associated with making it act this forcefully are considerable. Another shortcoming that the conscience addresses might be called the 'European' problem. Mill believes that on the Continent one finds less selfishness and greater willingness to promote disinterested ends, but also a willingness to choose whatever means will best promote the particular unselfish end that people have in view, with little compunction about mistreating anyone outside of the particular people they aim to help. Mill fears that do-gooders who are loose cannons do more damage to the general happiness than they do to advance it, because they undermine the sense of security upon which everyone's happiness depends.[37] (More will be said about the importance that he attaches to the notion of security in the section below on justice.)

In principle, it is possible that some day the benefits of relying on the conscience will no longer exceed the costs because some superior means of control will be found. Mill acknowledges that if some day 'a more expedient' means than punishment can be found for steering people's behaviour then at least one part of morality – the part that comprises rules of justice – would become obsolete.[38] Indeed, in a typical example of his adulation of Harriet, he says that if only everyone were as highly developed as she is then there would be no need for moral rules at all: 'morality might be very different from what it must now be, or rather it would not exist at all, as morality, since morality and inclination would coincide.'[39]

Mill seems to assume that moral codes do and will continue to exist at the level of individual societies, so that what society a given individual belongs to determines what moral code is authoritative for him or her. This means that he is a social or cultural relativist about morality. We see evidence of this in many places, such as his assertions about the different types of moralities that are appropriate to societies at different levels of civilization or development.[40]

In chapter 4, we saw that while Mill is a 'maximizing' utilitarian, he believes that happiness will be maximized only when we create conditions under which only victims of very bad luck fail to lead genuinely happy human lives. After the stretch of text in *Utilitarianism* in which Mill describes the higher quality pleasures, there is a seldom-remarked-on passage that ties this aspect of his thought to his rule utilitarianism:

> According to the Greatest Happiness Principle . . . the ultimate end, with reference to and for the sake of which all other things are desirable . . . is an existence exempt as far as possible from pain, and as rich as possible in enjoyments, both in point of quantity and quality. . . . [M]orality . . . may accordingly be defined, the rules and precepts for human conduct, by the observance of which an existence such as has been described might be, to the greatest extent possible, secured to all mankind. . . .[41]

Admittedly, it has taken a considerable amount of work to show that the best interpretation of Mill's moral theory seems to be a rule-utilitarian one. One might well wonder why he was not more explicit about the details of his view. The question is a fair one. Mill's obscurity on this point is partly exculpated by the fact that the terms 'act utilitarianism' and 'rule utilitarianism' were apparently only coined in 1959.[42] Additionally, Mill is writing in the period when utilitarian ideas are just beginning to gain wide currency with the thinking public. It would not be unreasonable for him to suppose that his energies could best be expended on promoting the general utilitarian approach, with the task of hashing out the details being left to later generations of utilitarians. With all of this said, though, it is neither unfair nor anachronistic for us to wish that Mill had been a bit more forthcoming about the details of his own favoured interpretation of utilitarianism. George Berkeley was able to see the difference between act and rule utilitarianism well enough to make it clear that he favoured the latter, and he was writing over a century before Mill, before even the word 'utilitarianism' had been coined.[43]

One possible objection to the rule-utilitarian view that has been ascribed to Mill here is that it has the unsettling implication that no action that will result in the agent's death can be wrong. If 'ought' implies 'can', as is usually assumed, then no agent ought to feel guilty for an act he or she cannot feel guilty about, which makes it false to say that someone who is dead ought to feel guilty.[44] If Mill's view is that an action is wrong if and only if an agent ought to feel guilt for it after the fact, then this seems to entail that no action which will lead to the agent's death is contrary to morality. One way for Mill to meet this objection would be for him to reformulate his analysis of what it is for an action to be wrong, framing it generally in terms of the appropriateness of the conscience enforcing a rule forbidding the action rather than in terms of the appropriateness specifically of after-the-fact guilt. The conscience can certainly enforce rules that prohibit actions which would result in the agent's death, by causing the agent to confront what Mill so aptly describes as a 'mass of feeling' as soon as he or she contemplates doing them.[45]

The question of whether Mill's rule utilitarianism is vulnerable to the incoherence objection is too large an issue to take on here, but it is at least worth pausing a moment to think about specifically what form this objection takes when directed against Mill's utilitarianism.[46] When directed against Mill, the incoherence objection states that there is no justification for why the department of Morality should dominate the department of Prudence, that is, why the reasons generated by the former should trump those generated by the latter. C. L. Ten steers our attention to this concern when he writes that 'There is nothing in Mill's analysis of the concept of morality to show that the requirements of morality must take precedence over all non-moral considerations.'[47]

The ideal code and moral reform

It is entirely fair to ask just what rules Mill takes the ideal moral code of some real-world society, such as his own, to comprise. And it must be said that he is in the company of every other rule utilitarian in being unable to produce a complete list of the contents of any society's ideal code. That does not mean, though, that he has nothing to contribute on the subject.

To begin with, Mill claims that a society's received morality deserves to be regarded as an approximation of its ideal code – a loose approximation, admittedly, but an approximation nonetheless. Explicitly utilitarian reflection on the question of which moral rules would best promote the general happiness may have played virtually no role whatsoever in the development of any community's positive morality. Nevertheless, the desire for happiness has everywhere 'had a large share in forming the moral doctrines even of those who most scornfully reject its authority.'[48]

Despite the fact that utilitarianism has so few supporters, then, utilitarian considerations inevitably exert a significant, albeit tacit, influence on the development of societies' moralities. Yet Mill hardly believes that communities are likely to 'accidentally' arrive at their ideal codes, which is why work is always available for 'moral reformers' who aim to 'revise' received morality and bring it closer to the ideal code. He understands the project of moral reform to involve two tasks: first, discovering ways in which the received morality might be improved and, second, publicizing and advocating these improvements. The latter of these activities could include both persuading people to alter the moral rules that they have themselves internalized, insofar as this is in their power, and persuading them to inculcate a morality in the next generation that is better than the one they internalized themselves. He sees this as a job primarily for the most educated members of society, particularly those with the greatest knowledge of the social sciences. Both general empirical knowledge of human nature and specific knowledge of the condition of the specific society in question at that time are required.

To ascertain what the ideal code of a society says on any given question, therefore, we should take the rules of its received morality to provide the default answer, but we should stand ready to modify that answer in light of the input of sages who are in a position to fashion useful reforms: 'That philosophers might easily do this, even now . . . I admit, or rather, earnestly maintain. The corollaries from the principle of utility, like the precepts of every practical art, admit of indefinite improvement, and, in a progressive state of the human mind, their improvement is perpetually going on.'[49]

There are a variety of factors that explain why a society's positive morality is likely to depart from its ideal code, and hence why moral reformers are needed. One is obvious: the content of every society's morality has also been influenced by factors that have little to do with the promotion of anyone's temporal happiness, such as 'the servility of mankind towards the supposed preferences or aversions of . . . their gods'.[50] Mill points out a variety of other general reasons, though, several of which bear mentioning.

The first is that it is rather unlikely that a society's positive morality will reflect an equal concern for everyone's happiness. It will best promote the interests of those with the most power, and so 'Wherever there is an ascendant class, a large portion of the morality of the country emanates from its class interests, and its feelings of class superiority.'[51] Sometimes marginalized social groups may still be able to influence the received morality so that it offers them some protection, as the women of the Middle Ages introduced 'the spirit of chivalry' into the accepted moral code.[52] Nevertheless, opportunities for exerting this kind of influence will never be equally distributed, and most societies' moral codes could be changed in ways that would better promote total net happiness through taking better account of the interests of marginalized groups.

Another reason that moral reformers are needed is that our conceptions of human nature and of the nature of happiness can be improved. Mill could justifiably take himself to have made some valuable contributions in these areas, and to have drawn out some of their implications for the improvement of morality. We will see one example of this when we consider the principle of liberty in the next chapter. An important part of his argument for this principle depends upon his account of the higher quality pleasures.

A third consideration is that as a society changes in various respects, its ideal code – the moral code that it would be optimific for its members to internalize, recall – will change also. Moral reformers are engaged in the two-part task of trying to figure out what their society's positive morality should be – what its ideal code is, in other words – and of trying to win acceptance for their discoveries. The first of these tasks is complicated by the fact that the changing nature of the ideal code means that they are aiming at a moving target. Mill provides a nice illustration of how the ideal code itself can change in *Auguste Comte and Positivism*. Just after his discussion of supererogation, which was quoted earlier, he adds that actions that were once supererogatory can become obligatory once they become common enough that it begins to make sense for people to count upon their being done. Once people begin to take for granted that others will act a certain way, the consequences of a failure to do so may be much worse than in the past, and this means that it may become worthwhile to instil a rule requiring this sort of action.[53] Mill's observation that the liberty principle is a fit moral rule only for societies that have reached a certain stage of development, about which more in the next chapter, is another clear example of how changes in other aspects of a society may necessitate changes in its morality.

Finally, a society's positive morality may stand in need of reform in order to resolve conflicts between its constituent rules. Mill does not go into great detail about his view of the structure of moral codes, but the picture that emerges from what he does say is that they include a relatively small number of primary rules. Because these primary rules are fairly sweeping, in the sense of requiring or forbidding very broad classes of actions, they will frequently conflict. In other words, situations will frequently arise in which the different moral requirements that these rules impose upon an agent cannot all be satisfied. In these cases, Mill writes, an exception has to be made to one of the rules, and the nature of this exception must be determined by asking how happiness can best be promoted: 'There exists no moral system under which there do not arise unequivocal cases of conflicting obligation. . . . If utility is the ultimate source of moral obligations, utility may be invoked to decide between them when their demands are incompatible.'[54]

At this point, one could be forgiven for wondering whether Mill's recognition of the possibility of conflicts between moral rules, conflicts that necessitate an appeal to the standard of 'utility', undermines the rule-utilitarian interpretation of his moral philosophy. This would be the case if what Mill had in mind was that when primary moral rules conflict, agents should set the rules aside and do whatever will produce the most happiness in the particular case at hand. This sort of view might be described as a hybrid of act and rule utilitarianism.

In fact, however, Mill makes abundantly clear that even when exceptions to primary moral rules exist, these exceptions are themselves governed by what we might describe as auxiliary rules:

> At all events, the existence of exceptions to moral rules is no stumbling-block peculiar to the principle of utility. The essential is, that the exception should be itself a general rule; so that, being of definite extent, and not leaving the expediencies to the partial judgment of the agent in the individual case, it may not shake the stability of the wider rule in the cases to which the reason of the exception does not extend.[55]

Auxiliary moral rules are thus justified in the same way as primary ones, namely by belonging to the set of rules that it would be optimific for the members of a society to internalize.[56] One task for moral reformers will be formulating appropriate auxiliary rules to resolve conflicts between primary rules. What auxiliary rules a given society needs will depend on what sorts of situations involving conflicts between primary rules its members are most likely to encounter.

So Mill hardly attempts to provide a comprehensive account of the ideal code of his society or any other. In fact, he does not provide us with any basis for hoping that we ever will know exactly what code would be ideal for a given community; at best, we can only reasonably expect to arrive at better and better approximations of it, with ongoing work being needed just to keep these approximations up to date. The fact that we will never know precisely what the ideal code of our own society is raises the question of whether it is really this ideal code itself that determines what our moral obligations are or only the best approximation to it that we have discovered. Mill's remark that a society's received morality represents 'the rules of morality for the multitude, and for the philosopher until he has succeeded in finding better' even raises the intriguing possibility that he might think that whether a given individual is bound by a moral rule depends on whether it is reasonable for that individual, given his or her own level of knowledge, to believe that the rule in question is part of that individual's society's ideal code.

This would introduce a degree of intrasocietal relativism into the view, and in particular it might mean that the moral duties of the moral reformers differed from those of the masses.[57] Even if this is Mill's view, though – and the only suggestion being made here is that this is a possibility – it bears emphasizing that this would still mean that a person is obligated to obey a rule if and only if it is reasonable for him or her to believe that it is part of the code whose *general* acceptance would best promote total net happiness. Moreover, Mill hardly suggests that aspiring moral reformers should be reticent about transmitting their discoveries to the rest of society. His utilitarianism is not of what has been called the 'Government House' variety, in which an intellectual elite keeps moral truths – including the truth of utilitarianism itself – from the masses.[58]

Justice

The final chapter of *Utilitarianism* treats 'the connexion between justice and utility'. Mill's ostensible aim in the chapter is to rebut the widespread perception that the 'phenomenology' of the sentiment of justice – the outrage we feel when an injustice is committed, the intensity of our desire for injustices to be rectified, the pleasure we feel when those who have perpetrated injustice are punished

– reveals to us that justice must be grounded on something other than its contribution to the promotion of well-being. He takes this perception to render moral intuitionism more plausible to many minds, so he is anxious to challenge it. Of equal or greater interest to us, though, is his account of what distinguishes justice from the remainder of the wider sphere of morality.

We will begin with this latter question. Mill's theory of justice is continuous with the rest of his rule-utilitarian moral theory. Rules or principles of justice are a subset of moral rules. Rules of justice, in contrast with other moral rules, require those they bind to engage in or to abstain from some line of conduct towards a specific individual. The 'perfect' obligations to which rules of justice give rise are correlated with individual rights.[59] The contrast is with duties of 'imperfect' obligation, 'which we are indeed bound to practise, but not towards any definite person, nor at any prescribed time'. This conception of justice, according to which every violation of a right is an injustice and vice versa, may not quite correspond with our ordinary way of speaking. It is not so revisionary, though, as to render the concept of justice unrecognizable to us as such.[60]

Interpreters who take Mill to be an act utilitarian face a challenge in explaining how he can attach any real moral significance to justice so understood, since we have already seen that this moral theory is in serious tension with the notion of rights. For the act utilitarian, rights can at most figure in a decision procedure. The act utilitarian can recommend acting as if others have certain rights, in other words, but must still regard the violation of those 'rights' as a moral duty whenever this would yield even slightly more happiness on balance.

If we read Mill as a rule utilitarian, however, then there is nothing problematic about his talk of rules of justice and of rights. On the reading being proposed here, Mill thinks that for X to have a right to Φ from Y is simply for Y to have a moral obligation to give X Φ – that is, for a rule requiring Y to give X Φ to be part of the authoritative moral code. Φ here could be anything, including freedom from some sort of interference in X's life. That this is Mill's view is confirmed by his analysis of what it is to have a right: 'When we call anything a person's right, we mean that he has a valid claim on society to protect him in the possession of it, either by the force of law, or by that of education and opinion.'[61]

It may look here as if Mill thinks that more than one moral rule must be justified in order for it to be the case that X has a right to Φ from Y: first, of course, a rule requiring Y to give X Φ, but also some further rule or rules requiring other individuals or (somehow) society at large come to X's aid if Y refuses to do so (at least if X should demand that it do so). Note, though, that Mill refers to society's protecting a rights-holder through 'education'. This suggests that he thinks it suffices for an individual to have a right to Φ that it be expedient for society to instil in its members a rule requiring them to give him or her Φ. We have already seen that he believes that when a rule has been widely internalized people will tend to impose informal external sanctions on people who violate it, in the absence of a particular reason not to; this accounts for his lumping together of 'education' and 'opinion'. Mill may well believe that certain moral rules obligating us to help people whose rights are being violated are justified; he just does not seem to make the justification of such rules a conceptual requirement on the existence of rights.

Mill's account of what distinguishes justice from the rest of morality is purely formal or conceptual. It does not rest on any claims about the content of the rules of justice, about what rights he takes individuals to possess or about utilitarianism. Mill also advances certain substantive views about what rights people have.[62] In *Utilitarianism*, he implies that the only rules of justice that can be justified are those that protect individuals against having certain things done to them. In the most general of terms, these are '[t]he moral rules which forbid mankind to hurt one another (in which we must never forget to include wrongful interference with each other's freedom).'[63] At first glance, at least, this may suggest that we have only 'negative' as opposed to 'positive' rights, where the former are rights to be left alone in one way or another and the latter are rights to have other people make a positive effort for our benefit. (Notice that this is a different sense of 'positive' from the one in the term 'positive morality'.) On closer inspection, though, this is not quite so clear.

One line that might appear to complicate the claim that Mill recognizes no positive rights appears in *Utilitarianism*, where he writes that '[I]t is confessedly unjust to *break faith* with any one: to violate an engagement, either express or implied, or disappoint expectations raised by our conduct, at least if we have raised those expectations knowingly and voluntarily.'[64] This passage could be read as expressing a belief in the existence of positive rights, at least in situations in which something in the conduct of the agent who owes the right's correlative obligation has encouraged the bearer of the right to count on receiving the benefit in question. But breaking faith with someone in the manner that Mill describes is really an instance of doing something to a person; it requires encouraging his or her expectations. The right not to be treated in such a way can therefore be regarded as a negative right. The real complications in determining whether Mill believes in the existence of true positive rights stem mainly from certain passages in *On Liberty*. Thus the question is best postponed until the next chapter.

Primary rules of justice could conflict with each other or with the moral rules that generate imperfect obligations. As always, Mill insists that the promotion of happiness is the appropriate criterion to use in selecting auxiliary rules that specify how to resolve these conflicts. He offers a variety of examples of conflicts between primary rules of justice. The first is the three-way debate between those who maintain that punishment is justified only when it benefits the very person being punished, those who hold that punishment is justified for the protection of others, and the Owenites who insist that punishment is never justified:

> All these opinions are extremely plausible. . . . For in truth every one of the three builds upon rules of justice confessedly true. The first appeals to the acknowledged injustice of singling out an individual, and making a sacrifice, without his consent, for other people's benefit. The second relies on the acknowledged justice of self-defence, and the admitted injustice of forcing one person to conform to another's notions of what constitutes his good. The Owenite invokes the admitted principle, that it is unjust to punish any one for what he cannot help. Each is triumphant so long as he is not compelled to take into consideration any other maxims of justice than the one he has selected. . . .[65]

Mill concludes his series of illustrations by writing 'From these confusions there is no other mode of extrication than the utilitarian.'[66] So the specific moral rules that ought to govern the infliction of punishment in a society can be regarded as auxiliary rules of justice – rules that carve out exceptions to these primary rules and specify how the conflicts between them should be resolved.

Matters get a little murky when it comes to conflicts between the rules of justice and the moral rules that give rise to imperfect obligations. On the surface, Mill's points are reasonably straightforward. On the one hand, the rules of justice usually trump other moral considerations: 'Justice is a name for certain classes of moral rules, which concern the essentials of human well-being more nearly, and are therefore of more absolute obligation, than any other rules for the guidance of life. . . .'[67]

It is no surprise that Mill would think we are seldom justified in making exceptions to rules of justice. When rules that forbid the infliction of significant harms are violated then the immediate victims will suffer serious direct blows to their happiness, but Mill believes that there is even more at stake than this. The more frequently that these rules are violated, the more that people's subjective sense of security will be diminished. This, in turn, seriously limits anyone's ability to derive happiness from life, even someone whose rights have not actually been violated. Mill regards security as

> to every one's feelings the most vital of all interests. . . . [S]ecurity no human being can possibly do without; on it we depend for all our immunity from evil, and for the whole value of all and every good, beyond the passing moment; since nothing but the gratification of the instant could be of any worth to us, if we could be deprived of anything the next instant by whoever was momentarily stronger than ourselves.[68]

For this reason, Mill maintains, the 'machinery for providing' security – the institutions and practices associated with the enforcement of rules of justice – must be 'kept unintermittedly in active play'.

On the other hand, though, Mill seems not to think that the rules of justice *always* take priority over other moral rules:

> Particular cases may occur in which some other social duty is so important, as to overrule any one of the general maxims of justice. Thus, to save a life, it may not only be allowable, but a duty, to steal, or take by force, the necessary food or medicine, or to kidnap, and compel to officiate, the only qualified medical practitioner.

However, he continues:

> In such cases, as we do not call anything justice which is not a virtue, we usually say, not that justice must give way to some other moral principle, but that what is just in ordinary cases is, by reason of that other principle, not just in the particular case. By this useful accommodation of language, the character of indefeasibility attributed to justice is kept up, and we are saved from the necessity of maintaining that there can be laudable injustice.[69]

The implication here is that sometimes imperfect obligations are to be satisfied in preference to perfect ones, but that in ordinary language we find ways to camouflage these rare occurrences.

At first inspection, this may appear to be sufficiently clear to let pass, but there is a puzzle lurking underneath the surface of the entire discussion. In precisely what sorts of scenarios *could* rules of justice conflict with rules that give rise to imperfect obligations? Imperfect obligations are obligations that leave the agent some discretion about how to fulfil them. That you have an imperfect obligation to provide some help to those in need, for instance, does not entail that you must help this specific person on this specific occasion in this specific way; you must simply do 'enough' over a period of time. If fulfilling an imperfect obligation on one specific occasion would violate a rule of justice, then it will typically be possible to find some other way to fulfil it that would not.[70] If you can do this, though, then the case is not one of conflicting rules, strictly speaking. A true case of conflict would have to involve a scenario in which for some extended period of time there was no way for a person to do enough to satisfy a particular imperfect duty without violating someone's rights. Situations like this must be rare, and in any case they are not the kinds of scenarios that Mill seems to have in mind when he talks about stealing food and kidnapping doctors. These sound like cases in which there is a duty to offer a specific kind of assistance to a specific person on a specific occasion (and not just because this is your last chance to do 'enough' to satisfy an imperfect duty that you could have satisfied in some other way previously). But this would mean that the duty is not an imperfect duty but a perfect one. Perhaps Mill is simply not his own best expositor here, and despite his seeming claim to the contrary he really does not believe that non-justice rules of morality can overrule rules of justice after all. Perhaps, in other words, he is really only giving examples of one rule of justice being overruled by another.[71]

In fact, we have already encountered a rule that Mill takes to be a primary rule of justice that – as least as he understands it – would appear to give a person in urgent need a right to assistance in the form of food, medical treatment and so on – at least in many situations. '[I]t is confessedly unjust to *break faith* with any one: to . . . disappoint expectations raised by our conduct, at least if we have raised those expectations knowingly and voluntarily.' The proposition that we have an obligation to follow through when we 'knowingly and voluntarily' cause someone to expect that we will benefit them in some way does not, at first glance, look like an especially sweeping principle. It seems to cover no more than cases in which one individual makes an explicit or implicit promise directly to another. For Mill, though, it is of much wider application than this. He takes it to underwrite a general obligation of reciprocity:

> Good for good is also one of the dictates of justice; and this, though its social utility is evident, and though it carries with it a natural human feeling, has not at first sight that obvious connection with hurt or injury, which, existing in the most elementary cases of just and unjust, is the source of the characteristic intensity of the sentiment.[72]

Nor does the duty of reciprocity to which this principle gives rise obligate you only to return good to those particular individuals from whom one has received it. Recall that, in a passage from his book on Comte quoted earlier in this chapter, Mill contends that 'every one, who avails himself of the advantages of society, leads others to expect from him all such positive good offices and disinterested services as the moral improvement attained by mankind has rendered customary. . . .' Just by living in society and accepting the benefits of social life, we automatically encourage others to expect certain customary kinds of help from us, and we commit the injustice of disappointing expectations that we have raised if we fail to provide this help when needed. Those who stand in need of it have a right to it. Helping to save the life of a person in mortal danger seems to qualify as a customary disinterested service, at least when the person needing to be saved is in close proximity and when you can offer this assistance without paying too high a price or putting yourself in too much danger. This rule of justice appears to cover the cases that Mill has in mind, and so we must conclude that he has not provided us with any clear examples of non-justice moral rules overriding rules of justice. (Do notice, though, that this reasoning would not apply in situations in which the person in need is a member of a different society. Accepting the benefits of life in your own society could not possibly be construed as encouragement for a member of a different society to expect help if it is needed.)

Mill, by the way, also believes that society as a whole can be bound to make good on expectations that it has raised in individuals. Even when society has created a 'right' that should never have been created, its doing so encourages expectations that it cannot disappoint without providing compensation. One clear illustration of this concerns slavery. Mill is second to none in his appreciation of the evils of modern slavery, and on a personal level he despises slave owners. Once society has created the expectation that slavery will be permitted, however, and encouraged individuals to consider slaves a legitimate 'investment', then according to Mill slave owners must be compensated when slaves are emancipated.[73] This genuinely is a matter of justice for Mill, not merely an expedient way of trying to end slavery without a fight. This, by the way, is how emancipation was effected in the British slave colonies in the Caribbean and in Washington, DC.

We can now turn to the sentiment of justice. Mill feels compelled to discuss the psychological basis of the sentiment of justice, as noted earlier, because its 'peculiar character and intensity' had been cited as evidence that 'the Just must have an existence in Nature as something absolute – generically distinct from every variety of the Expedient.'[74] The likely source of this claim is the moral intuitionist, who would assert that this sentiment is an original part of our constitution (which may suggest to many people that it was given to us by God) and that we have a priori knowledge of the rules or principles with which the sentiment is connected.

Mill's competing account of the sentiment of justice is, predictably, associationist. The sentiment of justice is rooted, he maintains, in the animal instinct that drives us to 'repel or retaliate, any harm done or attempted against ourselves, or against those with whom we sympathise'.[75] This is the source of the sentiment's intensity. Whereas in a lower animal this instinct might only be responsible for self-defence or the defence of offspring, in humans it can have a much wider scope. We are capable of sympathizing far more widely than any animal. We can also apprehend intellectually how the interests of other people are connected with our own. And so, Mill concludes: 'The sentiment of justice, in that one of its elements which consists of the desire to punish, is thus, I conceive, the natural feeling of retaliation or vengeance, rendered by intellect and sympathy applicable to those injuries, that is, to those hurts, which wound us through, or in common with, society at large.'[76] But, he continues: 'This sentiment, in itself, has nothing moral in it; what is moral is, the exclusive subordination of it to the social sympathies. . . .'[77] This psychological aspect of Mill's treatment of justice leads us back to the topic of moral intuitionism.

Moral intuitionism revisited

In chapter 2, we saw that Mill has a four-point critique of moral intuitionism.

1 Associationism better explains the existence of the moral feelings.
2 Moral intuitionism impedes moral progress.
3 Moral intuitionism is pluralistic to the point of being indeterminate.
4 Moral intuitionism by itself has no power to explain why the rules of morality are what they are.

The first of these points was discussed in chapter 2 itself, but it is now possible to say more about the remaining three. The doctrine of moral intuitionism impedes moral progress, Mill maintains, because it encourages people to regard the present deliverances of their consciences as unimpeachable sources of moral truth, at least so long as the prompting of their consciences agree with those of their neighbours. Moral progress, after all, begins with the recognition that positive morality may not be what it should: 'If it be true that man has a sense given him to determine what is right and wrong, it follows that his moral judgments and feelings cannot be susceptible of any improvement; such as they are they ought to remain.'[78] Mill repeatedly points to the 'the inability of persons in general to conceive that feelings of right and wrong, which have been deeply implanted in their minds by the teaching they have from infancy received from all around them, can be sincerely thought by any one else to be mistaken or misplaced' as an obstacle to social reform.[79]

Mill's third reason for rejecting intuitionism is its indeterminacy, that is, the fact that it is frequently unable to tell us what our moral duties are. According to Mill, there is little difference between the utilitarians' primary rules and the intuitionists' moral first principles. The real difference between these moral theories only becomes apparent in cases in which these rules conflict.[80] According to Mill, there are two things that intuitionists could say about how these conflicts are resolved. They could claim that there is an even more general 'master' moral principle, also self-evident, that entails all other moral principles, and that this principle can be appealed to in order to decide which moral principles should take precedence in cases of conflict. Alternately, they could say that there are a number of more specific self-evident moral principles that spell out which of the more general principles take precedence over others in different classes of cases. In fact, though, Mill claims, they say neither.[81] In contrast, while rule utilitarianism's primary rules frequently come into conflict, the theory also contains auxiliary rules that resolve these conflicts, rules that (like the primary ones) are justified by the contribution they make to promoting happiness.

This leaves Mill's claim that intuitionists are unable to explain *why* actions are wrong, at least without making an appeal to utilitarian considerations. '[T]o all those a priori moralists who deem it necessary to argue at all, utilitarian arguments are indispensable', he asserts. Unfortunately, Mill chooses to illustrate this point with a reference to Kant's moral philosophy, alleging that Kant fails 'to show that there would be any contradiction . . . in the adoption by all rational beings of the most outrageously immoral rules of conduct. All he shows is that the consequences of their universal adoption would be such as no one would choose to incur.'[82]

Mill is no Kant scholar. Kant's moral theory is not best regarded as a form of moral intuitionism, despite his belief that moral knowledge is a priori. Moreover, while Mill's criticism may have a certain amount of force when it is construed as a criticism of Kant's examples of the application of his 'Categorical Imperative' in the *Groundwork of the Metaphysics of Morals*, it would take far more work than Mill devotes to the matter to show that this objection cuts to the quick of Kantianism.[83] This does not mean, though, that Mill's point does not have force against those thinkers who really do espouse intuitionist views. He may agree with nearly everything they say about the content of the primary rules of morality, but he can take the explanation of why those rules are what they are a step further. And while his explanation has to end somewhere, too, with his defence of the utility principle, his account of how we can know this principle intuitively is arguably more successful than any account the intuitionists can give about our intuitive knowledge of moral rules. At a minimum, his claim that there is universal agreement on the desirability of pleasure is surely more plausible than the claim that there is universal agreement on any particular rule of morality.

Part III

Mill's Social and Political Thought

7

Mill on Liberty and Individuality

This and the following two chapters will address different aspects of Mill's social and political philosophies, the branches of moral philosophy concerned specifically with the ethical questions that surround social life and government respectively. This chapter in particular will examine certain themes in his rousing defence of individual freedom, *On Liberty*. Rather than attempting a comprehensive analysis of *On Liberty*, the chapter will focus on a narrower set of topics. In the interest of brevity, many parts of the essay on which other commentators have written at length – Mill's claim that the state is justified in refusing to enforce 'slavery contracts', for instance, and even the essay's celebrated defence of the freedoms of belief, speech and the press – will be treated cursorily, if at all.

An overview of *On Liberty*

Mill opens *On Liberty* with an epigraph drawn from *The Spheres and Duties of Government* by Wilhelm von Humboldt, which was first published in 1810.[1,2] Although Humboldt would go on to become the minister responsible for the Prussian system of public education, in this volume he argues that the only legitimate task for the state is that of keeping citizens safe from each other and from external enemies: '[T]he State is to abstain from all solicitude for the positive welfare of the citizens and not to proceed a step farther than is necessary for their mutual security and protection . . .'[3]

Although he does not believe that the proper functions of the state are quite so tightly circumscribed as Humboldt maintains, Mill shares Humboldt's concern with the dangers posed by an excessively powerful or active government. Yet whereas Humboldt restricts his attention to the threat that the state poses to freedom and diversity, Mill is equally if not more concerned by the threat posed by 'informal' or extra-legal compulsion, through which a society can practise 'a social tyranny more formidable than many kinds of political oppression, since . . . it leaves fewer means of escape, penetrating much more deeply into the details of life, and enslaving the soul itself.'[4]

Mill's liberty principle demarcates a boundary between cases in which the use of coercion may be legitimate and cases in which it is always illegitimate. He depicts this 'one very simple principle' as 'entitled to govern absolutely' society's use of 'compulsion and control, whether the means used be physical force in the form of legal penalties, or the moral coercion of public opinion':

> That principle is, that the sole end for which mankind are warranted, individually or collectively, in interfering with the liberty of action of any of their number, is self-protection. That the only purpose for which power can be rightfully exercised over any member of a civilised community, against his will, is to prevent harm to others. His own good, either physical or moral, is not a sufficient warrant. He cannot rightfully be compelled to do or forbear because it will be better for him to do so, because it will make him happier, because, in the opinions of others, to do so would be wise, or even right.[5]

Mill may never be so far wrong as when he describes the liberty principle as 'very simple'. As will soon become apparent, it is anything but simple to interpret and apply. In fact, even his description of it as 'one' principle may be misleading, for later in the essay he restates it in terms of a pair of 'maxims': '[F]irst, that the individual is not accountable to society for his actions, in so far as these concern the interests of no person but himself. . . . Secondly, that for such actions as are prejudicial to the interests of others, the individual is accountable. . . .'[6]

Mill takes his opponents to be animated by a variety of motives for limiting freedom. One of these motives is the simple hatred of difference for its own sake. Another is paternalism, the notion that adults ought to be made to do things for their own good. A third motive might be described as 'overreaching moralism'. The term is not Mill's, but it is one way to describe the desire to compel people to conform to 'aesthetic' ideals of conduct within (speaking loosely) parts of their lives that concern only themselves. Even when the ideals in question are true, he objects to the attempt to back them with external sanctions. First and foremost among Mill's targets in *On Liberty* is the spectre of puritanical Calvinism, a view he takes to be 'held, in a mitigated form, by many who do not consider themselves Calvinists'.[7] He interprets the Calvinists as believing that we should seek to root out and destroy all strong impulses and desires, and he views them as being animated by all of the different motives enumerated above at once. So far has the Calvinist spirit already settled into the 'general average of mankind' that anyone with strong feelings is likely to be the target of those who resent deviations from the ordinary as such.[8] Calvinism is paternalistic inasmuch as it regards the rooting out of people's stronger desires and impulses as contributing to their 'prudential' as well as their 'moral' improvement.[9] Finally, he believes that a 'strong movement has set in towards the improvement of morals' and, while he would hardly complain about the improvement of morals as such, in this case he takes the putative reform movement to amount to an over-reaching moralism that is campaigning to impose the straitened Calvinist ideal on those few remaining uncustomary and energetic characters.[10] This ideal he assuredly does consider false.

Chapter 1 of *On Liberty* is where Mill introduces the liberty principle. He opens the chapter, though, with a potted history of the development of the idea of liberty. On his reading of history, the demand for liberty began as a demand for protection against tyrannical monarchs that eventually took the form of the demand for political democracy. When and where the demand for democracy was met, some people began to believe that as long as government is in the hands of the citizens there is no need for its power to be limited – a view that finds philosophical expression in the work of Rousseau. By falsely assuming the homogeneity of the citizenry, however, this view overlooks the danger of the 'tyranny of the majority'. Having reviewed both volumes of Alexis de Tocqueville's *Democracy in America*, in which the French author describes the vulnerability of minorities to majorities in America's young democracy, Mill is intimately familiar with the concept of democratic despotism.[11]

The second chapter of *On Liberty* is where Mill makes his case for the freedoms of speech, the press and thought. He distinguishes between three possible types of views that a society might attempt to censor – true views, false ones and views that contain partial truths – and argues that in each instance it is a mistake to prevent people from discussing views of that type freely. If the accepted views are false, then suppressing contrary views will deprive people of the truth, and, Mill claims, only someone who maintains that society or some of its members are infallible could deny that the received views could possibly be false. Yet even if the views that society accepts are entirely true, it still makes a mistake if it prevents alternative views from being expressed. A society in which received opinions cannot be challenged will be one in which those opinions become 'dead dogmas' that receive universal lip service but that make no impact on the average person's feelings and so have little effect on his or her conduct.[12] (There are some obvious echoes of Aristotle in Mill's thought, for example in the higher pleasures doctrine and in Mill's concern with character development. Here is a slightly less obvious one. The person who holds a view as a dead dogma is something like the 'incontinent' individual who can say that something is good or bad without being 'penetrated' by the knowledge.) Finally, if the received views contain only partial truths, then censorship makes it impossible for dissenting views to be analysed and mined for whatever comple-mentary nuggets of truth *they* may contain. This last point looms large in Mill's mind, of course, given his firmly held belief that most intellectual advances are made by one-eyed men whose doctrines contain some 'fractional truths' admixed with much that is false.[13] Mill himself came out of his depression aspiring to be a complete thinker, but there can only be complete thinkers where it is possible to debate the claims of one-eyed ones freely.[14] While he spends most of the chapter making the case that a wide-open marketplace of ideas is efficacious as a way of getting truths accepted more widely, Mill also criticizes censorship on ethological grounds, for its ten-dency to foster cowardice in the thinking class: '[T]he price paid for this sort of intellectual pacification is the sacrifice of the entire moral courage of the human mind.'[15]

Chapter 3 of *On Liberty*, titled 'On Individuality, As One of the Elements of Well-Being', is where Mill makes his case for liberty in the sense of freedom of action. In chapters 4 and 5, 'Of the Limits to the Authority of Society over the Individual' and 'Applications', he attempts to elucidate the liberty principle – first in the abstract and then, ostensibly, by example. Since the material in these chap-ters will be discussed in detail below, however, there is no need to say anything more about it now (except to remark that chapter 5 might have been more appropriatcly titled 'Borderline Cases and

Related Matters', since there are surprisingly few straightforward applications of the liberty principle to be found there).

Mill's conception of harm

This and the following two sections will grapple with some, although hardly all, of the interpretive puzzles that surround the liberty principle. The first is that of how Mill conceives of harm. Before we turn to this, though, a few preliminary matters must first be mentioned.

At a minimum, the liberty principle states a necessary condition for the use of coercion to be justified, that is, for society to be entitled to interfere forcibly with the conduct of some of its members. The next section will be concerned with precisely what this necessary condition is. Initially, though, it will simplify matters if we assume provisionally that this condition is that the conduct to be interfered with harms someone besides the agent – and without the consent of the one suffering harm, although this proviso will sometimes be left unstated in what follows.

It is important to guard against two elementary misunderstandings of Mill here. One is the assumption that he believes that society is always justified in coercively interfering with any behaviour that would harm someone besides the agent. The liberty principle does not specify a sufficient condition for the use of coercion. Even when society has jurisdiction over someone's conduct, it might not always be warranted on balance in exercising it. '[I]t must by no means be supposed, because damage, or probability of damage, to the interests of others, can alone justify the interference of society, that therefore it always does justify such interference.'[16] In essence, Mill believes that decisions about whether interference with someone's conduct is justified involve two steps. The first step is deciding whether the necessary condition contained in the liberty principle is met. If it is, then the costs and benefits of interfering must still be weighed, and in many cases the costs may outweigh the benefits. The second misunderstanding against which it is important to be on guard is the supposition that Mill believes that it is always wrong for people to harm each other without their consent or that society should try to prevent all harmful behaviour. He recognizes that people cannot live in society together without frequently harming the people around them. But since society has jurisdiction over conduct that harms unwilling others, it may legitimately decide which harmful conduct will be permitted and which cannot be tolerated.

With these preliminaries out of the way, we can now move to consider Mill's conception of harm. Since he believes that painful experiences are the only things that are intrinsically bad, one might initially assume that he must equate harming someone with causing pain. A moment's reflection, though, should be enough to see that this is not his position. Given Mill's externalist view of pleasure and pain, any unwelcome subjective experience – even any slight distaste or other mild negative emotion – is painful. If causing people to have subjective experiences that they would rather not have is all it takes to harm them, then the liberty principle loses its point which is, after all, to protect unpopular behaviour from interference. Admittedly, there may be a broad colloquial sense of 'harm' in which anything that makes people worse off in any way harms them, and when the word is used in this sense then Mill may have to agree that anything that causes a person pain does harm. However, since reading this conception of harm into *On Liberty* would vitiate the entire essay, and since the fact that it would do so is sufficiently obvious that it is highly unlikely that it would have escaped Mill's notice, then in order to read him charitably we must suppose that he is using 'harm' as a term of art in *On Liberty*, giving it a special and more restricted meaning. It is then up to us to discover what this meaning is, which we will have to do in part by considering whether different possible meanings would generate the implications that Mill evidently takes the liberty principle to have.

John Rees is responsible for an important insight that may hold the potential for resolving this problem. Rees points out that Mill sometimes connects the idea of harm with that of a person's interests. Some examples of his doing this have already been quoted, such as the passage in which Mill restates the liberty principle in terms of two maxims; another comes when he writes that 'As soon as any part of a person's conduct affects prejudicially the interests of others, society has jurisdiction over it.'[17] Rees therefore proposes that Mill equates doing harm to another with damaging another person's interests.[18] As long as it is possible for people to have unwelcome experiences without their interests automatically being damaged, this proposal makes it possible to say that not every unwelcome effect amounts to a harm. This conception of harm might be broadened, using a phrase of Mill's from a passage quoted above, to causing 'definite damage, or a *definite risk* of damage' to their interests. The liberty principle would not be plausible if it did not allow society to prevent individuals from engaging in activity that was likely but not certain to hurt unwilling others. (This raises the question, which cannot be pursued here, of how high a risk Mill would think that conduct has to pose to someone's interests for society to be entitled to interfere with it.)

Still, Rees's proposal explicates one unclear concept, that of harm, in terms of another, that of interests. Just as Mill does not define 'harm' in *On Liberty*, neither does he define 'interests' there. He does offer characterizations of interests elsewhere, in other works roughly contemporaneous with *On Liberty*, but they are of no help for understanding the liberty principle. In *Utilitarianism*, he implies that people's only interest is their interest in happiness, saying that 'laws and social arrangements should place the happiness, or (as speaking practically it may be called) the interest, of every individual, as nearly as possible in harmony with the interest of the whole' and equating 'private utility' with 'the interest or happiness of some few persons'.[19] In *Considerations on Representative Government*, he says that 'A man's interest consists of whatever he takes an interest in. Everybody has as many different interests as he has feelings; likings or dislikings, either of a selfish or of a better kind.'[20] The problem with reading either of these characterizations into *On Liberty* should be obvious. If we must say that anything that detracts from people's happiness or that they dislike damages their interests, then Rees's proposal would not do anything to solve the interpretative problem that we faced initially, the one that led to the introduction of the notion of interests into the discussion. The liberty principle still would not protect unpopular behaviour from interference, and we should resist ascribing any conception of interests to Mill that so obviously leads to this result. (Notice that there is a cautionary lesson here against the assumption that Mill uses technical terms with consistent meanings in different works.)

Rees's own suggestion as to how we should understand Mill's references to interests with *On Liberty* suffers from a different problem. Rees writes that

> To bring out the distinction I am trying to make between interests and effects, but with no pretence at offering a definitive account of the nature of interests, one might say that interests . . . depend for their existence on social recognition and are closely connected with prevailing standards about the sort of behaviour a man can legitimately expect from others.[21]

Rees's claim that Mill makes interests depend upon social recognition renders the Liberty Principle, as Richard Wollheim notes, 'conservative and relativistic'.[22] Mill is willing to turn a critical eye upon prevailing social norms and what they have to say about which effects constitute damage to interests. He contends that the prevailing norms may recognize interests where none exist, as in those parts of the Islamic world where a person who eats pork and thereby provokes 'unaffected disgust' in his or her neighbours is taken to do damage to their interests (or so Mill believes).[23] Mill also recognizes that the prevailing norms can fail to recognize interests where they do exist, as the norms of his own society do where the suffering of animals is concerned: 'It is by the grossest misunderstanding of the principles of liberty, that the infliction of exemplary punishment on ruffianism practised towards these defenceless creatures, has been treated as a meddling by government with things beyond its province; an interference with domestic life.'[24]

A different approach that holds more promise is to suppose that what Mill has in mind when he talks about interests in *On Liberty* are things that are useful to people regardless of what specific goals, desires or plans for their lives they happen to have – things that can serve as means to a variety of ends, or at least that are preconditions for realizing a variety of ends. In the abstract, at least, this would make interests rather similar to John Rawls's notion of 'primary goods', which 'normally have a use whatever a person's rational plan of life'. Among his primary goods Rawls lists 'rights, liberties, and opportunities', 'income and wealth', 'health and vigor, intelligence and imagination' and the social bases of self-respect.[25] This account of interests resembles the influential twentieth-century account developed by Brian Barry. Barry writes that something 'is in a man's interests if it increases his opportunities to get what he wants' for himself.[26] In order to establish the historical pedigree of his account, Barry approvingly quotes Locke, who among people's 'civil interests' lists 'life, liberty, health, and indolency of body; and the possession of outward things, such as money, lands, houses, furniture, and the like', and a commentary on the work of the Italian sociologist Vilfredo Pareto, according to which the latter used 'interests' to refer to things like money and power that are 'generalized means to any ultimate ends'.[27]

While there is admittedly little direct evidence that Mill is operating with something like this 'generalized means' conception of interests in *On Liberty*, several factors weigh in favour of attributing it to him. First, it is a plausible account in its own right. Second, not all conduct that a person happens to dislike will damage his or her interests when interests are so construed. If we assume that Mill is equating harm with damage to a person's interests so understood, therefore, then the liberty principle can perform its intended function of protecting certain unpopular behaviour from interference. Third, some specific interests that Mill either states or assumes that people have, in *On Liberty* and other works, are consistent with this account. (The next paragraph will say more about this.) Finally, this account avoids the relativism that is built into Rees's proposed alternative. Differences between societies may make some difference to what counts as an interest, inasmuch as they may affect what can serve as a means to an end, but something does not have to be recognized as an interest by prevailing social norms in order to be one. On the whole, there is enough reason to conclude that *On Liberty* is premised on this conception of interests for the discussion that follows to presuppose that this is the case.

Were Mill to enumerate the interests that he has in mind in *On Liberty*, his list might bear some resemblance to both Locke's list and Rawls's list of primary goods, but it would be distinctively his own. For Mill, for example, our paramount interest would surely be that of security, 'to every one's feelings the most vital of all interests', in his extended sense of security that includes not only life and health but also freedom and the ability to count on others not to 'break faith'. Another vitally important interest for Mill would be the interest in opportunities for mental development. These are the 'permanent interests of man as a progressive being' that Mill references in chapter 1 of *On Liberty*. The other interests that he recognizes, such as wealth or income, he deems much less significant.[28]

So there is a way to define 'interests' such that it makes sense to suppose that Mill understands what it is to harm someone in terms of making them worse off with respect to one or more of their interests, that is, damaging their interests or subjecting them to a sufficiently high risk of such damage. This treatment falls short of a full account of his conception of harm, since only a partial list of the interests that Mill takes humans to have has been given, but it sheds at least some light on this conception. Notice that one implication of this way of understanding what it means to harm someone is that whenever you succeed in a competition, you harm those whom you best, at least assuming that what is at stake in the competition affects their interests. This is entirely true to Mill's comments on economic competition and competitive examinations.

While he ardently supports both types of competition, he makes no bones about the fact that the losers are harmed by the winners.[29] This is why, despite Mill's support for a market-oriented economy, he does not believe that the liberty principle itself entails the doctrine of free trade. Mill generally opposes restrictions on competition, but only because he believes that the costs of these restrictions outweigh the benefits. This decision is made at the second step of the aforementioned two-step process.

The one exception to the claim that Mill does not believe that the liberty principle entails that society must allow competition involves competition between workers. Mill condemns as a violation of liberty the fact that bad workers of a socialistic bent 'employ a moral police, which occasionally becomes a physical one, to deter skilful workmen from receiving, and employers from giving, a larger remuneration for a more useful service'.[30] This curious exception must be regarded as an inconsistency on his part. If the success of superior workers in a competitive labour market means that inferior workers earn less, then the latter's interests are damaged, however willing society ought to be to permit this damage in the name of greater economic efficiency. So the liberty principle says nothing about the case.

Harm prevention versus harmful conduct prevention

Now it is time to revisit the earlier provisional assumption that Mill believes that society can justifiably interfere with a person's conduct only when that conduct would itself cause harm to someone besides the agent. It may seem surprising that there could be any question about this. After all, Mill says that for society to be justified in using compulsion against an agent, 'the conduct from which it is desired to deter him must be *calculated to produce evil* to someone else', and in offering what appears to be a simple restatement of the principle, he writes that 'If any one does *an act hurtful to others*, there is a prima facie case for punishing him, by law, or, where legal penalties are not safely applicable, by general disapprobation.'[31]

Yet the following passages fit uneasily with this assumption:

> If any one does an act hurtful to others, there is a prima facie case for punishing him. . . . There are also many positive acts for the benefit of others, which he may rightfully be compelled to

perform; such as, to give evidence in a court of justice; to bear his fair share in the common defence, or in any other joint work necessary to the interest of the society of which he enjoys the protection; and to perform certain acts of individual beneficence, such as saving a fellow creature's life, or interposing to protect the defenceless against ill-usage, things which whenever it is obviously a man's duty to do, he may rightfully be made responsible to society for not doing.[32]

[E]very one who receives the protection of society owes a return for the benefit . . . This . . . consists, first, in not injuring the interests of one another . . . and secondly, in each person's bearing his share (to be fixed on some equitable principle) of the labours and sacrifices incurred for defending the society or its members from injury and molestation.[33]

In these passages, Mill suggests that society can be justified not only in preventing its members from harming each other but also in requiring them to go out of their way to provide each other with various sorts of positive assistance. Most of his examples are of things that people can be required to do in order to protect one another from third parties or from 'nature', either through participating in 'protective social institutions' like the military and the court system or through acting individually to rescue people in danger. Mill is even more specific about society's ability to compel its members to protect one another in some of his other work. He is, for example, strongly in favour of replacing Britain's standing army with a 'citizen army' or militia: 'Henceforth our army should be our whole people trained and disciplined.'[34] This would involve mandatory military training for (at least) every male citizen and conscription in the face of imminent invasion.[35]

This raises the question of whether it would be better to reject the provisional assumption made earlier and adopt a different reading of the liberty principle instead. This alternative reading would say that the principle permits society to use compulsion on us in any way that would serve to protect someone else from harm, which could mean either forcibly preventing us from doing something that would harm another or forcibly compelling us to help to protect someone else from harm even when what we would have done if left to our own devices would not itself have harmed anyone. When read along the lines of our earlier provisional assumption, the liberty principle can be described as a 'harmful-conduct-prevention principle'. On the alternative reading, it is a 'harm-prevention' principle.[36]

Which of these readings of the liberty principle is best is at issue in an important exchange between D. G. Brown and David Lyons. On the basis of passages like the one in which Mill asserts that a person can only 'rightfully be compelled to do or forbear' when 'the conduct from which it is desired to deter him' is 'calculated to produce evil to someone else', Brown maintains that Mill must intend the liberty principle as a harmful-conduct-prevention principle.[37] Brown, though, argues that requiring people to bear a share in the common defence, protect the defenceless against assault, and so on goes far beyond preventing harmful conduct. Thus Brown concludes that Mill actually misapplies his own principle. While Brown is a sympathetic reader of Mill, he concedes that the liberty principle (as he understands it) places too many restrictions on society's power to require its members to cooperate and to assist one another. In other words Brown thinks that Mill would have done better if he *had* offered a harm-prevention principle or, better still, a principle that would allow society to employ coercion even more freely still.

Lyons, in contrast, reads the liberty principle as a harm-prevention principle. He offers three reasons for this. First, he observes that Mill does sometimes word the principle this way, including his first and apparently most 'official' statement of it: 'That the only purpose for which power can be rightfully exercised over any member of a civilised community . . . is *to prevent harm to others.*' So the text is at least equivocal. Second, he points out that on this reading the liberty principle is generally consistent with Mill's more specific claims about the kinds of individual and collective positive assistance that the liberty principle permits society to compel its members to render to one another. Finally, Lyons contends that this reading of the principle is more charitable, since a principle that limited society to interfering with conduct that was itself harmful would be too restrictive.[38] Brown finds much to agree with in all three of these points, but he attaches more weight than Lyons to those passages in which Mill does seem to say specifically that society may only interfere with conduct that is itself harmful.[39]

Complicating the choice between these readings is the fact that Mill may well believe that a person harms his fellow citizens when he fails to take part in his polity's harm-preventing institutions or when he fails to perform those particular 'acts of individual beneficence . . . [that] he may rightfully be made responsible to society for not doing'. Thus he may not consider it consequential whether we read the liberty principle as a harmful-conduct-prevention or harm-prevention principle. The key to understanding how Mill might arrive at the conclusion that failing to prevent harm to our compatriots can itself be harmful comes when he writes: 'Though society is not founded on a contract, and though no good purpose is answered by inventing a contract in order to deduce social obligations from it, every one who receives the protection of society owes a return for the benefit. . . .'[40] Consider this line in light of what he says in chapter 5 of *Utilitarianism* about 'good for good' being 'one of the dictates of justice' and the 'important rank, among human evils and wrongs, of the disappointment of expectation': 'He who accepts benefits, and denies a return of them when needed, inflicts a real hurt, by disappointing one of the most natural and reasonable of expectations, and one which he must at least tacitly have encouraged, otherwise the benefits would seldom have been conferred.'[41] Remember also the passage from the Comte volume, quoted in the last chapter, in which Mill says that 'every one, who avails himself of the advantages of society, leads others to expect from him all such positive good offices and disinterested services as the moral improvement attained by mankind has rendered customary. . . .' When these passages are taken into account, Mill very much seems to be suggesting in *On Liberty* that by accepting the benefits of social life we encourage the other members of our society to expect that we will participate in the institutions and practices that are responsible for producing those benefits, and that if we disappoint this expectation then we *ipso facto* harm them.

But is this plausible? In certain situations, it is quite clear that we can harm people through failing to protect them after having fostered the expectation that we would. Take a case of the clearest sort first. Jason is a novice swimmer. Jordan actively encourages Jason to get into the pool, promising him that he will help him if he gets into trouble. Then, when Jason begins to struggle, Jordan does nothing. Here, Jordan harms Jason as surely as if he had pushed him into the deep end himself. There are variations on this case where similar reasoning seems to hold, albeit perhaps not quite as obviously. Cody takes a job as a lifeguard, but when Sonya gets into trouble in the pool, Cody idly watches her struggle. The claim that Cody harms Sonya is quite plausible, given that the presence of a lifeguard may have been a factor in Sonya's decision to enter the water. Or consider Hanna and Jacob. Hanna sits by the side of the pool, reading. No one else is present. Jacob arrives and dives in, but after a few minutes he begins to struggle. Hanna does nothing, even though she could easily and at no risk to herself throw him a life preserver. The claim that Hanna harms Jacob is more plausible than it might at first appear. She has not gone out of her way to signal him to expect any help from her. Nevertheless, it is 'customary' for people to make an effort to help in these circumstances, at least to the extent of tossing a life preserver, so perhaps it is reasonable for Jacob to infer from Hanna's mere presence that he can count on her to come to his assistance if necessary. If so, then merely by being there she is tacitly encouraging him to expect her help (unless, at least, she warns him not to).

In each of the above scenarios, one person needs to be rescued by another, and in each scenario the people needing help might not have been in danger in the first place had they not been encouraged to expect help if needed. All of these cases tap into what is very right in Mill's point about the disappointment of expectations in *Utilitarianism*: when someone encourages us to expect them to act in a given way, and we make plans that are premised on their doing so, then they harm us if they do not follow through. This is not only true when what they have led us to expect is that they will pull us out of a dangerous situation if necessary, but it is at least as true then as ever. It is not their mere failure to help alone that harms us, but the compound action of their encouraging us to expect help and then withholding it. The wrongness of this failure is embodied in the common law doctrine of 'detrimental reliance'.

But how widely does this reasoning apply? Consider Paris and Jennifer. Paris goes swimming alone in a deserted quarry and develops a sudden cramp, so that she is in danger of drowning. She believes that there is no one within miles. Unbeknownst to her, though, Jennifer is hiking in the vicinity and happens to see her flailing. It is in Jennifer's power to save Paris, by throwing her the end of a rope that Jennifer conveniently carries. Jennifer would obviously protect Paris from harm if she threw her the rope. Most people would probably be comfortable with saying that Jennifer has a moral obligation to throw Paris the rope. Many would even be willing to say that this is a perfect obligation and that Paris has a correlative positive right to assistance.[42] But all of this might be true and yet it still not be the case that if Jennifer fails to act then she will harm Paris. Paris's decision to go into the water was in no way premised on the expectation of Jennifer's help. Given this, it seems much less plausible in this instance that Jennifer's failure to act would be the cause or even a cause of the harm that would befall Paris.

Notice that this example does not question Mill's assertion that your accepting benefits from someone constitutes encouragement for them to expect similar benefits from you in the future, in similar circumstances. Questions could be raised about this as well, but nothing in the Paris/Jennifer example changes if we suppose that a week earlier Paris had somehow rescued Jennifer from a similar danger. What makes the claim that Jennifer would be doing harm to Paris if she did not rescue her dubious is the fact that Paris's being in this perilous position is in no way the result of her having counted on getting help from Jennifer or anyone else. For the same reason, the general claim that we cause harm to people when we fail to do our fair share to participate in our society's collective institutions and practices for protecting people against harm – the military, the court system and so on – is also dubious. Take the institution of the criminal jury, which by distinguishing the innocent from the guilty serves to protect both individuals from the harm of wrongful imprisonment and the public from the danger of criminals loose in their midst. Suppose that Rudolph shirks jury duty. Further suppose that his absence actually makes some difference to the disposition of a case: a defendant is set free because her right to a speedy jury trial could not be satisfied, perhaps, or a more attractive plea bargain is offered to a defendant to obviate the need for a trial. Someone might be harmed who would not have been had Rudolph done his duty, perhaps because a predatory criminal is released who would otherwise be behind bars. Even if we think that Rudolph bears some of the moral responsibility for this harm, though, that does not make him the *cause* of it. In particular, it is not likely that anyone would be harmed specifically as a result of relying on an expectation that Rudolph encouraged that he would show up for jury duty if summoned. This is not to deny that stories can be told in which A encourages B to believe that A will somehow participate in some protective social institution or practice, A fails to follow through and B is harmed as a result of having relied on this belief, but these stories would describe special cases. Even if the very fact that we live in society can be construed as encouraging our compatriots to expect us to do our part in the collective social institutions and practices that protect us all against harm, it will not be true as a rule that our failure to make good on these expectations makes us the cause of any harm that results.

So even if Mill should happen to think otherwise, it does matter which reading of the liberty principle one adopts. Unfortunately, the considerations that favour each reading are so closely balanced that it is difficult to choose between them. While Lyons's reading makes the principle both intrinsically more plausible and more consistent with Mill's examples, there are passages in which Mill does seem to specify that society can only interfere with harmful conduct. In addition, if his talk about what we owe in return for the benefits of social life is intended as an argument that many failures to protect people from harm are themselves harmful, then the very fact that he sees the need to make this argument may suggest that he is thinking of the liberty principle in harmful-conduct-prevention terms. Perhaps the harm-prevention reading enjoys slightly greater support on balance, but this is a very close call.

If the liberty principle is read as a harm-prevention principle then it is misleading to suggest, as Mill admittedly does, that there is a 'sphere of action' within which society can never justifiably interfere, a sphere made up of activities that are sufficiently private in nature that anyone except the agent has only an 'indirect' interest in them.[43] No matter what someone was doing at a given time, after all, compelling them to drop it for the present and do something else instead might help to protect another person from harm. On the harm-prevention reading, the liberty principle distinguishes not between types of conduct with which society can and cannot interfere but rather between kinds of restrictions that it can and cannot impose – namely those that do and do not contribute to harm prevention respectively. So instead of saying, for instance, that society can in principle regulate wages since the decisions that employers make about how much to pay their workers do cause harm, if one adopts Lyons's reading then one has to say instead that society can in principle regulate wages as long as the regulation in question would serve to protect people from being harmed without their consent. The difference is subtle yet significant.

On the harm-prevention reading, the liberty principle itself would not preclude a scheme that would require people to participate in some very demanding protective social institution, one that would take up much of their time. It would not preclude a society from drafting people who write books defending unpopular views into the army, for instance, so they would have no time to write. Nor would it preclude a society from requiring its members to spend 12 hours a day at home staring out of their windows, so that they could quickly call the police if they saw a crime on their block. Yet while the liberty principle itself would not rule such schemes out, on the harm-prevention reading, Mill would still consider them justified only if they passed two further tests. First, other principles of justice require that people not be forced to contribute more than their 'fair share' to harm-prevention institutions, that is, the burdens they impose have to be distributed equitably. A plan to stamp out some unpopular activity by drafting everyone likely to do it into the army would fail this test. Second, since the liberty principle does not state a sufficient condition for interference to be justified, no scheme requiring people to take part in some protective institution is justified unless its benefits outweigh its costs. The neighbourhood watch plan detailed above would surely fail this test.

The next section considers this cost-benefit analysis in more detail.

Is harm all that matters?

As noted earlier, Mill believes that decisions about whether society is justified in interfering with someone's actions in a given case must be made in two steps.[44] The first step is to determine whether the proposed interference would contribute to the prevention of harm. (We will assume henceforth that Lyons's harm-prevention reading is the right one, but anyone who favours Brown's reading can read harm-prevention talk as harmful-conduct-prevention talk in what follows; this will not alter the points being made here.) If the interference would prevent harm, though, then the second step of comparing the costs and benefits of interference is still necessary.[45] Two brief clarificatory remarks should be made here. First, one could say that a third step belongs on the list, namely that of making sure that the burdens of any positive demands made on people are fairly distributed. Many uses of social coercion involve no positive demands, though, so this step is not always necessary. Second, Mill's language in the passage just quoted may imply that the costs and benefits of interference are always to be compared on a case-by-case basis, but where government interference is concerned it is important to remember that the rule of law, in which Mill assuredly believes, restricts the state to using its power only in accordance with general laws. The state might decide that it would not be worthwhile to, say, enforce a particular criminal law in a given exceptional case. But it cannot use coercion except where a general law authorizes it to.

Society is only justified in exercising coercion when the benefits of doing so outweigh the costs. But what costs and benefits are to

be taken into account? One possibility is that in addition to impos-
ing a necessary condition for the use of compulsion to be justified,
the liberty principle also restricts the factors that can be taken into
account in this cost-benefit analysis, so that only benefits that flow
directly from the prevention of harm can be considered. A different
view is that as long as a proposed interference has been shown
to contribute to harm-prevention, any and all benefits that would
flow from the interference should be considered in deciding whether
or not it would be worthwhile. These might include both paternalistic benefits to the agent whose conduct is being interfered with
and the pleasure that the interference would give to anyone who
just wants it to happen for whatever reason (perhaps because it
would keep people from engaging in an activity that he or she
simply happens to dislike). The first view holds that the liberty
principle says that the only good reason for coercively interfering
with anyone's behaviour is the prevention of harm, and so it might
be labelled the 'reason-restricting' reading of the liberty principle.
The second view might, for contrast, be described as saying that
whatever collection of reasons can be mustered in favour of a given
interference is insufficient unless harm prevention is among them.
Since it says that the liberty principle only imposes a necessary
condition for interference to be justified, this can be labelled the
'mere necessary condition' reading.

Several passages clearly favour the reason-restricting reading.
After all, Mill says that harm prevention is the 'sole end for which
mankind are warranted, individually or collectively, in interfering
with the liberty of action of any of their number' and that it is 'the
only purpose for which power can be rightfully exercised over any
member of a civilised community, against his will'. These passages
do indeed suggest that, as Ten writes: 'Mill's point is that the case
for intervention must rest on reasons other than, for example, the
mere dislike or disapproval of the conduct. If these other reasons
are insufficient, no additional weight is given by citing the dislike
and disapproval.'[46]

What is more, if we take the liberty principle to impose a mere
necessary condition on the use of compulsion then it would not
prevent a society from adopting some restriction on freedom that
made a relatively minor contribution to preventing individuals
from harming each other but was primarily recommended by the
fact that it kept them from harming themselves. A ban on cigarettes
might be an example: there would be fewer people encountering
second-hand smoke without their consent, but most of the benefit

would come from the fact that smokers would no longer be harming themselves. This reading does render the liberty principle very weak. The principle may also appear to be somewhat arbitrary, on this reading, since it is not readily apparent why reasons unconnected with preventing harm to others should count for nothing in the absence of a harm-preventing reason but have weight if a harm-preventing reason is present as well. Where paternalistic considerations are concerned, for instance, one might agree with the spirit of Richard Arneson's question when he asks: '[W]hy is it any more legitimate to deprive me of liberty *for my own good* when my act affects others than when it does not? The fact that my behavior affects others may introduce good reasons to limit my freedom for their sakes, but it can hardly affect the legitimacy of paternalism one way or another.'[47]

Certain passages, though, do appear to call the reason-restricting account of the principle into question. When Mill himself argues for various uses of compulsion by society, he sometimes gives the appearance of adducing paternalistic considerations in favour of them. This is true in particular of his arguments in favour of requiring people to participate in protective social institutions, such as juries and the militia, on the grounds that this would contribute usefully to their education (in his extended sense). In *On Liberty* itself, he notes that while

> In many cases, though individuals may not do the particular thing so well . . . as the officers of government, it is nevertheless desirable that it should be done by them . . . as a means to their own mental education – a mode of strengthening their active faculties, exercising their judgment, and giving them a familiar knowledge of the subjects with which they are thus left to deal.[48]

Likewise, in arguing elsewhere in favour of mandatory military training, he claims that 'the loss of productive power by withdrawing from industry for a short time young men of that age would . . . be more than compensated by the good effects of military training in making them more steady and vigorous for the ordinary pursuits of life.'[49]

In these passages, Mill claims that requiring adults to perform mandatory public service helps them to cultivate capacities and character traits that will serve them well in the 'ordinary pursuits' of their private lives. Ethological arguments are not the only arguments that could be given for juries or militias, nor are they the only arguments that Mill does give. For instance, he contends that if Britain were to replace its standing army with a citizen militia then it would be both less likely to fall into despotism and less likely to become involved in foreign wars.[50] Still, though, at first glance Mill seems to be making his case for mandatory public service at least partly on paternalistic grounds. That is precisely the kind of argument that, on the reason-restricting reading, the liberty principle forbids.

On closer examination, though, these passages do not force us to adopt the very weak mere necessary condition account of the liberty principle.[51] First, Mill's ethological arguments are not purely paternalistic. He believes that a large part of what makes the capabilities and character traits that mandatory public service will foster valuable is that they will make people both more likely and better able to act in ways that will conduce to protecting other people from harm – especially, if not exclusively, when they are in the voting booth. Chapter 9 will deal with this point in more depth. Second, while Mill's assertion that military training would make individuals more 'steady and vigorous for the ordinary pursuits of life' does seem to be primarily concerned with how much it would improve them as workers, and while this may not necessarily have anything to do with protecting anyone else from harm, Mill is not citing this putative benefit as a positive merit of the scheme. He is instead merely saying that this effect would at least be great enough to counterbalance any negative effects of briefly taking workers away from their work periodically, so that on the whole the impact of mandatory militia service on productivity would be 'a wash'.

The value of freedom

> Though I hold the good of the species (or rather of its separate units) to be the *ultimate* end . . . I believe with the fullest Belief that this end can in no other way be forwarded but by . . . each taking for his exclusive aim the development of what is best in *himself*.[52]

Chapter 3 of *On Liberty* is where Mill makes his case for the value of individual freedom of action. While he leaves it largely to the reader to disentangle the chapter's various strands of argument, this case might be seen as having two main parts, one concerned with the value to each individual of his or her own liberty and the other with what can be called the social benefits of liberty. The first part of this case comprises three main lines of argument, of which two can be stated succinctly. The most straightforward is that people have 'diversities of taste': 'A man cannot get a coat or a pair of boots to fit him unless they are either made to his measure, or he has a whole warehouseful to choose from: and is it easier to fit him with a life than with a coat?'[53] Every restriction on conduct will make it harder for someone to satisfy their preferences, unless no one has any interest in performing the proscribed conduct anyway – in which case the restriction is unnecessary.

A second argument is that the very act of choosing the course of one's own life is an opportunity to use and develop the distinctly human faculties: 'He who chooses his plan for himself, employs all his faculties. He must use observation to see, reasoning and judgment to foresee, activity to gather materials for decision, discrimination to decide, and when he has decided, firmness and self-control to hold to his deliberate decision.'[54] Every time that individuals are deprived of the chance to make a choice about how to live is eliminated, they are *ipso facto* deprived of a chance to further their own development through making it.

A third argument builds on the second. It concerns the necessity of liberty for the development of the quality that Mill calls individuality. This argument is Mill's way of appropriating Humboldt's doctrine

> that 'the end of man, or that which is prescribed by the eternal or immutable dictates of reason, and not suggested by vague and transient desires, is the highest and most harmonious development of his powers to a complete and consistent whole'; that, therefore, the object 'towards which every human being must ceaselessly direct his efforts, and on which especially those who design to influence their fellow-men must ever keep their eyes, is the individuality of power and development'; that for this there are two requisites, 'freedom, and variety of situations'; and that from the union of these arise 'individual vigour and manifold diversity', which combine themselves in 'originality'.[55]

The central feature of the chapter, this argument calls for more comment than the first two.

Even if everyone had very similar psychological constitutions, there would still be some value in allowing, or even forcing, individuals to choose the course of their own lives. As we have seen, though, Mill denies that people are so similar. Even James Mill would admit that the inevitable differences in our early experiences will produce deeply rooted mental associations that are unique to each individual. And John Mill goes even further, as we saw in chapter 2, for unlike his father he recognizes that there are physiological differences that would prevent even two people who underwent the same experiences from the very start of their lives from forming the same associations. Thus, as John Gray writes, 'According to Mill, each man has a quiddity or peculiar endowment, the development of which is indispensable to his happiness.'[56] Each person's development must follow a unique path. The destination of this path should not be thought of simply as the cultivation of a unique assortment of abilities. It is the formation of a distinctive character, the set of 'dispositions, and habits of mind and heart' most congruent with the more deeply rooted aspects of one's unique psychology, and in particular the character that results in one's making the best overall use of the higher faculties given one's unique allocation of abilities or powers. 'Individuality' is the term that Mill uses to describe a character that fits its bearer's endowments in this way.

Mill takes for granted that individuality is a quality that each person must acquire for him- or herself through a deliberate process of self-formation. He even asserts that a person who has not undergone this kind of self-culture will have 'no character' at all, 'no more than a steam-engine has a character', although since elsewhere he understands the character simply in terms of the sum-total of a person's habits (however acquired) this has to be regarded as an exaggeration.[57] If pressed, he would presumably defend this assumption on epistemological grounds. While some people may know particular things about us that we do not know ourselves, the only person who could have enough insight into your nature to know what combination of character traits would suit you best is you yourself. Individuality could never be 'distributed' by society. To the extent that a society attempts to play an active role in the character development of its citizens, it is inevitably going to push their personalities in the direction of greater uniformity, not greater uniqueness. This is not to deny that Mill considers it appropriate for society to play such a role, within limits, nor to deny that he believes that there are certain elements that should be a part of each individual's character. There are virtues ranging from courage to truthfulness to cleanliness that everyone should possess.[58] So too, he insists, are there traits that should have no place in any person's character, the 'moral vices' that 'constitute a bad and odious moral character': 'Cruelty of disposition; malice and ill-nature; that most anti-social and odious of all passions, envy; dissimulation and insincerity, irascibility on insufficient cause, and resentment disproportioned to the provocation; the love of domineering over others' and so on.[59] Still, when one considers how many elements make up a person's character, it is readily apparent that Mill's list of virtues and vices that people should share leaves ample room for variation and hence for individuality.

Not only will someone who possesses individuality have the character that best facilitates his or her own enjoyment of the higher pleasures, but that character, exhibiting as it does the harmonious development described by Humboldt, is literally a thing of beauty. This makes it an object worthy of aesthetic appreciation and thus a source of higher quality pleasure to everyone in a position to observe it: 'It is not by wearing down into uniformity all that is individual in themselves, but by cultivating it, and calling it forth, within the limits imposed by the rights and interests of others, that human beings become a noble and beautiful object of contemplation. . . .'[60]

This suggests that the process of self-culture through which a person acquires individuality is one of artistic creation. As Mill puts it, 'Among the works of man, which human life is rightly employed in perfecting and beautifying, the first in importance surely is man himself.'[61] The notion that we should all regard our characters as works of art is a recurrent theme in Mill's work. In the essay 'Bentham', he criticizes the earlier utilitarian for failing to see that man is 'capable of pursuing spiritual perfection as an end; of desiring, for its own sake, the conformity of his own character to his standard of excellence, without hope of good or fear of evil from other source than his own inward consciousness', and, in the speech he gave to mark his being named Rector of St Andrews University, he contends that a person who appreciates beauty will 'keep before himself a type of perfect beauty in human character, to light his attempts at self-culture'.[62] In thinking about how we want to shape our own characters, we must think about how best to realize our abstract conceptions of beauty in human characters, starting with the raw materials we find in their own unique natures. Each of us is, in some respects, in the position of a sculptor who has been handed a piece of stone to work more or less at random and who must do the best with it that is possible.

People shape their characters – the sum-total of their mental habits, remember – through the choices they make and the circumstances in which they place themselves. If each person is to fashion a bespoke character for him- or herself, it follows that people require both freedom of choice and a broad range of different environments in which they might live. Personal freedom of action can be regarded in part as a kind of artistic freedom, and every restriction on this freedom narrows the range of characters that it is possible to create.

There are several respects, then, in which individuals willing to take advantage of freedom are made better off. Mill further believes – and here begins the second part of his case for freedom – that freedom offers benefits to society as a whole, benefits that can in principle be enjoyed even by people with little interest in deviating from conventional social norms themselves. He discusses three of these in particular in chapter 3. The first of these benefits is the existence of people with strong impulses and energetic characters, or rather the good that such people can do. Against the Calvinist fear of the danger posed by strong impulses, Mill contends that those with strong feelings can have strong consciences as well: 'Energy may be turned to bad uses; but more good may always be made of an energetic nature, than of an indolent and impassive one.'[63] Even people of a passive nature are better off for having people with energetic characters in their society. But people will only possess this vital energy, Mill claims, when they have acquired individuality: 'Whoever thinks that individuality of desires and impulses should not be encouraged to unfold itself, must maintain that society has no need of strong natures – is not the better for containing many persons who have much character – and that a high general average of energy is not desirable.'[64]

Mill never makes the nature of the connection between individuality and active characters explicit. He might hold the relatively strong view that individuality is both necessary and sufficient for strong impulses, but there is no obvious reason to believe that every person who is truly him- or herself will be especially energetic. More plausible, if still not obviously true, is the weaker view that individuality is necessary for an energetic character, so that only a person whose habits of doing, thinking and feeling are consonant with his or her own unique inner nature will move through life vigorously and vibrantly (even if some people's inner natures will turn out not to be so vibrant). In addition to arguing that society must embrace the liberty principle if its members' characters are to be energetic, by the way, Mill also admonishes against letting the government take on too much responsibility, even in matters that the liberty principle permits society to control. He asserts that a society will never be composed of active characters if its members habitually turn to the government for the solution of all of their problems; when all activity comes from the state, the most active and talented people become civil servants, and then they are eventually robbed of their energy by the bureaucratic system.[65] Mill believes that this is the trap into which France has fallen, with the result that when 'anything goes amiss' the French tend to say 'It takes patience,' and passively endure it.[66] Indeed, he considers the same to be true of all or nearly all of the nations of the Continent.[67]

A second social benefit to freedom is that as individuals' characters become more beautiful, so too will social life. Where people lack individuality, the tapestry of social life is a pale thing but, as they realize their individual natures, it fills with striking and vibrant shades and hues:

> [A]s the works partake the character of those who do them, by the same process human life also becomes rich, diversified, and animating, furnishing more abundant aliment to high thoughts and elevating feelings, and strengthening the tie which binds every individual to the race, by making the race infinitely better worth belonging to.[68]

Finally, people who do deviate from custom – who engage in 'experiments in living', to use Mill's famous phrase – will sometimes hit upon forms of behaviour that are worthy of becoming customs in their own right.[69] While this is an important point, though, a quibble is in order. Only people willing to deviate from custom will ever discover ways in which custom might be improved, but it is possible to agree with Mill about this and yet to question whether he puts rather too much emphasis on the idea that only 'persons of genius' are likely to discover 'better modes action, and customs more worthy of general adoption'.[70] Perhaps the lives that would be best suited for the development of singular and unusual people would not be good models for the lives of ordinary folks. In that case, the greatest source of improvement to a society's customs over time would likely be the incremental accumulation of smaller departures from custom by people who are creative but not too atypical.

The concern that Mill shows for the improvement of custom demonstrates that, contrary to the way in which he is sometimes depicted, he is no enemy of custom as such. '[I]t would be absurd', he writes, 'to pretend that people ought to live . . . as if experience had as yet done nothing towards showing that one mode of existence or of conduct, is preferable to another.' Yet he then adds: '[I]t is the privilege and proper condition of a human being, arrived at the maturity of his faculties, to use and interpret experience in his own way. It is for him to find out what part of recorded experience is properly applicable to his own circumstances and character.'[71]

Mill's ideal society would not be bereft of customs, but it would be a society in which customs would never be unreflectively followed and one in which the fact that a certain form of behaviour was customary would in and of itself never be regarded as a reason to force people to practice it. Individuals would feel free to ignore particular customs when they had sufficient reason to believe that following them would hamper their development. Mill may consider his and Harriet Taylor's deportment before their marriage as a model in this regard. He might well acknowledge that there is considerable wisdom embodied in the custom that prohibits close contact between people of different sexes who have other spouses and that most people would do well to follow it, at least until the general level of development reaches a level at which people are far less preoccupied with sexuality. Even so, on reflection it seemed clear to Mill and Taylor that the reasons behind this customary prohibition had little weight in their own case and that only by setting the custom aside could they realize their mental potential. And so they did.

In chapter 1 of *On Liberty*, Mill announces in no uncertain terms that his case for individual freedom will rest on a utilitarian foundation:

> It is proper to state that I forego any advantage which could be derived to my argument from the idea of abstract right, as a thing independent of utility. I regard utility as the ultimate appeal on all ethical questions; but it must be utility in the largest sense, grounded on the permanent interests of man as a progressive being.[72]

All of the arguments considered in this section are completely consistent with this methodological constraint. While some thinkers might take the development and exercise of the distinctly human faculties to matter independently of their contributions to happiness, nothing that Mill says in *On Liberty* suggests that he has abandoned his commitment to the utility principle. In fact, his case for the importance of liberty is consistent not only with utilitarianism but also with hedonism. We have seen that Mill has a hedonistic account to give of why it matters, not just how well people can satisfy their preferences, but also to what extent they can develop their higher faculties.[73] Everything that he says in *On Liberty* is consistent with this account. Two bits of text in particular might seem to call the claim that *On Liberty* is consistent with hedonism into question. One is the title of chapter 3, where he refers to individuality as an 'element of well-being'. Construed in the most literal sense, this description of individuality would be at odds with hedonism. The other is his criticism of the fact 'that individual spontaneity is hardly recognised by the common modes of thinking as having any intrinsic worth, or deserving any regard on its own account'. As we saw in chapter 4, though, Mill is not always careful to distinguish between something's being intrinsically valuable in the most literal sense and its being valuable because it gives rise to happiness in an especially direct manner.

Mill fails to spell out how he moves from the arguments sketched above to his specific formulation of the liberty principle. The principle that these arguments support most directly is what Brown has called the 'Principle against Restraint, according to which there is a prima facie case against all interference', or, as Brown puts it elsewhere, 'All interference with the liberty of action of the individual is prima facie wrong.'[74] This is not a principle that Mill explicitly formulates anywhere, but it is, as Brown says, an implicit part of his theory of liberty. It amounts to what was called in the last chapter a primary rule or principle of justice, which makes the liberty principle an auxiliary principle or rule, one that emerges as a way of resolving conflicts between primary principles. Note, though, that the Principle against Restraint contains the qualifier 'prima facie' (which in this case mean that there is prima facie reason to believe that any given interference is wrong, not that there is a prima facie duty of the 'Rossian' sort not to interfere). This means that, strictly speaking, it does not conflict with the other primary principles that limit it, which must include principles intended to protect people against harm.

Despite being an auxiliary principle, the liberty principle is still rather sweeping in scope. One might wonder why Mill does not think that a finer-grained or more nuanced rule, one that allows for the use of compulsion in a wider range of circumstances, would be preferable. It is important to remember that his endorsement of the liberty principle does not imply that he believes that uses of coercion that are contrary to the principle will never be optimific.

It simply means that he believes that there is no better principle for people to internalize. This can be true even if there are some situations in which a use of social power that is contrary to the liberty principle actually would maximize total net happiness. Even if such situations exist, it could easily be the case that getting people to internalize the 'original' liberty principle would have better consequences than getting them to internalize a modified version that incorporates exceptions allowing coercion to be used in them. This is especially true if there is no easy way to characterize these situations in terms of common features, because Mill believes that exceptions to a moral rule have to be subsumed under rules themselves. The harder these situations are to characterize, the more convoluted these exceptional rules and the alternative principle that incorporates them would need to be. Imagine the liberty principle with a list of complicated exceptions appended that are either extremely detailed or extremely vague. It would probably be harder to get people to internalize this more nuanced principle in the first place, and they would certainly be more likely to apply it incorrectly. (This issue will crop up again in the section below entitled 'Conservative Caveats'.)

There is little room to doubt that Mill would consider a considerable measure of individuality to be a necessary part of a genuinely happy life. This implies that genuine happiness requires a considerable measure of liberty. One might wonder why, if Mill considers individual freedom so necessary for genuine human happiness, he explicitly states that the liberty principle only applies to societies which have reached a sufficiently high level of civilization: 'Despotism is a legitimate mode of government in dealing with barbarians, provided the end be their improvement, and the means justified by actually effecting that end.'[75] Is Mill being inconsistent here, first making trenchant arguments for the value of liberty and then blithely asserting that it would be better not to extend this liberty to the citizens of countries that are less developed by his lights – which, while he is not specific, presumably includes most of the non-Western world? If so, then it is not only this point from his writings that is inconsistent with chapter 3 of *On Liberty* – so too is his entire career spent helping to run the British colonial empire. Yet Mill sees no worrisome tension here, let alone any outright inconsistency, for he takes societies to move through distinct stages of development. At the most primitive level, that of savage or barbaric society, the prospects for cooperation are very limited: 'The savage cannot bear to sacrifice, for any purpose, the satisfaction of his individual will.'[76] Societies can only move past this stage when their members are subjected to thoroughgoing domination so that their spirits can be broken: 'law and discipline' must assert 'a power over the whole man, claiming to control all his life in order to control his character'.[77] If liberty is a prerequisite for a genuinely happy human life, it is not the only one, and it is no blessing to a people not yet ready to take advantage of it.

Contemporary readers will rightly be troubled by Mill's easy description of other societies as savage or slavish (another early stage of social development, one at which the people can be controlled externally but are incapable of self-control).[78] Mill's image of the non-Western world cannot conceivably do its inhabitants justice. Some points made in chapter 2 are worth reiterating at this juncture, though, in his partial defence. As much as Mill may believe that the West, and some parts of it in particular, have outstripped the rest of the world in terms of the growth of civilization, he does not believe that the West deserves to be called highly civilized in absolute terms, that its greater relative level of development is due to anything more than historical accident, or that it will always be ascendant. In particular, he denies any important role to race in explaining why the countries of Europe and their former colonies are generally ready for liberty while the rest of the world generally is not.

Conservative caveats

The critical literature on *On Liberty* is so vast that there is no prospect of presenting even summaries of all of the different objections that have been made, possible responses and so on. It will therefore be necessary to be selective, and the most interesting objections to consider will be ones that contend that there is something fundamentally awry with *On Liberty*, accept Mill's utilitarian starting point rather than departing from him at the level of first principles, and have contemporary relevance. One set of objections that meets these criteria comes from the conservative James Fitzjames Stephen, one of Mill's contemporaries. Stephen purports to be not only a utilitarian (of a sort) but also a devotee of Mill's earlier work, especially the *System of Logic*. He claims, though, to have little sympathy for Mill's later work in moral philosophy, in particular *Utilitarianism*, *On Liberty* and *The Subjection of Women*.[79] His brother Leslie quotes a letter in which Stephen writes that 'I am falling foul of John

Mill in his modern and more humane mood – or rather, I should say, in his sentimental mood – which always makes me feel that he is a deserter from the proper principles of rigidity and ferocity in which he was brought up.'[80]

Despite sharing Mill's utilitarian orientation, if not necessarily the details of his moral theory, Stephen differs from Mill on several points of fact. There is a fundamental difference between their views on human nature, and more specifically on the ability of education to modify human nature. Stephen writes that Mill's liberalism 'proceeds upon an exaggerated estimate of the power of education. Society cannot make silk purses out of sows' ears, and there are plenty of ears in the world which no tanning can turn even into serviceable pigskin.'[81]

Another difference, or so at least Stephen believes, concerns their views on the nature of the relations between people living in society. Stephen takes Mill to understate both the intimacy of these relations and the extent to which anything that affects one person's life will affect the lives of others as well: 'The strong metaphor that we are all members one of another is little more than the expression of a fact. A man would no more be a man if he was alone in the world than a hand would be a hand without the rest of the body.'[82]

While Mill believes that most individuals will still be able to work out for themselves how to lead decent lives, even genuinely happy ones, in a society governed by the liberty principle, Stephen questions this. His primary line of argument begins with an observation about what he takes to be an immutable fact about human nature, namely that most people would fall victim to one 'vice' or another – sloth, alcohol, lust and so on – unless society somehow played upon their fears to prevent this from happening:

> Men are so constructed that whatever theory as to goodness and badness we choose to adopt, there are and always will be in the world an enormous mass of bad and indifferent people. . . . The only way by which it is practically possible to act upon them at all is by compulsion or restraint. [T]he utmost conceivable liberty which could be bestowed upon them would not in the least degree tend to improve them.[83]

Stephen's rationale for why society ought to use coercion more freely than the liberty principle would permit is not purely paternalistic. So tightly are people connected, he maintains, that whenever anyone succumbs to the temptations of substance abuse, the avoidance of work, or sexual excess, this lowers the quality of life of others, even if it does not mean that they are harmed in Mill's sense of 'harm'. Society would be poorer, both materially and spiritually, with people who could have been active contributors to its economy and its culture incapacitated:

> Men are so closely connected together that it is quite impossible to say how far the influence of acts apparently of the most personal character may extend. . . . Still less can we assign limits to that indefinable influence which they exercise over each other . . . by the spirit which shines through their looks and gestures, to say nothing of their words and thoughts.[84]

Moreover, their example would make it even more difficult for others to resist the same temptation for, as Stephen continues, 'Vice is as infectious as disease . . .'[85]

Something may seem to be amiss here. If people are worse off than they might be as a result of their neighbours' licentious behaviour – even economically worse off, so that their interests are definitely affected – then does this not mean that they are being harmed and that the liberty principle would therefore permit society to step in? Not necessarily. Mill understands harm in terms of damage to someone's interests (or the risk of damage, although this can be ignored here). But what counts as damage? This, it seems, has to mean being pushed below some 'baseline level' with respect to one or more of one's interests. The difficulty is in saying what baseline is the appropriate reference point. When thinking about an interaction between two people A and B, it will often make sense to say that A harms B by making B worse off with respect to one or more of B's interests than B would have been if this interaction had never taken place. This formula appears to work in the 'drowning' cases that were discussed above ('Mill's Conception of Harm'), for instance. In the scenarios involving the swimming pool, the interaction begins when the prospective rescuer encourages the swimmer to expect help if needed. Since quite possibly the swimmer would not be in the pool in the first place if not for that encouragement, it makes sense to say that he or she is worse off than would be the case had the interaction never occurred. In contrast, if Jennifer lets Paris drown, then Paris will still be no worse off than if Jennifer had never even been born. This formula may not always work as a way of setting the appropriate baseline when people are interacting, though, and some other formula will clearly be needed in cases in which we want to be able to say that a person is suffering harm but no one else is involved (such as when someone is having a heart attack). Perhaps further fleshing out Mill's account of harm would involve appending an account of basic needs and of normal bodily functioning which would make it possible to say that a person is below the appropriate baseline (and so is suffering harm) whenever those needs are going unmet or that functioning is interrupted, whatever the cause.

In any case, it must be possible to draw a line between harming people and merely failing to benefit them. If someone gives you a monetary gift, they have benefited you in virtue of improving your position with respect to your interests. If they do not give such a gift when they could have, then you are worse off than you would have been if they had. But if the appropriate baseline just is the state of affairs in which they leave you entirely alone, then this would not damage your interests. If they have not promised you the money, then there would seem to be no grounds on which to say that their failing to gift it to you harms you. Stephen, then, can be understood as saying that, unless society can use the power of compulsion more freely than the liberty principle would permit, people would not do as much to benefit one another as they might, even if they would be no more prone to harm each other.

An example may help to illustrate this distinction. One argument that is sometimes made against legalizing the use of drugs like marijuana is that this would make the workforce less productive. That firms can replace workers who do not meet their standards for productivity is not a complete answer to this objection, since there is always the hypothetical possibility that so many people will abuse the drug that firms will not be able to find enough good workers. If this possibility materializes, though, then can one say that an employer – call her Ellen – who is unable to attract enough sober employees has been harmed? Probably not, strictly speaking. That is not to deny that Ellen is worse off than if her prospective employees were more temperate, but only to say that a state of affairs in which these prospective employees both keep themselves fit for employment and apply for the positions offered does not seem to be the appropriate baseline for judging whether she has been harmed. The appropriate baseline would instead seem to be a state in which Ellen has no meaningful interaction with them at all. This is precisely the state that Ellen will be in vis-à-vis prospective workers whom she never hires, which means that people she never hires cannot be responsible for pushing her *below* the appropriate baseline. So Ellen is worse off than she would be if her prospective employees were more temperate, but that is because they would be benefiting her (and presumably themselves) if they kept themselves in a suitable condition to work, not because they are harming her by failing to do so. (If Ellen hires employees who allow drug use to prevent them from performing at the promised level then she likely *will* be harmed, in contrast, because she will probably be worse off than if she had never hired them.)

Therefore, it is not nonsensical for Stephen to say that concern for the welfare of people who make sensible decisions themselves, in addition to paternalistic concern for the welfare of those who cannot, favour giving society a freer hand in the use of coercion than the liberty principle would allow. So as not to give the wrong impression, it is worth emphasizing that Stephen is far from being an advocate of totalitarianism. He says, though, that decisions about whether a particular intervention or use of coercion is appropriate ought to be made by asking three questions: '1. Is the object good? 2. Are the means proposed likely to be effective? 3. What is the comparative importance of the object secured and of the means by which it is secured?'[86] Among the examples that Stephen gives of social controls on individual behaviour that he would endorse but that Mill would have to oppose are the use of the law to prevent the publication of a seduction manual and to fine the owner of 'a house of entertainment' that is 'specially provided' for 'a set of lads and girls to get drunk of an evening' and 'other purposes'.[87]

The relevance from a utilitarian perspective of Stephen's three questions is obvious. Stephen's phrasing may sound a bit too act-utilitarian for Mill, but the questions are still pertinent from the rule-utilitarian perspective. If there is a general type of interference that is intended to accomplish something desirable, would in fact accomplish it, and would do so in a cost-effective manner (producing more happiness than unhappiness), then Mill would have to take there to be a prima facie justification for society's moral rules to permit this kind of interference. If the liberty principle would preclude such interference, then Mill would have to acknowledge that there is a prima facie case for replacing it with a different principle governing the use of coercion, one that would permit the type of interference in question.

Mill did not live long enough to reply to Stephen, but he read at least some parts of *Liberty, Equality, Fraternity* when it first appeared in serial form in the *Pall Mall Gazette*. Bain quotes him as saying that 'the author "does not know what he is arguing against; and is more likely to repel than to attract people." '[88] It is evident that Mill is not going to disagree with Stephen about the undesirability of people's living thoroughly debauched lives, either from their standpoint or that of society as a whole. Even if his attention were restricted to people who are and forever will be incapable of enjoying higher quality pleasures, Mill would hardly consider excessive indulgence in alcohol or other chemicals, in sexual activity, or in idleness to be the best or happiest form of life. Even if we all ought to have custom-made characters that we fashion for ourselves, these are among the habits that Mill believes should not be part of anyone's character. While he does write that a person's 'own mode of laying out his existence is the best . . . because it is his own mode', this is only true if the person in question has a 'tolerable amount of common sense'.[89] So what response can Mill make to Stephen?

One point that Mill might make and indeed does make in *On Liberty* is that the threat of bad habits spreading by example is easily exaggerated:

> [W]e are now speaking of conduct which, while it does no wrong to others, is supposed to do great harm to the agent himself: and I do not see how those who believe this can think otherwise than that the example, on the whole, must be more salutary than hurtful, since, if it displays the misconduct, it displays also the painful or degrading consequences.[90]

There is some force in this response, although it is not completely satisfying. Not only is the danger posed by bad examples only a part of Stephen's case, but we know that people, especially young people, often do follow the example set by the self-destructive behaviour of others. Mill fails to acknowledge that the 'painful or degrading consequences' of self-harming behaviours may some-times be years in the future, so that for a time a person engaged in them can appear to be leading a life worth emulating.

A more promising approach for Mill or a contemporary Millian may be to question how well punishment and coercion work as a response to the types of vice with which Stephen is concerned. This means questioning whether the marginal benefits of the strategies for responding to vice that the liberty principle takes off the table outweigh their marginal costs. While Mill emphasizes just how capably society can squelch unconventional behaviour, it is still open to him to acknowledge that it is quite difficult to deter people from engaging in certain behaviours via the threat of punishment due to, perhaps among other factors, the strength of their motives and the difficulty of catching them.

As one case in point, albeit one from which we admittedly should generalize only with great caution, consider the United States' 'war on drugs'. The prisons in this country overflow with those convicted of violating the country's rather strict drug laws. The US puts its citizens behind bars at a higher rate than any other country in the world: 756 out of 100,000, which is a rate more than 20 per cent greater than that of 'second-place' Russia.[91] Drug laws are in no small part responsible. In 2005, approximately 19.5 per cent of prisoners under state jurisdiction had been convicted of a drug offence, and in 2007 over half of the inmates in federal prisons (95,446 out of 179,204) had a drug crime as their most serious offence; this second statistic, in other words, does not include individuals who were convicted of a drug crime in addition to an assault or a property crime.[92] Nor is drug use generally condoned by the American public. Known drug users are liable to be met with informal social sanctions from many people also, ranging from expressions of contempt to denials of employment opportunities. The United States incurs a heavy cost for its drug laws. Over and above the suffering imposed on those who are being punished, which is a significant cost from the utilitarian perspective, mass incarceration is an expensive proposition. Moreover, there is evidence that drug offenders who are sent to prison are more likely to offend again than those who are not.[93] Plus, millions or billions of dollars of commercial transactions go untaxed, and violent criminal organizations, and perhaps even terrorists, are enriched. Yet despite all of the above, narcotics of all kinds are still readily available.

While drug use may in some respects be a special case, some of the features that limit the efficacy of punishment as a response to it apply to most or all of the types of vice that Stephen discusses: they are behaviours that can be carried out in relative privacy and that are prompted by fairly strong urges. This is not to deny that social coercion may make some difference to the level of vice in a society, and it certainly may help to push it underground, out of the sight of respectable society. Nonetheless, when the conduct in question causes no real harm to anyone except the agent, the suggestion that this price may not be worth paying is entitled to serious consideration. The use of coercion as a response to vice may well fail the third of Stephen's own criteria, and perhaps even the second. If the use of coercion in this context is not justified on utilitarian grounds, then there is no reason for Mill to carve out an exception permitting it to the liberty principle.

One might be tempted to respond on Stephen's behalf that, even if punishment is not an ideal means of discouraging licentious behaviour, it is better than nothing. But even if a society were to adopt the principle of abstaining from the use of force against vices that only harm those who participate in them, there would still be other avenues by which it might address this behaviour. Even if we limit our attention to steps that the government might take, various options are fully compatible with the liberty principle. In the *Principles of Political Economy*, Mill draws a distinction 'between two kinds of intervention by the government'. Government interferes 'authoritatively' when it requires or forbids. In contrast,

> There is another kind of intervention which is not authoritative: when a government, instead of issuing a command and enforcing it by penalties, adopts the course . . . of giving advice and promulgating information; or when, leaving individuals free to use their own means of pursuing any object of general interest, the government . . . establishes . . . an agency of its own for a like purpose.[94]

The liberty principle restricts authoritative but not 'unauthoritative' uses of the state's power. This means, first, that it allows a society to provide treatment and counselling. Second, it allows a society to combat vice through eliminating some of the underlying conditions that make it so tempting in the first place. People frequently turn to substance abuse as a way of deadening the pain of lives characterized by extreme deprivation or hardship, and the liberty principle does not forbid forms of assistance meant to ameliorate these conditions. Idleness is only attractive when people are able to support themselves without working, and the liberty principle hardly requires that this be possible. Third, and finally, the principle permits a society to try to give its members an education that would enable them to steer clear of self-destructive conduct. How successful a society can hope to be at this is in dispute between Mill and Stephen, but it is at least important to recognize that nothing in Mill's philosophy precludes the making of the attempt. Certainly the liberty principle does not prevent a society from seeing to it that children are taught the consequences of different choices that they might make about the shape of their lives: 'Society has had absolute power over them during all the early portion of their existence: it has had the whole period of childhood and nonage in which to try whether it could make them capable of rational conduct in life.'[95]

Nor, under Mill's liberalism, is society's instruction limited to a value-free curriculum of cause and effect. Some recent liberal philosophers, including most notably Rawls and Ronald Dworkin, have espoused a view according to which the state has to maintain 'neutrality' between different views about what sort of life is best, over some wide range of views.[96] Mill's liberalism, though, is not neutral in this sense. Skorupski has helpfully distinguished between 'permissive neutrality', which forbids compelling people to adopt certain forms of life and avoid others, and 'persuasive neutrality', which forbids advocating some forms of life in preference to others.[97] Mill's liberalism is permissively but not persuasively neutral. Society in general and the state in particular can actively encourage people to choose temperate and productive ways of living. It can even encourage them to develop their higher faculties and cultivate their individuality.

It is a fair point that societies do these things already without great success. No doubt they could do them better than they do at present, but it may not be realistic to hope that these kinds of methods could ever prevent a certain percentage of the population from squandering away their lives. Bear in mind, though, that making an answer to Stephen on Mill's behalf does not require showing that the social problems under discussion can be cured without the use of compulsion, since there is no sign that they can be cured *with* it, either. It is only necessary to show that coercion and punishment are not part of the optimal mix of strategies for dealing with them, that is, that the costs of their use exceed the benefits. If neither Mill nor his contemporary followers are able to establish conclusively that this is case, then it is equally true that neither Stephen nor contemporary social conservatives are able to prove that it is not. Much rests on whom one decides bears the burden of proof. Stephen's social conservative heirs – if not conservatives of the more contemporary libertarian variety, who if anything owe a larger debt to Mill – will tend to say that those who would seek to overturn tradition and place new limits on the use of social power face the burden of proving that the institutions and practices they are criticizing fail to achieve their intended aims. Liberals will tend to say that every use of coercion requires justification, so that those who favour any restriction have the burden of showing that its use would be worthwhile. ('[T]he initial onus of justification' lies, Stanley Benn writes, 'not with the person interfered with, but with the interferer.'⁹⁸) This debate is too large to try to settle here, but surely the liberal account of where the justificatory burden lies has at least as much prima facie plausibility as the conservative one.

Paternalism

This line of argument developed in the previous section is intended specifically as a response to Stephen. It may not be nearly as applicable to a variety of other uses of social coercion that have been much discussed of late, such as laws requiring seat belts to be worn in cars, laws requiring helmets to be worn on motorcycles and laws placing restrictions on the use of tobacco. There is no way to distinguish sharply between these measures and the kinds of social control that Stephen is advocating, but the arguments that are usually given for the former probably place somewhat more emphasis on paternalistic considerations, that is, on the supposed benefits to individuals of having their own freedom of action restricted. There is this difference, as well: on the whole the costs of enforcing these restrictions are probably lower than the costs of enforcing restrictions on alcohol, drugs or sex, and the rate of compliance that enforcement yields is likely much higher.

Many people are unconvinced that the general considerations that Mill adduces in favour of the liberty principle in chapter 3 of *On Liberty* suffice to show that no purely paternalistic laws could be justified on utilitarian grounds. Even some of Mill's most sympathetic readers think that he may underestimate how prone people are to make unwise decisions that jeopardize their own safety and well-being at risk for no adequate reason. Hart, for example, writes:

> Mill carried his protests against paternalism to lengths that may now appear to us fantastic. . . . Underlying Mill's extreme fear of paternalism there is perhaps a conception of what a normal human being is like which now seems to us not to correspond to the facts. Mill, in fact, endows him with too much of the psychology of a middle-aged man whose desires are relatively fixed, not liable to be artificially stimulated by external influences; who knows what he wants and what gives him satisfaction or happiness; and who pursues these thing when he can.⁹⁹

What might Mill or a contemporary Millian say in defence of his opposition to laws that are recommended only by their putative paternalistic benefits? How can a utilitarian like Mill reject such laws out of hand, without careful consideration of their costs and benefits?

Several possible lines of response might be available to Mill. One answer is that, once the door is opened for paternalistic legislation to be passed, it is sure to be carried eventually to ridiculous lengths. There may be some truth in this. The United Kingdom has perhaps gone a bit further down this road towards the 'nanny state' than the United States: one British newspaper recently mentioned reports that teachers were instructed to wear goggles while handling 'Blu-Tack'.[100] Still, 'slippery slope' arguments like this must always be viewed sceptically. There is no necessity that a society that allows itself some paternalistic laws will eventually pass absurd ones.

Another possible response is that laws like these often fail to attain their stated objectives. When it comes to seat belt laws, for instance, there is some question about whether they save lives on balance.[101] It has been hypothesized that some drivers might tend to drive more aggressively when they are wearing a seat belt. Drivers themselves may still be safer on balance when seat belt laws are in place, even those with this tendency, but when fatalities to rear-seat passengers, pedestrians and so on are taken into account, the claim that seat belt laws save lives is not without controversy. This response, though, is not applicable to every possible paternalistic law.

A third possible answer is that the benefits that people get out of the activities that paternalists want to restrict generally outweigh the risks they are taking. Someone taking this line will want to insist that individuals are the best judges of when the benefits of their behaviour make the risks worthwhile. Maybe the pleasure that some motorcyclists get from riding without a helmet really is sufficient to justify the risk they take, for example.[102] Maybe non-riders just are not even entitled to an opinion about this. Again, though, this response will be more plausible in some cases than others; it would be hard to take seriously someone who said that the thrill of driving without a seat belt made the extra risk worthwhile, for example.

If Mill indeed needs to buttress his arguments in *On Liberty* in order to make a stronger case against paternalistic legislation, then it would be desirable for him to be able to offer a general argument that applies against all paternalistic laws. In addition, it needs to be an argument that is rooted in his utilitarianism. One argument that might fill this need is the ethological argument that holding people personally responsible for choices about the trade-offs between risks and rewards fosters habits that should be part of each person's character. The reasoning would run that when the government or society more generally begins to prevent individuals from doing things on the grounds that they might hurt themselves, people are less likely to be vigilant about life's dangers. They will be prone to assume that if something is allowed, then it must not be too bad for them. But there will always be vastly more imprudent (in the self-regarding sense) choices than can be legislated against, so it is desirable for people to be habitually on their guard. Better, then, for adults never to be prevented from doing anything simply on the grounds that they might hurt themselves, so that an unequivocal message is sent that the person primarily responsible for preventing a person from harming themselves is themselves. This is at least part of what Albert Jay Nock is contending when he writes that any enlargement of the region of government subject to control by law

> reduces the scope of individual responsibility, and thus retards and cripples the education which can be a produce of nothing but the free exercise of moral judgment.... The profound instinct against being 'done for our own good'... is wholly sound. Men are aware of the need of this moral experience as a condition of growth, and they are aware, too, that anything tending to ease it off from them, even for their own good, is to be profoundly distrusted.... The practical reason for freedom, then, is that freedom seems to be the only condition under which any substantial moral fibre can be developed.[103]

Economists have referred to the tendency of safety regulations to make people lower their guard and behave less cautiously as 'the lulling effect'.[104]

Needless to say, not everyone is going to find this argument persuasive. It might, though, hold particular appeal for Mill. It parallels his observation that one general consideration that counts against any expansion of government power is the fact that the more the government does, the more the public tends to assume that the state is responsible for solving every problem that crops up and the more passive their characters become.[105]

As a final point, it is important to recognize that Mill's anti-paternalism is not as thoroughgoing as it might initially seem. There are at least two respects in which his liberalism still permits society and even the state to act paternalistically. First, it permits what is sometimes called 'soft paternalism'. 'Soft paternalism', according to Joel Feinberg, 'holds that the state has the right to prevent self-regarding harmful conduct . . . *when but only when* that conduct is substantially nonvoluntary, or when temporary intervention is necessary to establish whether it is voluntary or not.'[106] 'Hard paternalism', in contrast, is the view that people can be prevented from engaging in 'self-regarding harmful conduct' even when it is fully voluntary. Mill endorses soft paternalism not only when he exempts children and 'barbarians' from the scope of the liberty principle but also when he allows that it is permissible to stop a person from crossing an unstable bridge in order to make certain that he knows the risk. Although note that he adds here that as long as the traveller has the 'full use of the reflecting faculty', he has to be allowed to continue once he is apprised of the danger he faces.[107]

Second, given that the liberty principle places no restrictions on the so-called unauthoritative uses of government power, it does not prevent the state from advising people about various dangers, leaving them free to choose for themselves whether to heed that advice. Admittedly, if Mill would indeed credit the argument that the use of authoritative paternalism tends to make people insufficiently cautious, then he might take the use of 'unauthoritative paternalism' to pose the same danger. In other words, perhaps merely warning people against dangers can give rise to a lulling effect. Insofar as this worry is real, it would be a reason for the state to use its power to advise against self-harming behaviour sparingly. Humboldt, it is interesting to note, takes this concern very seriously.[108]

8

Millian Normative Political Economy

In his own day, Mill was celebrated nearly as much for his accomplishments in political economy as those in philosophy.[1] The economic historian Mark Blaug describes the *Principles of Political Economy* as the 'undisputed bible of economists' in the latter half of the nineteenth century. He notes that it was still used as a standard textbook in British and American universities until 1900.[2]

'Political economy' may sound like an old-fashioned name for the field of economics, but this overstates the degree of continuity between the way that this field was studied before the twentieth century and the way it is approached today, namely as a self-contained subject pursued by specialists, distinct from related fields such as political science, sociology or social philosophy, and dominated by abstract mathematical models. Mill defines 'political economy' as 'The science which traces the laws of such of the phenomena of society as arise from the combined operations of mankind for the production of wealth, in so far as those phenomena are not modified by the pursuit of any other object.'[3]

As a descriptive science, as distinct from a normative art, political economy says nothing about what decisions should be made within the economic sphere; it only describes what effects will follow from given causes. Mill makes many contributions to the science of political economy, among the most important of which were those concerning the theories of demand, international trade and pricing.[4] Yet he also has much to say about economic matters from a normative perspective; indeed, the subtitle of the *Principles* is *With Some of Their Applications to Social Philosophy*. For the lack of a better term we can refer to the art that corresponds to the science of political economy as normative political economy. This chapter will concentrate on some specific aspects of Mill's normative political economy, especially the question of where he stands in the debate between proponents of capitalism and defenders of socialism.

Nineteenth-century capitalism

If Mill ever uses the term 'capitalism' he does so very rarely, although he does use 'capitalist' (as a noun). Still, it is a fitting label for a system of economic organization about which he has much to say, even if he never happens to apply a name to it. Capitalism, as Mill understands it, comprises two elements. The first is the system of private or individual property:

> The institution of property, when limited to its essential elements, consists in the recognition, in each person, of a right to the exclusive disposal of what he or she have produced by their own exertions, or received either by gift or by fair agreement, without force or fraud, from those who produced it. The foundation of the whole is, the right of producers to what they themselves have produced.[5]

Jonathan Riley has labelled the principle that ownership on these terms is permissible the 'desert principle'.[6] Capitalism's second element is the distinction between capitalists and workers. Under capitalism, large-scale capital is worked by people who do not own it and, usually, not worked by the people who do. Other characteristic features of capitalism can be viewed as the upshot of one or both of these elements.

Mill had the opportunity to become acquainted with the work of a number of socialist critics of capitalism as it existed in Victorian Britain and other countries of the time, although he seems not to be aware of the work of Marx.[7] The socialists with whom Mill is acquainted are of the sort derided by Marx as 'utopian' or unscientific, such as Louis Blanc, Robert Owen, Henri de Saint-Simon and Charles Fourier. He has considerable sympathy with some of their complaints.

One of the socialists' leading criticisms is that capitalism impoverishes labourers, an outcome that is all the more unjust because they work harder than those with more. Mill concurs with both points. 'It is unhappily true that the wages of ordinary labour, in all the countries of Europe, are wretchedly insufficient to supply the physical and moral necessities of the population in any tolerable measure', he writes.[8] Moreover, he admits that 'the produce of labour' is divided 'almost in an inverse ratio to the labour', so that 'the largest portions' go 'to those who have never worked at all', while those who do 'the most fatiguing and exhausting bodily labour cannot count with certainty on being able to earn even the necessaries of life'.[9]

Another socialist complaint that Mill endorses is that capitalism warps the workers' characters, turning them into 'slaves to toil in which they *have* no interest, and therefore *feel* no interest – drudging from early morning till late at night for bare necessaries, and with all the intellectual and moral deficiencies which that implies. . . .'[10] Nor do the labourers have much of a work ethic: 'We look in vain among the working classes in general for the just pride which will choose to give good work for good wages; for the most part, their sole endeavour is to receive as much, and return as little in the shape of service, as possible.'[11]

Mill does think that he sees slow improvement in the condition of the working class. Not only are wages rising, but 'there is a spontaneous education going on in the minds of the multitude' that is being propelled by developments like the advent of cheap newspapers.[12] Yet, at the time he is writing, it is clear that much of the working class is precluded from enjoying anything like genuinely happy lives. Their economic state makes it difficult for them to enjoy even the lower pleasures with much regularity, let alone a life rich in the higher quality ones.

Mill's concern with the damaging ethological consequences of capitalism is not limited to its effects on the working class, however. He shares the socialists' dim view of the characters of most members of the upper classes. While they have more formal education, the truly cultivated intellects in their number are still few and far between. Mill is utterly unimpressed even with the elite 'public' schools (which are not public in the American sense but are instead analogous to private American 'prep' schools) and 'Oxbridge' universities of the English aristocracy. While there were some reforms during his lifetime, the traditional curriculum included little beyond Greek, Latin and some mathematics. Middle-class students often enjoyed no better than a second-rate version of a public school education, although they might sometimes receive training in more practical subjects.[13] From the moral standpoint, in Mill's eyes, the selfish and superficial upper classes are little if any better than the workers. Their money they mostly fritter away on conspicuous consumption.[14] Moreover, if the workers see them as nothing more than a means to an end, the reverse is equally true; they see those beneath them as 'by a kind of natural law, their servants and dependents'.[15]

Yet while he agrees with much that socialists say against the capitalism of his day, Mill parts company with them over whether these problems are inherent in the system of private property. Socialist writers like Blanc place much of the blame for the woes of nineteenth-century capitalism on competition, alleging both that competition between workers for jobs hurts them economically and that competition 'is the parent of envy, hatred, and all uncharitableness; it makes everyone the natural enemy of all others who cross his path, and everyone's path is constantly liable to be crossed'.[16] While Mill acknowledges that there is a certain amount of truth in these points, he maintains that on balance competition does far more good than harm in both economic and 'ethological' terms. The ultimate reason wages are not higher is not that workers must compete for jobs, he asserts, but rather that the working class reproduces at too high a rate, and 'if the supply of labourers is excessive, not even Socialism can prevent their remuneration from being low.'[17] When it comes to the purported anti-social effects of competition on individuals' characters, Mill seems to think that any tendency that competition might have to make people less altruistic is more than compensated for by its tendency to make them more energetic, to overcome 'the natural indolence of mankind; their tendency to be passive, to be the slaves of habit, to persist indefinitely in a course once chosen . . . To be protected against competition is to be protected in idleness, in mental dulness; to be saved the necessity of being as active and as intelligent as other people . . .'[18]

Nor does Mill agree with those socialists who say that the private ownership of capital is an injustice in and of itself. The desert principle says that wealth belongs to those who produce it, but Mill denies that this means that all wealth must be owned by current workers. Capital exists because earlier generations of labourers did not consume everything that they produced but rather saved it and passed it on to others. As long as these transfers of their accumulated savings were legitimate, the accumulation of capital by present-day capitalists does not violate the desert principle. And Mill believes that capitalists contribute to production through investing their capital rather than consuming it, which he takes to be as deserving of reward as is productive labour.[19] The greatest exploitation that Mill sees in Victorian capitalism is not that of workers by capitalists, but rather that perpetrated by the landowning class. Landowners can grow richer without either doing productive work or investing, simply because population growth drives up the demand for food and hence the value of arable land. From Mill's (Ricardian) perspective, they, if anyone, are the true 'robber barons'.

Reforming capitalism

Mill believes that the real evils of nineteenth-century capitalism result not from its defining elements but rather from institutions and practices that happen to have grown up under it – institutions and practices that could be altered without abandoning capitalism itself. In an early debating speech, he observes that 'the same sum of money is of much greater value to a poor man than a rich one', which entails that 'the distribution of wealth which tends most to the general happiness is that which approximates nearest to equality.' He therefore concludes that, under capitalism, 'the legislator ought to favour the equal distribution of wealth in every way not inconsistent with the security of property but for which there would be no wealth to distribute.'[20] The great defect of nineteenth-century capitalism, as Mill sees it, is that its legislators have failed to heed this maxim:

> That all should indeed start on perfectly equal terms, is inconsistent with any law of private property: but if as much pains as has been taken to aggravate the inequality of chances arising from the natural working of the principle, had been taken to temper that inequality by every means not subversive of the principle itself . . . the principle of individual property would have been found to have no necessary connexion with the physical and social evils which almost all Socialist writers assume to be inseparable from it.[21]

Mill describes a variety of reforms that would be necessary in order to give capitalism its fair trial.

The first of these concerns the inheritance of property. Mill distinguishes the right to give or bequeath property from the right to receive or inherit it, and says that limitations on the latter (though not the former) are entirely consistent with the desert principle. He advocates limiting the amount of property that any person can inherit. He would still allow people to leave all of their wealth to their designated heirs, but no single heir could receive more than a certain amount.[22] This limitation is primarily intended as a means of spreading the wealth, and Bain remarks that Mill expects it to 'pull down all large fortunes in two generations'.[23] In addition, Mill believes that a person's character is seldom improved by inheriting so much money that he or she can live without working.[24] (The headlines of contemporary tabloids may bear this opinion out.)

Another set of reforms concerns property in land. The desert principle does not apply to 'the raw material of the earth', for 'No man made the land. It is the original inheritance of the whole species.'[25] While he takes this idea of common ownership of the land quite seriously, Mill recognizes that, in a private property economy, it will probably be necessary to allow individuals to enjoy most of the legal rights associated with landownership in order to provide them with a sufficient incentive to make the land productive. Still, he would extend no more rights to landowners than necessary for this purpose.[26] He believes that the state ought to tax at a one hundred per cent rate any future increases in the rents landlords receive that derive from natural causes such as an increase in population instead of improvements by the landlords.[27]

A third area in which reform is necessary if capitalism is to be just is the provision of education. Mill is committed to the proposition that '*Laisser-faire* . . . should be the general practice,' and that 'every departure from it, unless required by some great good, is a certain evil,' and in the *Principles* he offers several reasons for why anything that can be done by private entities should be.[28] Nevertheless, he also recognizes a number of exceptions to this general presumption against state interference in the economy, and education is one of these. The state is justified in seeing to it that educational opportunities exist at all levels.[29] It is also justified in requiring parents to see to it that their children receive at least elementary instruction.[30] While the state may need to provide subsidies to ensure that education is affordable, Mill is sufficiently committed to the *laisser-faire* principle to say that it should not seek to become the exclusive or even the chief educator itself: 'A general State education is a mere contrivance for moulding people to be exactly like one another: and . . . the mould in which it casts them is that which pleases the predominant power in the government.'[31] He therefore favours a system something like that proposed today in the United States by advocates of 'educational vouchers' or 'school choice'.

One specific economic benefit that Mill believes would flow from universal education is that it would help to address the problem of population control. A just capitalism would do everything possible to prevent the working class from sinking into poverty, but no society can avoid poverty, regardless of its economic system, unless it can impose 'a due limitation on the numbers of the community'.[32] While some argue that this can only happen under socialism, Mill believes that capitalistic societies can convince the working class to practise self-restraint as long as two conditions are met: workers must receive enough of an education to grasp the connection between a high population and low wages, and something must happen to effectively eliminate poverty for at least one generation so they can get a taste for the comforts that higher wages make it possible for them to enjoy.[33]

A further reform, lifting restrictions on the jobs that are available to women, would both contribute to this same end and yield numerous other benefits. Allowing women more opportunities to work outside the home would have, 'among its probable consequences', 'a great diminution of the evil of over-population. It is by devoting one-half of the human species to that exclusive function . . . that the animal instinct in question is nursed into the disproportionate preponderance which it has hitherto exercised in human life.'[34]

Allowing women to enter the labour market would also improve their prospects for happiness. It would open up more opportunities for them to develop and exercise their abilities. By making it economically feasible for them to choose not to marry (an option that Mill does not expect large numbers of women to prefer for its own sake), it would also allow them to refuse to marry men who would not treat them as equals. For society to stop putting women in a situation in which their only real option is to subject themselves to a petty tyrant in the home would promote the moral development of women and men alike, with the latter benefiting more since 'It is wholesomer for the moral nature to be restrained, even by arbitrary power, than to be allowed to exercise arbitrary power without restraint.'[35] Other changes to the marital relation would be needed as well for this reform to have its full effect, in particular changing the law so that husbands no longer become the owners of all property that their wives brought into the marriage. Finally, a more general social benefit to allowing 'women the free use of their faculties, by leaving them the free choice of their employments . . . would be that of doubling the mass of mental faculties available for the higher service of humanity'.[36] While some might object that women ought to be prevented from entering certain lines of work on the grounds that they are in general less suited for them,

Mill answers that employers can judge whether individual women are capable of performing particular jobs, just as they do with male applicants.[37]

After this brief rehearsal of Mill's great defence of the employment rights of women, however, there is no way to avoid mentioning an unfortunate passage in *The Subjection of Women* that undermines much of his stance:

> If, in addition to the physical suffering of bearing children, and the whole responsibility of their care and education in early years, the wife undertakes the careful and economical application of the husband's earnings to the general comfort of the family; she takes not only her fair share, but usually the larger share, of the bodily and mental exertion required by their joint existence. . . . In an otherwise just state of things, it is not, therefore, I think, a desirable custom, that the wife should contribute by her labour to the income of the family.[38]

Mill is certainly right to worry about what is today sometimes called the 'second shift problem', where women work full-time outside of the home but still bear a disproportionate share of the domestic duties. Yet these lines reveal a serious failure of imagination on his part. The idea that a husband might take on a significant part of the household chores or the care of the children seems not to have occurred to him. Nor does he consider that, when they are both earners, a couple can afford to pay someone else to do some of their domestic chores. He may well be guilty of assuming, against his own admonitions about the difficulty of knowing how men's and women's characters differ, that men on the whole are less well suited emotionally for raising young children. You cannot easily plead in Mill's defence that his sense of what is possible is limited by the customs of his own time, since the entire purpose of the *Subjection* is to show that those customs do not constitute the necessary state of things and that other arrangements are possible. While for any given heterosexual couple the arrangement in which the wife stays home might well be the most sensible choice, there is no adequate excuse for Mill's eagerness to endorse it as the general rule.

A final set of reforms to Victorian capitalism that Mill advocates concerns changes in the laws of partnership. These include removing restrictions on limited liability joint-stock and so-called *en commandite* partnerships, and rectifying the legal system's failure to provide an adequate method for resolving disputes amongst partners.[39] His reason for advocating these rather technical changes to the law, some of which were adopted in his lifetime, is that they will facilitate a sweeping and fundamental alteration of the relation between capitalists and workers. He is confident that the strides the working class is making in its moral and intellectual development will continue even without his reforms, although they – in conjunction with certain political reforms, which will be the subject of the next chapter – would accelerate it markedly.[40] The growing intelligence of the working class and its growing consciousness of its own political power will, he feels certain, eventually lead it to reject anything that smacks of dependence on other classes. In the workplace, this will mean a demand to be more than mere labour for hire. Initially, at least, this demand will take the form of a demand for 'a piece of the action'; workers will insist upon a partnership with capitalists in which they receive a share of their firm's profits. Where this has been tried, 'it has very materially increased the remuneration of every description of labour.'[41] Mill believes that, once the moral and intellectual improvement of the workers has reached a stage where they are ready to demand this kind of partnership, capitalists ought to find the arrangement attractive as well, so that everyone benefits; he discusses several early experiments with profit-sharing that actually resulted in capitalists earning a larger return because of the greater zeal and care with which workers approached their tasks.[42]

Socialism

While capitalism could be vastly improved, however, it is still possible that some form of socialism might be preferable. And there is some prima facie evidence for the view that Mill believes this to be the case. According to his *Autobiography*, the 'ideal of ultimate improvement' that he shared with Harriet, at least during one period of their lives, 'went far beyond Democracy, and would class us decidedly under the general designation of Socialists'.[43] Mill uses 'socialism' to designate 'any system which requires that the land and instruments of production should be the property, not of individuals, but of communities or associations, or of the government'. It is characteristic of socialistic systems that the division of the produce of labour is a 'public act, performed according to rules laid down by the community'.[44] This is a very broad definition, one that does not require even partial government ownership of the means of production. It may well be *too* broad, although it will become clear below that it is only in terms of an extremely inclusive definition such as this one that Mill can be labelled a socialist.

There is room within Mill's definition for distinctions between different varieties of socialism. One distinction that comes directly out of the definition is that between the different 'levels' at which socialism can be established. First, there is socialism at the level of the individual firm, which means the full ownership of a firm by an association comprising its workers. Second, there is socialism at the level of the village or community; this is the level of the schemes of Blanc, Owen, Saint-Simon and Fourier.[45] Finally, there is socialism at the level of the nation-state, 'the management of the whole productive resources of the country by one central authority, the general government'.[46] Mill describes this as 'revolutionary socialism', since its advocates typically favour its being established *now*, 'at all costs'.[47]

Mill draws a second, cross-cutting distinction between communistic and non-communistic socialism. This distinction concerns the distribution of the product of labour. Communistic versions of socialism, like those advocated by Blanc or Owen, divide it either equally or on the basis of need, whereas non-communistic socialism allows for the distribution to take account of the 'different kinds or degrees of service to the community' that different individuals give.[48] Non-communistic versions of socialism, for example those of Saint-Simon and Fourier, permit individuals to be rewarded unequally as a way of providing incentives for greater effort of sacrifice. Although this is not Mill's language, it will sometimes be convenient to refer to this doctrine as 'incentivistic' socialism.

For the critics of capitalism to show that the institution of private property should be abandoned, they must show that socialism is superior not to capitalism as it is but to capitalism as it could be. For Mill, '[T]he question is which of these arrangements is most conducive to human happiness.'[49] Complicating his efforts to answer this question is the fact that the improved capitalism he sketches has never been tried, nor have there been many trials of socialism. There are only a few things that Mill thinks can be said with absolute certainty.

First, because 'For a long period to come the principle of individual property will be in possession of the field', social reformers should devote their time and energy primarily to improving capitalism.[50] Second, the centralized state control of the economy advocated by the revolutionary socialists is such a difficult undertaking that it is certain to fail: 'the very idea of conducting the whole industry of a country from a single centre is so obviously chimerical, that nobody bothers to propose any mode in which it should be done.'[51] Third, experiments in socialism at the level of the firm and the community are necessary: '[T]he thing to be desired, and to which they have a just claim, is opportunity of trial. They are all capable of being tried on a moderate scale, and at no risk, either personal or pecuniary, to any except those who try them.'[52] If these experiments seem to show that some form of socialism really is most conducive to human happiness, then they will be emulated by ever larger numbers of people; the question of what manner of organizing production *should* be adopted is really that of what manner *will* be adopted.

In advance of a systematic study of socialist experiments, all that is possible is to conjecture about how conducive to happiness different forms of socialism would be. In a discussion that first appeared in the 1852 edition of the *Principles*, however, Mill claims with some confidence that large numbers of workers would eventually insist upon being the full owners of their firms, 'on terms of equality, collectively owning the capital with which they carry on their operations, and working under managers elected and removable by themselves'.[53] Much of Mill's certainty on this score derives from the fact that he can point to some early examples of the successful operation of the 'co-operative system'.[54] Many of these workers' associations started by following the communistic principle of equal division, but then supplemented it by the incentivistic system of piecework.

Capitalist ownership of firms will therefore largely be displaced by firm-level socialism; capitalists will, at most, 'lend their capital to the associations' of workers.[55] Mill believes that this transformation can occur in a way that protects capitalists' property rights and that in order to be morally legitimate it must. Capitalists have been encouraged to base their expectations on their continued ownership of their factories, and for the state simply to turn these over to the workers, or to allow workers to take them for themselves, would be entirely incongruent with the value of security. In fact, Mill does not even call for the state to give the capital to workers and pay the former owners compensation. He never suggests that the government should have any more of a role in this process than perhaps the provision of loans to those making early experiments with workers' associations.[56] He expects workers to save enough money to buy existing companies or to start their own. 'In this or some such mode', Mill tells us,

> the existing accumulations of capital might honestly, and by a kind of spontaneous process, become in the end the joint property of all who participate in their productive employment: a transformation which, thus effected, (and assuming of course that both sexes participate equally in the rights and the government of the association) would be the nearest approach to social justice, and the most beneficial ordering of industrial affairs, which it is possible at present to foresee.[57]

Nor does Mill see this kind of socialism as incompatible in any way with competition. Worker-owned firms would compete with one another and with capitalist-owned firms. In fact, he thinks that for cooperative firms to face capitalist-owned competitors would yield some significant economic benefits. Capitalist-owned firms are more likely to run risks and originate improvements, for example.[58]

Yet Mill thinks that eventually, as 'associations multiplied, they would tend more and more to absorb all work-people, except those who have too little understanding, or too little virtue, to be capable of learning to act on any other system than that of narrow selfishness'.[59] Diminishing competition with capitalists might make socialistic firms less innovative, but Mill does not see that as a very worrisome consequence. Far more important, to his mind, is the 'moral revolution' that would result if the economy were to be predominantly organized along socialistic lines:

> the healing of the standing feud between capital and labour; the transformation of human life, from a conflict of classes struggling for opposite interests, to a friendly rivalry in the pursuit of a good common to all; the elevation of the dignity of labour; a new sense of security and independence in the labouring class; and the conversion of each human being's daily occupation into a school of the social sympathies and the practical intelligence.[60]

Mill has high expectations for the educational potential of worker-owned firms. If workers controlled their own enterprises, then there would no longer be two distinct classes of people who see their interaction, however wrongly, as a 'zero-sum game', that is, a situation in which every gain for one party must come at the expense of another. When people think they are in a zero-sum game, it is all too easy for them to acquire the habit of disregarding the interests of their 'opponents'. If workers controlled their own firms, there would no longer be a class of employers in a position of dominance that made them susceptible to the character-warping effects of power over others. For the workers, the need to make decisions about the operation of the firm would be an invaluable intellectual exercise, and the fact that these decisions would need to be made collectively would instil in them the habit of attending to the feelings of their colleagues.

Would this spontaneous process go any further, so that socialism at the level of the firm would be co-mingled with, or supplanted by, some other version of socialism? Mill does not think it is possible to have much confidence in any answer to this question, but he engages in some speculation. When he writes about the prospects for community-level socialism, Mill primarily focuses upon its communistic form. Communism demands a higher level of moral development than incentivistic socialism; it will only work if people display a high degree of unselfishness. Mill believes that some people already do, and that it might eventually be possible to cultivate that degree of unselfishness in a wide segment of the population: 'Communism would even now be practicable among the *élite* of mankind, and may become so among the rest.'[61] Yet this could only happen 'by slow degrees, and a system of culture prolonged through successive generations'.[62]

Mill's optimism about the prospects for community-level communism waxes and wanes across different texts. He is most optimistic in some of the later editions of the *Principles* (starting in 1852), and his correspondence with Harriet shows that this may be largely because of her influence.[63] In the 'Chapters on Socialism', however, an unfinished work that Mill started in his last years and that was published after his death, he is far more pessimistic. He worries in particular about whether people would enjoy sufficient liberty under communism.[64] He is concerned, for instance, that parents in a communistic community would find it difficult to agree upon the sort of education that their children should receive.[65] Arneson, though, points out that there is no clear reason why a communistic community could not decentralize its educational system to give parents more choices nor generally why communism requires political settlements to non-economic questions.[66]

What it is most important to recognize about Mill's views on socialism, though, is that he never advocates abandoning the desert principle. The types of socialism that attract him eliminate capitalism's division between workers and capitalists, but not only do they come into being without violating capitalists' property rights, they involve small-scale enterprises whose property is public with respect to their members but private with respect to everyone else (as with worker-owned firms today) and who can compete with one another.[67] The most fervent free-market foe of socialism as it is usually understood today could find relatively little to object to in Mill.

Notice also that, while he is confident that eventually most workers would want to be part of workers' associations of some kind, Mill is not committed to the claim that some day all workers would insist on joining socialistic enterprises. His reformed capitalism would make it possible for capitalists' employees to lead satisfactory lives, especially since the need to compete with cooperatives for workers would put a lower limit on the terms that employers could offer, and he never suggests any reforms to property laws, at the level of the nation-state, that would make it impossible for individuals to own productive property.[68] His arguments in *On Liberty* suggest rather strongly that no one means of organizing production would ever have the field to itself. Work is an important part of a person's life, and the choice of how and under what conditions to labour can be an important choice, not only because you find certain ways of working more pleasurable than others but because labour can be a means of self-expression. There is no more reason to think that every person will be satisfied labouring under the same conditions than to believe that they will be satisfied engaging in the same recreations or reading the same books. How far Mill himself appreciates this point is not clear, although starting in the 1860s the *Principles* makes slightly weaker claims than in the 1850s about just how universally cooperative ownership would be adopted.[69] Oskar Kurer writes that 'It seems that Mill in the end came to believe a fully cooperative society was neither necessary nor very likely to occur.'[70]

There is not likely to be one simple explanation for why Mill's prediction that the vast majority of workers would some day refuse to work for capitalists did not come to pass. The barrier is surely not to be found in any of the small number of reforms to capitalism that he advocated that were never made. One part of the story, no doubt, is that he underestimated the logistical difficulties that groups of workers trying to pool their capital to create a firm or to purchase an existing one would face.[71] A deeper reason, though, is that he seems to overestimate rather dramatically how much appeal the idea of being part-owners of the firms where they work would have for workers, especially in the United States. Some might find that they do not want the responsibilities and extra duties that would come with being involved in a worker-owned firm; they may simply want to be able to go home or to pursue personal projects after working all day, rather than going to meetings. Such people might find working for a capitalist liberating.[72] Some might be sceptical about whether they would enjoy any more control over the workplace than they do under capitalist ownership, as just one vote among many (especially if they anticipate that the firm would still need to hire professional managers to oversee its day-to-day operation, even if those managers were ultimately answerable to the employee).

The problem of the poor

The question of what should be done to aid the poor was controversial in the nineteenth century as it is now. Mill's approach to this question involves trying to strike a balance among competing concerns. On the one hand, providing 'poor relief' promotes the security of the poor themselves by ensuring they will not face starvation, and that of everyone else by easing the temptation of the poor to turn to crime (which they are especially likely to do, Mill realizes, when life in prison is easier than life out of it).[73] On the other hand, though, poor relief creates disincentives to labour; the more comfortable the life that it is possible for people to lead without working, the less motivated they will be to work. For Mill, the disutility associated with these disincentives to labour goes beyond the mere economic cost of lost productivity. For people to fall into the habit of relying on others 'for the means of subsistence' saps their vigour, 'and unhappily there is no lesson which they more easily learn'. The importance of instilling energetic characters does not unambiguously argue against giving aid to the poor, however, because 'Energy and self-dependence are, however, liable to be impaired by the absence of help, as well as by its excess.'[74]

Taking all of this into consideration, Mill concludes that the state should provide no more and no less than minimal subsistence to paupers. The rest should be left to private charity which, when well administered, is capable of making fine distinctions between the deserving and undeserving poor that bureaucrats cannot.[75] As a way of minimizing disincentives to labour, he favours the basic approach to poor relief that was embodied in the British Poor Law of 1834.[76] This law offered a bare subsistence to the employable poor, but only upon terms that were meant to be so unpleasant that no one would accept them except as a last resort. As a rule, receiving relief required entering a workhouse.[77] Readers of *Oliver Twist* will be acquainted with just how unpleasant life in a Victorian workhouse could be.

The stationary state

Finally, we come to the notion of the so-called 'stationary state', which is attained when the rate of profit reaches the minimum that investors are willing to accept and economic growth ceases. Classical economic theory holds that such a state must eventually be reached. It assumes that periods of economic growth increase the demand for workers, which by the laws of supply and demand increases their standard of living. It also assumes that when workers' standard of living rises above a certain level they will choose to have more children. This means that the number of people competing for jobs in the next generation will be larger, and by the laws of supply and demand wages will sink again. So a few years after a period of economic growth, the working class will be larger but its standard of living will be just what it was before. However, population growth necessitates the use of less fertile land for agriculture, land on which the costs of producing food are higher. The larger the population, the more expensive food becomes as the marginal cost of producing more of it rises. As food becomes more expensive, capitalists have to devote a larger percentage of the share of the revenues of their enterprises to labour costs, leaving less for themselves. (Meanwhile, since it is the cost of producing food on the worst land being used for this purpose that determines the price of food, the people who own land on which food can be grown cheaply are growing incredibly wealthy – at least unless Mill's land reforms, described earlier, are adopted.) So capitalists' profits get smaller, and when they are small enough, investment is no longer worthwhile and growth ceases.[78] While this statement of the argument presupposes the existence of capitalism, by the way, note that adopting socialism would not change things. Classical economic theory recognizes no exception to the iron law that economic growth must eventually stop.

Mill does not dispute that the stationary state must inevitably arrive, but he does not see this prospect as a cause for gloom or despair. After all, as should be abundantly clear by now, his evaluations of economic systems are based more on what sorts of *people* they tend to produce than on how many widgets they turn out. A genuinely happy life, one rich in the 'higher pleasures', requires only a modest amount of material wealth. Indeed, it precludes an excessive concern with accumulation. Therefore a society of people leading happy lives can, and indeed perhaps must, have a stationary economy.[79]

A stationary state is only stationary in an economic sense, of course; in every other way, society can still move forward:

> It is scarcely necessary to remark that a stationary condition of capital and population implies no stationary state of human improvement. There would be as much scope as ever for all kinds of mental culture, and moral and social progress; as much room for improving the Art of Living, and much more likelihood of its being improved, when minds ceased to be engrossed by the art of getting on.[80]

It is necessary to stave off stationariness until sufficient abundance has been attained for everyone willing to work to enjoy at least a reasonable level of material comfort and the population has reached the level of moral and intellectual development necessary for them to turn their attention to the higher pleasures, to be willing to effect a distribution of property that allows everyone to enjoy a comfortable existence and to be able to practise the restraint necessary to keep the population from growing any larger. When these conditions are satisfied, there is no real need for further economic growth.

9

Millian Democracy

This chapter will consider Mill's views on democratic government, giving particular attention to one of the most contested questions about his political philosophy, namely the relative strength of his commitments to elitism and political equality.[1]

Mill's case for representative democracy

In chapter 2 of *Considerations on Representative Government* (*Representative Government*, for short), Mill considers what criteria should govern the choice of a form of government. Obviously his view is that this choice must ultimately turn on which form best promotes happiness, but he proposes two more specific criteria on the basis of which different alternatives can be compared:

> We may consider, then, as one criterion of the goodness of a government, the degree in which it tends to increase the sum of good qualities in the governed, collectively and individually; since, besides that their well-being is the sole object of government, their good qualities supply the moving force which works the machinery. This leaves, as the other constituent element of the merit of a government, the quality of the machinery itself; that is, the degree in which it is adapted to take advantage of the amount of good qualities which may at any time exist, and make them instrumental to the right purposes.[2]

While one criterion is that a form of government ought to conduce to the future improvement of the people who live under it, the other is that it ought to promote their interests effectively in the present, taking them as they are. The perspective of one criterion is dynamic, we might say, and that of the other static. Carole Pateman and Dennis Thompson name these criteria the 'educative' and 'protective' goals respectively but, if the second criterion were really concerned only with *protecting* citizens' interests, then it would give us no reason to prefer a form of government that actively advances these interests over one that merely keeps them from being damaged.[3] This cannot be Mill's intent. He believes, after all, that governments should do whatever will 'conduce to general convenience'.[4] It is more accurate, if less specific, to say that Mill calls for forms of government to be judged based on how well they serve the twin goals of education and effectiveness. He never discusses what trade-offs between these two criteria are worth making, that is, how much effectiveness it is worth giving up in order to gain a given increase in educational potential. He is largely able to avoid this question since he believes that a properly designed democratic government can simultaneously satisfy both criteria quite well. Notice, by the way, that while Mill explicitly formulates these criteria in his argument for representative democracy, the cases he constructs for other institutions and practices – for the reforms to capitalism that he favours, for instance, or for individual liberty – can been understood in terms of the same two criteria.

There is a limit, Mill maintains, to how effective any form of government that is not popular or democratic can be. To be effective, government must take the interests of all citizens into account, but the interests of anyone who entirely lacks political power are likely to be disregarded or misconstrued: 'in the absence of its natural defenders, the interest of the excluded is always in danger of being overlooked; and, when looked at, is seen with very different eyes from those of the persons whom it directly concerns.'[5] One might assume that Mill holds this view because he presupposes a high level of self-interest in politics, so that individuals or groups who wield political power will use it to promote their own sinister interests exclusively, but this is only part of the story. While he realizes that at present self-interest – or at least class interest – predominates in the political sphere, he believes that the disinterested use of political power is a moral imperative. And with his characteristic optimism about the gradual improvement of human nature, he both hopes and expects that people will become more public spirited in the future. 'Public spirit' is an important term for Mill. It denotes a willingness to participate in public affairs disinterestedly, that is, to participate in order to promote not merely one's own good but the public good. It is another name for the quality that writers in the civic republican political tradition often call 'civic virtue'.[6]

Even if everyone with political power were assumed to be completely disinterested, however, Mill would still believe that the interests of those without power would not be well served. A case in point: by the 1860s, Mill feels able to say that Parliament is no longer entirely unconcerned about the well-being of the disenfranchised workers. Yet even when MPs sincerely try to promote the workers' interests, he observes, they do so based on their own conception of those interests. Lacking a voice in Parliament, the workers are not able to count on MPs to attend to their *own* conception of their needs. And while Mill may not believe that the workers are infallible judges of their own interests, he sees that Parliament cannot be expected to form a proper understanding of working-class interests unless what the workers themselves have to say on the subject is 'respectfully listened to, instead of being, as it is, . . . ignored'.[7]

Mill characteristically attaches even more importance to democracy's improving ethological effects than to its ability to promote the well-being of people as they are. Participation in public affairs, Mill believes, transforms individuals' characters. Participation fosters 'the various desirable qualities, moral and intellectual, or rather . . . moral, intellectual, and active' (or, as he says a bit further into *Representative Government*, 'intellectual, practical, and moral').[8]

Two of Mill's statements of this thesis, drafted roughly twenty years apart, are exceptionally powerful. In a comparatively early essay, a review of Tocqueville's *Democracy in America*, he writes:

> The private money-getting occupation of almost everyone is more or less a mechanical routine; it brings but few of his faculties into action, while its exclusive pursuit tends to fasten his attention and interest exclusively upon himself, and upon his family. . . . Balance these tendencies by contrary ones; give him something to do for the public, whether as a vestryman, a juryman, or an elector; and, in that degree, his ideas and feelings are taken out of this narrow circle. He becomes acquainted with more varied business, and a larger range of considerations. He is made to feel that besides the interests which separate him from his fellow citizens, he has interests which connect him with them. . . .[9]

He returns to this theme in *Representative Government*, where he argues that whereas despotism teaches passivity and submissiveness,

> Very different is the state of the human faculties where a human being feels himself under no other external restraint than the necessities of nature, or mandates of society which he has his share in imposing, and which it is open to him, if he thinks them wrong, publicly to dissent from, and exert himself actively to get altered.[10]

In addition to encouraging citizens to develop more vigorous characters, Mill continues, participation in public affairs also gives them the opportunity to grapple with intellectual problems of an order that most of them would never confront in their workaday lives, and so to develop new habits of thoughts. If a citizen's public duties are substantial enough – Mill is thinking here of service on juries and in local civic offices – 'it makes him an educated man'.[11] And of greater value still, he concludes, 'is the moral part of the instruction afforded by the participation of the private citizen, if even rarely, in public functions': 'Where this school of public spirit does not exist . . . [t]here is no unselfish sentiment of identification with the public.'[12]

As these passages show, when Mill talks about the educational benefits of civic participation he has multiple modes of participation in mind, not merely voting. The practice of political participation via popular elections has particular educational value, however, in large part because it leads to political discussion. It is through political discussion that the citizen

> is taught that remote causes, and events which take place far off, have a most sensible effect even on his personal interests; and it is from political discussion, and collective political action, that one whose daily occupations concentrate his interests in a small circle round himself, learns to feel for and with his fellow citizens, and becomes consciously a member of a great community.[13]

While it is possible in principle for people who are disenfranchised to talk about public affairs, this rarely happens, Mill contends: 'Political discussions fly over the heads of those who have no votes', because for the vast majority of people 'The only sufficient incitement to mental exertion . . . is the prospect of some practical use to be made of its results.'[14] Although many 'People find it fanciful to expect so much from what seems so slight a cause – to recognize a potent instrument of mental improvement in the exercise of the political franchise', Mill takes the American experience, as described by Tocqueville, to demonstrate its effectiveness empirically.[15]

In sum, civic participation contributes to citizens' mental development in a variety of ways. It forces them to take account of the viewpoints and feelings of people with whom they would normally not associate. Initially, this may be only a self-interested strategic necessity; they may pay attention to what others need only in order to negotiate with them for what they themselves want. Mill believes that paying close attention to the feelings of others tends to often lead to sympathizing with them, though, and regularly paying close attention to their feelings tends to lead to developing the habit of doing so. This, in turn, leads to becoming someone who can be counted upon to sympathize with them and participation thereby nurtures the growth of public spirit. Participation also presents citizens with greater intellectual challenges than they will typically be confronted with in their personal lives, especially if they do not have a role in managing a business of some sort. And since participation requires action, it fosters the development of active characters. One might worry that only people who already have active characters will take advantage of opportunities to participate. Remember, though, that some of the modes of participation that Mill discusses, like jury service and militia training, are compulsory. Besides, people's characters will be active to different degrees. Providing a person with some disposition towards activity with opportunities to become involved in public affairs will reinforce the habit. And of course, Mill does want to see society become participatory in ways that go beyond political or civic participation, since he advocates democracy in the workplace as well as in the *polis* (although Fourierist or Saint-Simonian villages blur the line between democratic control of the firm and local politics).

To maximize citizens' opportunities for civic participation, Mill calls for the greatest feasible decentralization of power. The more decisions that are made at the local level, the more opportunities citizens will have to participate in making them and in administering the policies that result.[16] Local government is especially important, Mill notes, because it gives many more citizens the opportunity to hold some sort of office at some point. Nevertheless, he holds, 'since all cannot, in a community exceeding a single small town, participate personally in any but some very minor portions of the public business, it follows that the ideal type of a perfect government must be representative.'[17]

Elitism

While this democratic and participatory strand of thought is a vital part of Mill's political philosophy, so too is a counterbalancing elitist strand. One line of thought that resurfaces at numerous points in Mill's writings includes the claims that what might be described as an 'intellectual elite' exists, that in his day and age this 'intelligentsia' is deeply divided on moral, social and political questions, and that we should both hope and expect that in the future the views of its members will converge and that the rest of society will then show them appropriate deference. This line of thought emerges most clearly in Mill's essay 'The Spirit of the Age':

> It is, therefore, one of the necessary conditions of humanity, that the majority must either have wrong opinions, or no fixed opinions, or must place the degree of reliance warranted by reason, in the authority of those who have made moral and social philosophy their peculiar study. . . . This state of things does not now exist in the civilized world. . . . [T]he first men of the age will one day join hands and be agreed: and then there is no power on earth or in hell itself, capable of withstanding them.[18]

'The Spirit of the Age' is an early essay, appearing in serial form in the newspaper *The Examiner* in 1831. When it was written, Mill was in the grip of an enthusiasm for the Saint-Simonian philosophy of history, according to which societies move through alternating 'organic' periods of intellectual consensus and 'critical' periods of disharmony, that later diminished.[19] Thus one cannot take Mill's continued adherence to all of the views he expressed in the essay for granted. In particular, his failure to include the essay in *Dissertations and Discussions*, the collection of his writings that he published in 1859 (with longer editions appearing after his death), might suggest a major change of mind on some points (although this might also be partly explained by his later disdain for the literary style of the essay).[20] Even if Mill eventually rejects the cyclical Saint-Simonian view, however, in his later work we still find the claims that we are moving towards a day in which the views of elite moral thinkers will converge and that when this happens the rest of society will and should defer to their views. For instance, Mill writes in *Auguste Comte and Positivism* that 'unless something stops the progress of human improvement', a day is sure to come when 'social inquirers would exhibit as much agreement in their doctrines as those who cultivate any of the sciences of inorganic life' and, when it does, 'mere deference' to their 'accordance of opinion' may produce 'universal assent' to a given form of social organization.[21] Mill does not expect the intellectual elite to reach this accordance any time soon; quite the contrary, he takes Comte to task for supposing that the day is nigh. But he continues to hold that there is a fairly distinct group of intellectual elites distinguished not only by their superior intelligence but also, more specifically, by their superior grasp of moral philosophy (including social and political philosophy), that some day their views will agree, and that when they do the rest of society should and will defer to their views in these areas.

Another type of elite also figures in Mill's political philosophy. This is a moral elite, one that comprises public-spirited individuals who have transcended both selfishness and short-sightedness. (It is overcoming the first of these that allows the second to be overcome as well, Mill believes, for 'It is only a disinterested regard for others . . . whether grounded on sympathy or on a conscientious feeling, which ever directs the minds and purposes of classes or bodies of men towards distant or unobvious interests.'[22]) So morally advanced are the members of this elite that, as we saw in the previous chapter, Mill has 'no difficulty in admitting that Communism would even now be practicable' among them.[23]

Mill sometimes singles out either the moral or the intellectual elite for attention in a manner that suggests that there is no particular relation between them at all, that is, that an individual's belonging to one group has no bearing on how likely he or she is to belong to the other. At points, however, it becomes apparent that he really thinks that there is just one elite, not two: one group of individuals who are distinguished both intellectually *and* morally. As Willmoore Kendall and George W. Carey put it, for Mill there are not 'two Fews but just one.'[24] One nice illustration of this comes when he writes that 'The constituencies to which most of the highly educated and public spirited persons in the country belong, those of the large towns, are now, in great part, either unrepresented or misrepresented.'[25] '[N]ot the highly educated on the one hand and the public spirited on the other', as Kendall and Carey point out, 'but the highly educated *and* public spirited'.

Mill gives no argument for why those members of the community who have the keenest insight into moral philosophy should also be the most public-spirited; he simply seems to take for granted that they will. He provides only sketchy details about this moral and intellectual elite, but we have seen how low an opinion he has of most of the formal education that his contemporaries receive; clearly no amount of formal education, even an Oxbridge degree, is sufficient by itself to make one a member. What is required instead, apparently, is the intelligent, intensive study of the right theoretical subjects. There is a sense in which a representative member of the upper classes who has had some formal schooling comes closer to belonging to the elite than a representative worker who has had none. The former may at least have read some of the right things. Mill does not seem to assume, though, that on the whole the upper classes possess any more genuine public spirit than the working class. The prototypical member of either is likely to have sympathies that at most extend only to other members of the same class, resulting in their being motivated by a class spirit or 'class-selfishness'.[26]

Mill's enlightened few does not seem to emerge exclusively from any one socio-economic class. In his references to the elite, we can hear an echo of his father's references to the 'middle rank'. James Mill describes the middle rank as 'the most wise and the most virtuous part of the community . . . , which gives to science, to art, and to legislation itself, their most distinguished ornaments, and is the chief source of all that has exalted and refined human nature', and notes that it 'is that portion of the community of which, if the basis of Representation were ever so far extended, the opinion would ultimately decide. Of the people beneath them, a vast majority would be sure to be guided by their advice and example.'[27] As Terence Ball explains, the middle rank is not co-extensive with the 'middle class' but rather 'cuts across the kinds of class divisions with which we are familiar today'.[28] While John Stuart Mill's elite may come out of the middle rank, however, it comprises only that subset of it that has made a true study of moral, social and political questions. And it is as yet too disunited to offer guidance to 'the people beneath' it. (We have already encountered other 'fews' in Mill's thought, such as the group of moral reformers who are able to see how society's positive morality might be improved and the select group of creative geniuses from whose experiments in living the rest of us may be able to learn. Mill's elite presumably contains or is co-extensive with the first of these 'fews'; how it relates to the second is a little less clear.)

The available evidence suggests that Mill considers the existence of an intellectual and moral elite to be a fixed fact about human society. Improvements in education may greatly narrow the gap between the bulk of humanity and its most advanced members, but it will not close it entirely. First, there will never be more than a few who specialize in theoretical studies.[29] Nor, second, does Mill seem to think that all people will ever be capable of precisely the same amount of sympathetic public spirit. He writes in *Utilitarianism* that 'Genuine private affections and a sincere interest in the public good, are possible, *though in unequal degrees*, to every rightly brought up human being.'[30] Some people, in other words, will always be capable of deeper friendship, deeper love or more public spirit than others. (There is another way to read this passage, according to which Mill is saying not that different people are capable of sympathy to different degrees but rather that the same person will never be equally capable of private affection and public spirit. But it is hardly plausible that he would claim without qualification that this is impossible so shortly after having inscribed on Harriet's tombstone that she was 'As earnest for the public good as she was generous and devoted to all who surrounded her.'[31])

In Mill's eyes, the existence of this moral and intellectual elite has major political ramifications, for greater virtue and greater knowledge are both reasons for one person's political judgements to be given more weight than another's: 'the opinion, the judgment, of the higher moral or intellectual being, is worth more than that of the inferior: and if the institutions of the country virtually assert that they are of the same value, they assert a thing which is not.'[32] Mill's theory of democracy can be understood as an effort to find a form of representative democracy consistent with this principle.

On one recent reading of Mill, that of Joseph Hamburger, Mill's real social-political agenda is to put the elite minority in a position to dominate the remainder of society via extra-political means.[33] The keystone of Hamburger's reading is the fact that in *On Liberty* Mill says that the liberty principle does not protect people against suffering the 'natural penalties which cannot be prevented from falling on those who incur the distaste or the contempt of those who know them':[34]

We have a right . . . to act upon our unfavourable opinion of any one, not to the oppression of his individuality, but in the exercise of ours. We are not bound, for example, to seek his society; we have a right to avoid it (though not to parade the avoidance), for we have a right to choose the society most acceptable to us. We have a right, and it may be our duty, to caution others against him. . . . We may give others a preference over him in optional good offices, except those which tend to his improvement.[35]

Hamburger portrays Mill as aiming to create social conditions within which the elite, when it arrives at intellectual consensus, can in effect shame the rest of society into acting on its views via these natural penalties. He seeks, then, to reveal Mill as an anti-liberal in liberal's clothing. This is not the first time that such an unmasking has been attempted, but the project is hopeless.[36] While there are many problems here, it should be obvious that it would be impossible for the tiny and geographically scattered elite to exert much influence over the rest of a country via the natural penalties Mill describes. If you are not likely to know any members of a group personally in the first place, then the fact that they are avoiding your company will not make much of an impact on you. Moreover, in his later work Mill is at pains to insist that any deference shown to the elite is to be rational and knowing, not blind; it is to be the 'intelligent deference of those who know much to those who know still more'.[37]

Plural voting and proportional representation

This section and the ones that follow will focus on different aspects of the workings of a properly designed democratic system as Mill conceives of it. He is primarily writing about the British political system for British readers, and he is writing in a particular historical context. Still, his arguments for the measures he favours are grounded on principles that he takes to be applicable to any democratic government. Even though some of these measures may strike contemporary readers as outlandish, in the absence of a specific reason to think otherwise we should read Mill as if he is seriously recommending them to us. (And we should keep in mind that among those of Mill's proposals that strike his own contemporaries as the most outlandish, several have long been adopted throughout the Western world.)

It will be useful, though, to introduce some elementary factual information about the period in which Mill is writing. The suffrage in Britain was extended through a series of reforms that stretched over the course of the nineteenth century and into the twentieth. Prior to 1832, a patchwork system of laws determined who was allowed to vote in the United Kingdom. In theory, there were two basic kinds of districts or constituencies, rural counties and municipal boroughs. No women could vote, of course, and substantial property qualifications and other requirements sharply limited the number of male voters. Because few changes had been made over the last several hundred years to which municipalities were constituted as borough constituencies, many were no larger than villages and some were much smaller even than this. With so few electors and in the absence of the secret ballot, which was not introduced until 1872, one powerful figure in a small borough constituency could effectively determine whom the borough would send to Parliament; this was the hallmark of a so-called 'rotten borough'. Meanwhile, many new industrial cities had no representation.

The first Reform Act passed in 1832, under the Whig Prime Minister Charles Grey, the second Earl Grey (in whose honour the tea was named). In addition to giving more representatives to the large cities at the expense of small boroughs, the Act lowered the property qualifications in both the counties and the boroughs, roughly doubling the number of voters. Most of the new voters it created were from the middle class, although in London a working man might qualify; five out of six males still lacked the vote.[38] The second Reform Act did not pass until 1867, when the Conservative Benjamin Disraeli was prime minister. It lowered the property qualification in the boroughs so that significantly more male industrial workers could vote. The third Reform Act was passed in 1884, when Disraeli's Liberal rival William Gladstone was prime minister, and it lowered the property qualifications in the county constituencies. (Both the second Reform Act and a piece of legislation passed the year after the third further contributed to the redistribution of parliamentary seats from less to more populated areas.) Legislation passed in 1918 eliminated property qualifications entirely for men, who could vote at age 21, and allowed women to vote for the first time, albeit only at age 30 and only if they met certain property qualifications. Only in 1928 did women gain the vote on equal terms with men.

Most of Mill's life, then, falls between the passage of the first and second Reform Acts. He is working at a time in which it seems likely that the entire working class is eventually going to be admitted to the franchise and readily apparent that more workers will be admitted to it relatively soon. This poses a dilemma for Mill. On the one hand, he is committed to both the proposition that government cannot be nearly as effective as it might as long as a large number of people are disenfranchised and the proposition that the opportunity to participate in politics would do more than virtually anything else to advance the workers' education. On the other hand, the working class is so large that if all of the workers were to gain the vote without anything else changing in the British political system, then the House of Commons would be utterly dominated by their representatives. This would spell disaster, Mill believes, because the workers' deficient educations leave them woefully unprepared, on the whole, to exercise power. He fears in particular that their representatives would be likely to enact short-sighted economic measures that would eventually work to their own disadvantage as well as to the disadvantage of the rest of the nation: the imposition of 'equality of earnings'; the abolition of 'piecework, payment by the hour, and all practices which enable superior industry or abilities to gain a superior reward'; and the passage of laws to 'raise wages', limit 'competition in the labour market', restrict 'machinery' and protect 'the home producer against foreign industry'.[39] What Thompson calls Mill's principle of participation collides with what he calls Mill's principle of competence.[40]

In an 1859 pamphlet titled 'Thoughts on Parliamentary Reform', Mill proposes two ways of resolving this collision. The ideal solution, he says, would be for the entire working class to be enfranchised – that is, for property qualifications to be eliminated – but for a system of 'plural voting' to be established whereby those with more education would receive more votes:

> If every ordinary unskilled labourer had one vote, a skilled labourer, whose occupation requires an exercised mind and a knowledge of some of the laws of external nature, ought to have two. A foreman, or superintendent of labour, whose occupation requires something more of general culture, and some moral as well as intellectual qualities, should perhaps have three. A farmer, manufacturer, or trader . . . should have three or four. A member of any profession requiring a long, accurate, and systematic mental cultivation, – a lawyer, a physician or surgeon, a clergyman of any denomination, a literary man, an artist, a public functionary . . . ought to have five or six. A graduate of any university, or a person freely elected a member of any learned society, is entitled to at least as many.[41]

He goes on to suggest that tests might be used to allow someone whose learning is greater than would be anticipated for his occupation or formal training to establish that he ought to receive additional votes.

Mill indicates in the pamphlet that he considers plural voting to be a necessary concomitant of the enfranchisement of the entire working class: its adoption would be desirable even before the entire working class gets the vote, but to allow all labourers to vote in the absence of its adoption would be completely unjustifiable. He recognizes that most workers are hardly likely to meet this plan with enthusiasm. Yet he flatly asserts that if they refuse to 'recognise a right in the better educated . . . to such plurality of votes as may prevent them from being always and hopelessly outvoted', then they 'must submit to have the suffrage limited to such portion of their numbers . . . as may effect the necessary balance between numbers and education in another manner'.[42]

In contrast with plural voting, Mill's second proposal is one that he thinks must be adopted in order for popular government to be justifiable, even if the franchise is never expanded. This is that a way must be found for political minorities to elect at least some members to the House of Commons. A political party might draw support from 30 or 40 per cent of the voters in every constituency, after all, and yet not manage to send a single one of its candidates to Westminster. Mill suggests that each constituency might elect three members, with each elector getting three votes that might all be given to the same candidate. This would let one third of the voters within a constituency ensure that a given candidate was elected, as long as they devoted all of their votes to the purpose.[43]

While only two years passed between the publication of 'Thoughts on Parliamentary Reform' and that of the far more substantial *Considerations on Representative Government*, Mill made a discovery in the intervening period that he takes to be of monumental importance. This is the 'Hare plan', that is, the system of proportional representation developed by Thomas Hare.[44] In contemporary parlance, the Hare plan is a transferable ballot system of proportional representation.[45] Instead of selecting a single candidate, voters list multiple candidates in order of preference. A quota is set for the number of votes that a candidate must receive in order to be elected. (Various formulas can be used for determining this quota. Hare's own proposal is the simplest of these, namely voters/seats.) If a candidate receives more first-place votes than necessary to secure a seat, then the 'excess' votes are redistributed to the candidates listed second on those ballots. (Again, various methods can be employed to determine which ballots are redistributed. Hare's own proposal involves random drawings, although Mill suggests to him in a letter that the ballots with the longest lists of candidates should instead be redistributed first.[46]) This process continues through one iteration after another until a point is reached at which redistribution does not result in any additional candidates reaching the quota. At this point, another process begins in which the candidates with the lowest number of votes are eliminated and those ballots are redistributed. This continues until the number of candidates remaining equals the number of seats left to be filled. As a means of ensuring the representation of minority views, Hare's system is vastly more efficacious than Mill's earlier proposal. While it may seem hopelessly complicated, today the single transferable ballot is used for elections at different levels of government in several countries.[47]

In *Representative Government*, Mill further develops the rationale for proportional representation that he gives in the 'Thoughts on Parliamentary Reform'. He still maintains, of course, that minority views are entitled to representation. He adds an additional point to his case, however, which is that under the Hare plan the moral and intellectual elite of the country could be assured of getting at least some of their number elected: 'In no other way which it seems possible to suggest would Parliament be so certain of containing the very *élite* of the country', for 'The minority of instructed minds scattered through the local constituencies would unite to return a number, proportioned to their own numbers, of the very ablest men the country contains.'[48] Even if only a few members of this group were to be elected, Mill is confident that their influence would be disproportionate to their numbers because of the force of their intellects. As long as some of the elite are in office, then their voices will be heard and their sagacity will give them considerable influence with the other representatives (and the public at large), especially as they approach unanimity:

> But if the *élite* . . . formed part of the Parliament, by the same title as any other of its members . . . their presence could give umbrage to nobody, while they would be in the position of highest vantage, both for making their opinions and counsels heard on all important subjects, and for taking an active part in public business. . . . The instructed minority would, in the actual voting, count only for

their numbers, but as a moral power they would count for much more, in virtue of their knowledge, and of the influence it would give them over the rest.[49]

So confident is Mill of the improving effects of the Hare plan on government that he concludes that if it were to be adopted then the entire working class could be enfranchised without undue risk even if plural voting were not adopted: 'I should not despair of the operation even of equal and universal suffrage, if made real by the proportional representation of all minorities, on Mr. Hare's principle.'[50]

However – and this is a large 'however' – the fact that Mill is grudgingly willing to accept the full enfranchisement of the working class without plural voting does not mean that he abandons the idea of giving more votes to the better educated. The line just quoted is followed by this one: 'But if the best hopes which can be formed on this subject [the Hare plan] were certainties, I should still contend for the principle of plural voting.'[51]

Insofar as plural voting would make it possible for the elite to get more of its number elected, it is clear why Mill would think that it is desirable. Members of the elite are distinguished by both superior 'knowledge and intelligence' and superior virtue. Even before they reach any sort of 'organic convergence' in their thinking, their presence in the legislature would at least elevate the level of debate.

It is also clear, though, that plural voting's effects would go well beyond empowering the elite. Anyone with an occupation any more intellectually demanding than manual labour will receive additional votes, after all, and while university graduates apparently stand to receive the largest number of additional votes, we have seen that Mill considers most of them to have anything but first-class minds. So he has to have reasons for proposing plural voting that go beyond getting elites into office.

We can distinguish at least three of these. First, while he never makes this point explicitly, Mill presumably believes that, despite the many deficiencies of the education that the upper classes have received, the average member of the middle class or aristocracy would still be a better voter than the average worker. If the upper classes have not thought about social or political questions in any depth, if they are in the grip of multiple prejudices, and if they are largely animated by class selfishness, at least many of them probably understand a little rudimentary economics. While they might still support bad economic policy – witness the Corn Laws – at least there is no need to fear that they might lean towards revolutionary socialism.

A second reason is pedagogical or ethological in nature. Mill thinks that the institutions of voting in a country will inevitably teach some moral lesson about the value of moral and intellectual development. He criticizes 'American institutions' in particular for teaching the 'false creed' that 'any one man (with a white skin) is as good as any other', a creed that invites people to infer that there is no real point in pursuing 'moral and intellectual excellence'.[52] Plural voting, in contrast, teaches that it is well worth pursuing these qualities. His point here is not that extra votes should be offered as an external incentive to pursue development, but rather that, by shaping the 'spirit of the institutions of a country' to reflect the value of development, it is possible to 'shape the national character' in the direction of esteeming it.

There is a further consideration which apparently factors in Mill's thinking as well. He is very much afraid that if property qualifications were dropped, then manual labourers would have 'the complete command of the House', which he believes would not bode well for the economy.[53] He seems to think that the Hare plan, which would allow the public-spirited elite to see to it that at least a few of its number are returned, would by itself do just enough to make matters tolerable. With their superior qualities giving them an influence disproportionate to the number of seats they hold, a small number of elite representatives could use the power of moral suasion to exercise some check over the representatives of the workers even if the latter controlled most of the seats in the legislature. It would be better, though, if the elite had even more influence than this, as they would if a rough balance in number existed between the representatives of the working class and of the upper classes. Even on the assumption that most of the representatives elected by the members of the working and upper classes alike would be motivated by class selfishness, achieving this balance would give the more public-spirited representatives of the elite the swing votes. And Mill's plural voting plan would help to establish this balance, since the individuals to whom it would assign more votes would virtually all belong to the middle class or aristocracy.

Mill does not raise this point while discussing plural voting in *Representative Government*, but a comment that he makes in an earlier chapter lays the groundwork for it so perfectly that it is inconceivable that it did not occur to him, and he does not disavow it:

[I]f the representative system could be made ideally perfect . . . its organisation must be such that these two classes, manual labourers and their affinities on one side, employers of labour and their affinities on the other, should be, in the arrangement of the representative system, equally balanced. . . . since, assuming that the majority of each class, in any difference between them, would be mainly governed by their class interests, there would be a minority of each in whom that consideration would be subordinate to reason, justice, and the good of the whole; and this minority of either, joining with the whole of the other, would turn the scale against any demands of their own majority which were not such as ought to prevail.[54]

While this balance would be disrupted in the opposite direction if the upper classes received too many 'extra' votes, Mill states in no uncertain terms that 'The plurality of votes must on no account be carried so far, that those who are privileged by it . . . shall outweigh by means of it all the rest of the community' or 'be able to practise class legislation on their own account'.[55]

It is no wonder that several interpreters have seen evidence in Mill's endorsement of plural voting for the claim that he intends for the elite to be in a position to control the political process. Arneson, for example, takes him to hold that 'it should be constitutionally required or a matter of practical necessity that majorities defer to the opinion of experts.'[56] Graeme Duncan, who describes Mill's position as 'democratic Platonism', says that Mill 'did favour political institutions in which the educated and disinterested – if temporarily divided – sections of the community were over-represented in relation to their numerical support. Consequently, his democratic credentials are thrown strongly into question.'[57]

The idea that Mill's preferred form of government, although putatively democratic, is in fact engineered to put the elite in a position of political supremacy is a far more plausible concern than Hamburger's somewhat fantastic worries about the elite's exercising control over the rest of society through shame. Further evidence might be found in certain other measures that Mill proposes, such as restricting the legislature's role to the approval or rejection of bills prepared by a commission of expert legislative draftsmen.[58]

Admittedly, Mill's plural voting scheme would result in majorities being forced to defer to the opinions of experts under certain conditions. If the number of representatives whose votes were determined by the perceived class interest of the lower class were roughly equal to the number whose votes were determined by the perceived class interest of the upper classes, and if on a given issue the representatives elected by Mill's elite joined with those of the upper classes and tipped the outcome in that direction, then one might say that the working-class majority was required to defer to 'experts'. On other occasions, though, the experts might tip the balance in favour of the majority. And if the lower and upper classes ever agreed about what should be done, then the small number of representatives selected by the instructed and public-spirited few would be hopelessly outvoted. So if Mill is not a democrat in the majoritarian, one-person-one-vote sense, neither is his elite 'unrestrained'.

Nor is his call for a 'Commission of Codification' made up of specialists to draft bills an avenue for the elite to dominate political decision making. Mill's intention is for legislation to be carefully crafted enough that it is free of the sorts of obscurities and paradoxes which Bentham so effectively criticized. This is consistent with its giving effect to the popular will, and Mill writes that 'The Commission, of course, would have no power of refusing instrumentality to any legislation which the country desired.'[59]

In truth, we cannot safely say that Mill is first and foremost either an elitist or a political egalitarian, for the elitist and egalitarian elements of his nuanced political philosophy temper one another with neither clearly predominating. Mill's theory of democracy is a product of his aspiration to be a complete thinker. It thoroughly synthesizes two perspectives that he regards as one-sided, both right in what they affirm but wrong in what they deny. According to one, 'the great mass of mankind' needs to be ruled 'by a degree of intelligence and virtue superior to their own'. According to the other, 'all governments in all ages' have been controlled by the sort of man who will, if he can, 'postpone the interests of other people to his own calculations or instincts of self-interest', and 'the only possible remedy is a pure democracy', since 'the people . . . can have no selfish interest in oppressing themselves.'[60] His plural voting scheme is the ultimate embodiment of this synthesis.

Some commentators call the wholeheartedness of Mill's endorsement of plural voting into question. They suggest either that his enthusiasm for it wanes after his discovery of the Hare plan or that he only intends it as a temporary transitional measure and does not believe that it will still be called for once the workers are better educated.[61] There is an element of truth in both of these suggestions, but on the whole each is more wrong than right.

It is certainly true that after his discovery of the Hare plan Mill does not regard plural voting as imperative in the way that he did earlier. In this sense, it is fair to say that he attaches less importance to it in *Representative Government* than he did previously. And he admits to being 'very sensible of the great practical difficulties' of plural voting and of having no hope 'of soon seeing what I think the true principles embodied in a specific plan likely to obtain any very wide acceptance', whereas he seems to think that it is realistic to hope for the Hare plan to be adopted relatively soon.[62] Nonetheless, his defence of plural voting in *Representative Government* is lengthy and passionate, so it hardly seems accurate to say that his interest in the subject has flagged.

Nor does the evidence support the claim that Mill regards plural voting only as a 'transitional' measure between a period in which many adult citizens are disenfranchised and one in which there is mass participation on the principle of one person, one vote. He anticipates that the day will come in which workers are no longer locked into an antagonistic relation with employers, since they will own their own firms. Whether this future society would truly be a 'classless' one is an interesting question. But in either case, insofar as the 'balancing argument' for plural voting pertains to the balance in numbers between the representatives of 'manual labourers and their affinities on one side, employers of labour and their affinities on the other', it will admittedly become obsolete. Yet this still leaves Mill's other rationales for plural voting in place. Even if everyone should eventually merit an equal number of votes – and we have seen that he does not expect that they will, even if he expects that some day virtually everyone will deserve more than one – he would still support maintaining the system of plural voting as a way of helping to impart a sense of the importance of education and development in each new generation: 'I should still contend for assigning plurality of votes to authenticated superiority of education, were it only to give the tone to public feeling, irrespective of any direct political consequences.'[63] In fact, he denies in the most explicit terms possible that he sees plural voting as a transitional measure: 'I do not propose the plurality as a thing in itself undesirable, which, like the exclusion of part of the community from the suffrage, may be temporarily tolerated while necessary to prevent greater evils.'[64]

Admittedly, there is a parliamentary speech in which Mill distinguishes between the Hare plan and plural voting by saying that the former, but not the latter, is 'equally desirable in any democratic constitution'.[65] However, Mill's point here is that plural voting would only be justified on the condition of universal suffrage, but the bill under discussion would leave most workers disenfranchised:

> It may be that I have suggested plurality of votes and various other checks as proper parts of a general system of representation; but . . . [t]he proposals I made had reference to universal suffrage. . . . Is there any danger that the working class will acquire a numerical ascendancy by the reduction of the franchise qualification to £7? It is ridiculous to suppose such a thing.[66]

Mill does not hold that plural voting is, like the Hare plan, desirable as part of every democratic constitution, but the state of affairs in which it is undesirable is his *present*, or any state resembling his present in keeping most workers away from the polls. He neither says nor implies that plural voting would be undesirable at any point in the future after property qualifications have been eliminated.

While it is unlikely that anyone would now want to go back to restricting the right to vote based on the value of a person's home and possessions, and while many Western democracies utilize some form of proportional representation, Mill's call for plural voting will probably not find a very receptive audience today. There are a variety of reasons for this. One is that, contrary to Mill's fears, the working class has never been a dominant political force, at least in the United States or United Kingdom. Another reason is that Mill's confidence that there are right answers to moral questions is not universally shared today. If there is no truth but only opinion, then what justification can there be for giving one person's opinion more weight than another's? While some people may doubt the existence of moral or political truth, others may question the proposition that more education translates into better political decision making. 'Intellectuals' as a group may be viewed with great suspicion in some quarters, on the grounds that their theoretical sophistication has somehow led them astray from simple truths. The prevalence of this thinking, at least in the United States, is shown by the fact that some politicians get considerable mileage out of positioning themselves as champions of the views of the 'heartland's' intellectually unpretentious hero 'Joe Sixpack' against those of the nation's 'intellectual elite'.[67]

Moreover, even people who are attracted to the abstract principle of giving more votes to those with more education may conclude that the practical obstacles to implementing it would be so great that it would not prove worthwhile. There might be interminable arguments over precisely how many votes different people should receive. Should all college graduates receive the same number, for instance, or should economics or political science students receive more than someone studying engineering on the grounds that their studies are more politically relevant? What about philosophy students? If we were to retain Mill's idea that some people should receive extra votes based on their occupations, regardless of how much formal education they have completed, then this would complicate the problem of assigning votes still further – exponentially so. Giving more votes to those with more education would also invite debate about whether more votes should be given on other grounds. Mill says that superior virtue should in principle merit additional political power, in addition to superior knowledge and intelligence. Should those who have done military service receive additional votes, then, on the grounds that they have demonstrated uncommon public spirit? What about those who have done some other form of community service?

Who gets to vote?

While Mill places some preconditions on the extension of the suffrage to the working class, his support for extending it to women on the same terms as men is unconditional: 'I consider [sex] to be as entirely irrelevant to political rights as difference in height or in the colour of the hair. All human beings have the same interest in good government; the welfare of all is alike affected by it, and they have equal need of a voice in it to secure their share of its benefits.'[68]

One of Mill's arguments for the enfranchisement of women is an argument from justice, which 'though it does not necessarily require that we should confer political functions on every one, does require that we should not, capriciously and without cause, withhold from one to give to another'.[69] (Mill, by the way, implies that to deny people the opportunity to vote because of the colour of their skin is just as unjust as to do so because of their sex.[70]) He also maintains that the same arguments from effectiveness and education that support the expansion of the franchise in general support its extension to women in particular. In making the argument from the effectiveness of government, Mill first observes that the notion that women as a class are inferior and ought to be placed in a subordinate position to men is completely at odds with 'the whole mode of thought of the modern world', which tends towards letting individual aptitude determine what each person can and cannot do. But even if this notion were accepted, he continues, it would not show that women should not have the vote, since even if they were not fit to govern they would still need to protect themselves against misgovernment. In fact, though, he points out, government is perhaps the area in which women have most effectively shown themselves equal in capacity with men, inasmuch as on average queens have ruled more effectively than kings.[71]

In making the educational argument, Mill notes that women of the upper classes characteristically tend to display a sort of 'family selfishness', judging every question from the perspective of what would be best for the family's social standing. As a result, he thinks, such influence as they have over their husband's conduct in the political sphere is typically exerted against the choice of any unconventional or unpopular course, even when this is motivated by public spirit, making it 'in 99 cases out of 100 destructive of public virtue in the men connected with them'[72]: 'I am afraid it must be said, that disinterestedness in the general conduct of life – the devotion of the energies to purposes which hold out no promise of private advantages to the family – is very seldom encouraged or supported by women's influence. . . . [W]omen's influence is often anything but favourable to public virtue.'[73]

The remedy to this state of affairs, Mill contends, is to stop teaching women 'both by institutions and by the whole of their education, to regard themselves as entirely apart from politics'.[74] The first step, the institutional one, is the step that Mill tried to take himself while in Parliament, when he attempted to amend Disraeli's Reform Bill by replacing the word 'man' with 'persons' and thereby give women the vote on equal terms with men. While this motion failed, as he knew that it would, Mill describes the attempt as 'by far the most important, perhaps the only really important public service I performed in the capacity of a Member of Parliament'.[75]

There are two significant restrictions on the franchise that Mill does endorse. One is educational: he maintains that any one who has not mastered certain basic skills should not be allowed to cast even one vote – even if society has failed them by not providing them with the opportunity to acquire a basic education.[76] While there might be no good reason for placing such a condition on voting today, a literacy requirement clearly made more sense in a period in which the written word was the primary means of conveying news about public affairs. Mill is sensitive to the potential for abuse in this kind of test, that is, the possibility that the people responsible for administering it could 'cheat' in order to disenfranchise qualified voters arbitrarily. In the British context, he considers the likelihood high that a straightforward test of the most rudimentary skills would be administered fairly, although he worries that making the test more demanding would increase the probability of arbitrary assessment. A few years after he is writing, literacy tests would be systematically and fraudulently misadministered in the American South as a pretext for disenfranchising freed slaves and their descendants.[77] In a context like that, in which the people charged with carrying out the testing had a powerful antipathy towards certain prospective voters, he would almost certainly reject the use of literacy tests altogether: 'It is better that the suffrage should be conferred indiscriminately, or even withheld indiscriminately, than that it should be given to one and withheld from another at the discretion of a public officer.'[78]

The second restriction on who can vote that Mill favours might be construed as a weak property qualification. This is that the receipt of public assistance 'should be a peremptory disqualification for the franchise'. Mill's argument for this restriction is that people who do not contribute to the wealth of the community should have no voice in how the public purse is spent:

> He who cannot by his labour suffice for his own support has no claim to the privilege of helping himself to the money of others. . . . Those to whom he is indebted for the continuance of his very existence may justly claim the exclusive management of those common concerns, to which he now brings nothing, or less than he takes away.[79]

Mill clearly regards it as unfair that those who do not do enough work to support themselves should receive a vote. Yet the fairness of disenfranchising them, at least under all circumstances, is itself quite questionable. For example, Mill does not distinguish between people who could support themselves and choose not to (a group that might be expanded to include those who are unable to support themselves because of their past choices, such as those incapacitated by substance abuse) and people with disabilities that render them unable to work. Even someone who considers it unfair to give the former group the opportunity to vote might consider it unfair to deny this opportunity to the latter group. There is a larger point to make here, though, which is that when he calls for people who cannot support themselves to be prevented from voting, Mill seems to be operating on the blatantly false assumption that elected officials do nothing except impose taxes and distribute the monies they collect. If wartime military conscription is in place, a practice that Mill endorses, then someone who has received public relief might still be in a position to be called up to fight. If so, then what justification could there be for denying him a say in decisions that might affect the likelihood of war? Legislatures decide what offences are to be criminalized. What justification could there be for denying any citizen a say in those decisions? In another passage, Mill himself seems to realize both that considerations of fairness militate in favour of giving people with a stake in political decisions a say and that people can have a stake for reasons that go beyond their economic contributions: 'If he is compelled to pay, *if he may be compelled to fight, if he is required implicitly to obey*, he should be legally entitled to be told what for; to have his consent asked, and his opinion counted at its worth, though not at more than its worth.'[80]

'The ballot'

In Mill's time, the term 'the ballot' was used for what we today call the secret or 'Australian' ballot. The ballot was generally considered to be a central plank in the radical platform, and in 1830 James Mill published a closely argued essay in defence of it in the *Westminster Review*. In *Representative Government* and elsewhere, however, John Stuart Mill argues against the ballot. It is tempting to frame this question in terms of 'Mill versus Mill', but that would be to oversimplify both of their positions.

In a brief mention of the ballot in his *History of British India*, James Mill states that there are circumstances in which the ballot is justified and circumstances in which it is not. When how people vote is made public, then other people are in a position to influence electors through various pleasant or painful inducements. This influence can be used by those with a sinister interest to make electors less likely to vote in the manner that would best promote the public weal. James Mill acknowledges, though, that in some situations it might be more likely to be used to counteract the electors' own sinister interest and make them better voters. What John Stuart Mill contends in *Representative Government* and other contemporaneous works is that over the course of his life Britain transitioned from the first sort of circumstances to the second. He does not look back on his own earlier advocacy of the ballot or that of his father as a mistake. Rather, he contends that while there was a point in time when the ballot would have been genuinely valuable, that time has passed and those who continue to agitate for it will do more harm than good if they succeed.

In 'The Ballot', James Mill argues that if how people vote is a matter of public record, many voters will not feel able to exercise individual judgement about what candidate to support but will instead be obliged to vote for wealthy members of the constituency or for the candidates favoured by the wealthy. To do otherwise is to risk the loss of one's house or farm if one is a tenant, one's job if one is an employee or one's customers if one is a shopkeeper. If votes are cast secretly, then worries about retaliation or bribery are alleviated: 'The power either of rewarding a prostitute vote, or punishing an honest one, is useless, whenever it has been made impossible to be known whether the prostitute or the honest vote has been given.'[81] To the objection that the ballot encourages mendacity or lying, since what it does in effect is to make it possible for people to lie safely if they are interrogated about how they will or did vote, James Mill makes three replies. First, he claims, there is nothing morally objectionable about lying to someone who demands information to which they are not entitled.[82] Second, the ballot will not in fact result in frequent lying, since people who know that they are likely to receive a lie in answer to their question are not likely to ask it in the first place. James Mill strikes a Kantian note here, writing 'If men never continue to do anything in vain, men will not seek promises from others, in circumstances in which the promise is of no use to them. Where there is no promising at all, there is no false promising.'[83] Finally, he points to the hypocrisy of those members of the upper classes who consider the ballot dishonest and yet who employ secret voting in their clubs to make it possible for someone to 'blackball' an aspirant without fear of consequences.[84]

To understand John Stuart Mill's argument against the secret ballot, it is useful to begin with the question of why members of Parliament or of Congress do not vote secretly. The answer, it seems, must be that their constituents are entitled to hold them accountable for how they vote. Mill maintains, though, that ordinary citizens are equally liable to be held accountable for their votes since they are obligated to their compatriots to cast their votes for the candidates whom they conscientiously believe will best promote the public good. For this reason, he strongly resists the notion that a vote is something to which an individual has a right. From Mill's perspective, to say that someone has a right to vote is to say that an individual can vote as he or she pleases. A citizen's vote, he insists, is rather a trust:

> If it is a right, if it belongs to the voter for his own sake, on what ground can we blame him for selling it, or using it to recommend himself to any one whom it is his interest to please? . . . His vote is not a thing in which he has an option; it has no more to do with his personal wishes than the verdict of a juryman. It is strictly a matter of duty; he is bound to give it according to his best and most conscientious opinion of the public good.[85]

If how citizens vote is known, Mill asserts, then their sense of shame (or of pride) will tend to motivate them to cast a public-spirited vote rather than a selfish one.[86] In addition, ethological or pedagogical concerns once again occupy a prominent place in his reasoning. Allowing citizens to vote in private sends the message that the vote is something to which they have a right, that is, something that they can dispose of as they wish. Requiring them to vote under the public gaze reinforces the point that their vote is to be disinterested.[87] For Mill, then, requiring public voting both provides citizens who may be lacking in public spirit with an external inducement to vote as a public-spirited person would and helps to instil genuine public spirit.

Mill is unconvinced by his father's assertion that people would not bother to ask questions when they knew that they could not rely upon the answers, so that the ballot would not lead to lying. On the contrary, he says, 'a man who thinks that he has power over another, and who is disposed to make tyrannical use of it, will question him about his vote, even when he has no guarantee for obtaining a true answer but the man's veracity, or his awkwardness.'[88] And he particularly fears his compatriots being put in a situation in which they would feel compelled to lie since he believes that a high regard for the truth is one of the finer aspects of the English national character and he does not want to see it diminished; in England, he writes, 'the higher classes do not lie, and the lower, though mostly habitual liars, are ashamed of lying. To run any risk of weakening this feeling . . . would be a permanent evil.'[89] (When addressing an audience of workers during his campaign for Parliament in 1865, Mill would be confronted by a placard bearing this statement that the English lower classes are habitual liars but ashamed of lying. When he was asked if he had written it and replied that he did, the audience broke out in applause. In his *Autobiography*, he explains that 'the working people were so accustomed to expect equivocation and evasion from those who sought their suffrages, that when they found, instead of that, a direct avowal of what was likely to be disagreeable to them . . . they concluded at once that this was a person whom they could trust.'[90]) Nor does he find the fact that the ballot is used in private clubs persuasive since the members of private clubs are entitled to consult their own preferences in deciding whether a prospective new member should be admitted.[91]

As noted earlier, Mill does acknowledge that within his lifetime a state of affairs existed in which the ballot was the lesser of two evils. This was a time when many Britons were personally dependent upon the good graces of members of the aristocracy or of the wealthier portions of the middle class and could not safely defy their wishes. By the mid-1850s, though, when he is beginning to draft 'Thoughts on Parliamentary Reform', Mill feels able to say that this time has passed: 'A good tenant can now feel that he is as valuable to his landlord as his landlord is to him; a prosperous tradesman can afford to feel independent of any particular customer. At every election the votes are more and more the voter's own.'[92]

Once the lower classes lost their dependence on the higher, Mill contends, the adoption of the ballot became unacceptable. Until the suffrage becomes universal, it is only through knowing how those with a vote use it that those without can exert any influence on political decisions. For instance, Mill says, suppose that a law should be proposed that would allow married women to retain the property that they brought into the marriage. In this case, he asks, 'Are not a man's wife and daughters entitled to know whether he votes for or against a candidate who will support these propositions?' But even if the suffrage were universal, Mill continues, the ballot should still be resisted, since it would still be the case that people would be less inclined to cast a selfish ballot if their vote would be exposed to their neighbour's eyes.[93]

It seems safe to say that Mill is wildly over-optimistic about the independence with which those without substantial means of their own could cast a ballot. In the United States today, people can be and have been terminated from their jobs simply for expressing political views (outside of the workplace) that differed from those of their employer.[94] It is difficult to imagine that the workers of the nineteenth century would have been secure against the same treatment, even if they made some effort to 'stand by one another' to resist coercion from their employers or landlords.[95]

But even larger problems loom here. One is that of outright corruption, that is, the buying of votes. Mill actually cites the growth of the practice of bribery as proof that citizens' votes are not determined by the use of coercion by the local grandee: 'The growth of bribery, so loudly complained of, and the spread of the contagion to places formerly free from it, are evidence that the local influences are no longer paramount; that the electors now vote to please themselves, and not other people.'[96] Surely, though, bribery is by definition voting to please another person.

Moreover, Mill's optimism about the ability of voters to make their own decisions about what to do is rather strange coming from the author of *On Liberty*. It seems incredible that individuals who are subject to so much social control over other parts of their lives could be completely autonomous in the polling place. Mill concentrates on the point that voters would not be subject to coercion from the members of classes higher than their own. What, though, about coercion from members of their own class? Suppose that, in a society in which the average level of public spirit is rather low and the average level of class selfishness rather high – characteristics that Mill takes his own society to have – a voter named Victor faces a choice between a candidate who is generally perceived to be a champion of the interests of Victor's class and a candidate who is at least believed to be a superior alternative from the standpoint of the public good. Even if Victor himself is enlightened or public spirited enough to opt for the latter if left to his own devices, will he be left to them? What sort of opprobrium will Victor face from the members of his social circle if he does not vote for the candidate they prefer, and what sort of treatment will he receive from them? Public voting would seem to make it very costly for people to display more public spirit than is common among their neighbours.

Public spirit and individuality

Some scholars claim to have found a larger inconsistency between *On Liberty* and Mill's democratic theory, namely his insistence on the importance of disinterested or public-spirited participation in public affairs. Gertrude Himmelfarb may be the best-known interpreter to suggest that Mill's liberalism should prevent him from making disinterested participation into a political ideal, let alone holding that it is sometimes obligatory. After quoting a passage from a letter to George Cornwall Lewis in which he praises Athenian voters for using their ballots to advance the public good – he writes that 'There will never be honest or self-restraining government unless each individual participant feels himself a trustee for all his fellow citizens and for posterity. Certainly no Athenian voter thought otherwise' – she comments: 'The idea that the individual should act, not freely, privately, in his own interests, but rather with self-restraint, on behalf of the public and of posterity, comes strangely from the author of *On Liberty* – almost as strangely as his appeal to the ancients.'[97]

Unfortunately, Himmelfarb's scholarship is loose here. First, it is not surprising that the author of *On Liberty* should refer approvingly to the ancient Athenians, given that he takes them to share his commitment to the value of toleration.[98] Moreover, Himmelfarb overlooks a passage in the final chapter of *On Liberty* where Mill emphasizes the desirability of requiring citizens to perform various public services on the grounds that this can have the effect of 'habituating them to act from public or semi-public motives, and guide their conduct by aims which unite instead of isolating them from each other'.[99] There is nothing strange about the author of *this* passage claiming voters should aim to promote the public good.[100]

Yet even if Himmelfarb is wrong to deny that the idea of disinterested participation can be located in *On Liberty*, she may still be right to deny that it is consistent with the essay's liberal doctrine. This is the position taken by Stewart Justman, who argues that *On Liberty* itself is internally inconsistent. One manifestation of this internal inconsistency, he states, is that Mill endorses contradictory precepts; Mill the liberal permits actions that Mill the advocate of public spirit proscribes. *On Liberty* is 'the pre-eminent defence of the individual's right to pursue his or her own good'; it tells us that 'we are to be free to do as we like, provided we scrupulously abstain from treading on the interests of others.'[101] But at the same time, Mill 'would have us *dis*interestedly serve the public good' and, as a consequence, his 'civic liberalism' (not Justman's term) both permits and forbids us to put our own interests ahead of the public interest.[102] In short, 'never does Mill explain how the code of obligation to the public can be squared with the freest possible pursuit of one's own good. If the word "obligation" means obligation then these values must conflict.'[103] A case in point: Mill reproaches hypothetical 'shipowners and lawyers' who are returned to Parliament but use their positions to secure 'special interest' legislation, even though, Justman says, they are merely putting into practice the liberal principle that 'people should be free . . . to act on their own interests as they themselves understand them.'[104]

Justman seems to believe that the inconsistency manifests in a second way, too, namely that disinterested participation requires citizens to have motivations that are incompatible with the motivations that Mill maintains that individuals should have in *On Liberty*. In the introduction to his book, he remarks on his surprise when he discovered his students read *On Liberty* as a 'philosophical charter of consumer values'.[105] Apparently, however, they convinced him. Not only does he read *On Liberty* as endorsing 'the pursuit of an exclusively private happiness', he even takes Mill to mount, 'more or less explicitly', a defence of 'unhindered consumption'.[106] For Justman, the foundation of Mill's liberalism is his high estimation of the satisfactions afforded by a consumerist lifestyle. While it may be logically possible for citizens to exhibit this particularly shallow egoism in their 'private lives' but to shed it the moment they take on public roles, this seems to require greater psychological flexibility than a healthy personality is capable of, and hence, Justman apparently concludes, Mill's civic liberalism is a psychological impossibility.

Justman's criticisms of Mill largely miss their target. As we saw in chapter 7, the liberty principle does not entail that a person is entitled to pursue his own good when this will affect the interests of unwilling others. This is the inevitable result of voting or other forms of political participation. This is the nature of political decision making; if representatives pass legislation which benefits a particular industry, as in Justman's example, then someone else, and perhaps the public at large, will be paying for those benefits. The liberty principle, therefore, cannot be used to justify self-interested political participation. Justman's claim that Mill is mounting a defence of unhindered material consumption is even wider of the mark; there is simply no textual basis for this claim. It is at odds with his sanguine attitude towards the stationary state and with his disapproval of the 'very secondary' materialistic objects on which the 'striving, go-ahead character of England and the United States . . . commonly expends its strength'.[107]

There is a grain of truth in Justman's second objection, though. There may be a psychological tension between the civic and liberal aspects of Mill's civic liberalism, inasmuch as public spirit involves sympathy with one's fellow citizens (including those in future generations) and sympathy can be an impediment to the exercise of liberty. Suppose that Susan sympathizes strongly with the rest of her family, and that while she believes that she would enjoy the life of a florist and be successful at it they want very badly for her to join the family's pipe-fitting business; any other career choice on her part will make them miserable. The unhappiness she would cause them by becoming a florist does not constitute a harm, in the relevant sense, but *ex hypothesi* their unhappiness is still a significant source of unhappiness for her. Even if she has the right to pursue the career that she prefers, in the sense that no one can force her to do otherwise, her sympathy with her family will still make it difficult for her to choose to exercise that right. This is a fanciful example, but sympathy with the distress that they would cause their parents no doubt causes people to decide against doing everything from leading an openly gay lifestyle to studying philosophy. If we sympathize fairly strongly with all of our fellow citizens, as Mill's conception of public spirit apparently requires that we should, then would not this sympathy inhibit us in the same way from doing anything unpopular, that is, anything that would distress the people around us? And if it would, then what good is our liberty to us?

There are various points that might be made on Mill's behalf here. One is that a person with an appropriate degree of sympathy with others might be willing to do something they will find offensive, for example, if that person takes him- or herself to have some good reason for it, but be unwilling to do so on a whim. This reluctance to cause others pain casually hardly imperils individuality. Another point, though, is that Mill's understanding of sympathy may be a bit too crude. Human psychology may be capable of more discriminating forms of 'co-feeling', that is, feeling what others are feeling because they are feeling it. If so, then one may be capable of acquiring the habit of co-feeling with one's fellow citizens while in the voting booth (or in other contexts in which one is acting in one's capacity as a citizen) without co-feeling with them (at least in the same way) when deciding about how to conduct oneself in contexts in which no unwilling other stands to be harmed.[108]

Part IV

Concluding Remarks

10

Mill's Utopian Utilitarianism

In a letter of 1863, Mill writes to a correspondent:

> I do not . . . take a gloomy view of human prospects. Few persons look forward to the future career of humanity with more brilliant hopes than I do. I see, however, many perils ahead, which unless successfully avoided could blast these prospects. . . .[1]

Here Mill expresses once again the optimism about the future that is so characteristic of his own moral, social and political thought and, more generally, of the moral, social and political thought of his century. (That anyone could describe him as 'deeply pessimistic', as does R. J. Halliday, is nothing short of astounding.[2]) Yet Mill's considerable optimism is tempered by his awareness of the future's contingency. In contrast with, say, Hegel (at least on one reading of Hegel), Mill does not believe that there is a predetermined 'plotline' that history will necessarily follow.[3] In short, we could still screw this up – just as certain non-Western nations were once the most highly developed parts of the world and then stalled or regressed. Spelling out some of Mill's hopes for the future and the perils that he fears could 'blast' them may help to tie together some of the threads running through this study of his thought.

The most brilliant of Mill's hopes, the sine qua non of the rest, is 'the improvement of mankind', that is, greater development of the various capacities that Mill describes at different points in his writings: our intellectual, aesthetic, active and moral faculties.[4] At this point, nothing remains to be said about Mill's views on the development of the first three faculties. Mill's views on moral improvement, though, do call for some further elaboration. While this has been a bit of an oversimplification, his understanding of moral improvement has been presented here primarily in terms of the overcoming of selfishness – an excessive or exclusive concern with one's own interests or those of one's family or class – and the formation of sympathetic attachments to a larger group of people. As with intellectual development, Mill thinks that he sees slow but steady movement in this area, and this is the most that anyone could hope for since each generation can make the next only a little better than itself. But where does Mill hope that this movement is heading? What is its ultimate destination?

The last chapter dealt at some length with the role that the idea of public spirit – a sympathetic attachment to one's fellow citizens that serves as a motive to promote the public good – plays in Mill's theory of democracy. While the public-spirited individual has transcended personal, familial or class-based selfishness, however, he or she might still lack any significant concern for anyone outside his or her own country's borders – and this is a kind of selfishness, too. Mill's utilitarianism is non-parochial; it says that a given amount of happiness has a particular value when it is experienced by anyone, anywhere. This does not necessarily commit him to the claim that it is desirable for people to sympathize strongly with everyone everywhere; if happiness would be better promoted if our sympathies were more circumscribed, then he should consider narrower sympathies preferable to broader ones. Prima facie, though, it seems that he should view the growth of public spirit as an improvement over the status quo but that he should hope that one day people's sympathies will be truly cosmopolitan. And so he does.

The work in which this is most readily apparent is the essay titled 'The Utility of Religion', part of the *Three Essays on Religion*. Here, Mill's aim is to argue that all of the temporal or this-worldly benefits of belief in a supernatural divinity could be produced to an equal or greater degree by a naturalistic 'Religion of Humanity'. He borrows the idea of the Religion of Humanity from Comte, although he rejects Comte's bizarre pronouncements regarding its forms and rituals.[5] Mill believes that the Religion of Humanity could, like any more traditional supernatural religion, provide adherents with both 'ideal conceptions' able to 'exalt the feelings' and motives for good conduct.[6] Its ideal conception, though, is an ideal conception of humanity itself, and the motive is sympathy with present and future generations of humanity in their entirety:

> Nor let it be thought that only the more eminent of our species, in mind and heart, are capable of identifying their feelings with the entire life of the human race. This noble capability implies indeed a certain cultivation, but not superior to that which might be, and certainly will be if human improvement continues, the lot of all. . . . A morality grounded on large and wise views of the good of the whole, neither sacrificing the individual to the aggregate nor the aggregate to the individual, but giving to duty on the one hand and to freedom and spontaneity on the other their proper province, would derive its power in the superior natures from sympathy and benevolence and the passion for ideal excellence: in the inferior, from the same feelings cultivated up to the measure of their capacity, with the superadded force of shame.[7]

So here is Mill's conception of humanity's ultimate moral destination. He does not refer to guilt or the feeling of duty as a motivation for moral behaviour here, which raises the question of whether what he is describing is really morality at all in the sense described in chapter 6. This may only be slack drafting on his part, given his references to the notion of duty. Although it may be intentional, and if so then this passage would fit well with the letter to Harriet (quoted in chapter 6) in which he says that in a society of people who approached her level of development 'morality . . . would not exist at all, as morality, since morality and inclination would coincide.' Obviously the reference to shame in the last sentence of this passage is, to venture a bad pun, grist for Hamburger's mill. However, it is important to bear in mind the first sentence, too. Everyone will some day sympathize with the entirety of humanity, if 'human improvement continues'. An ethical vanguard, which is to say the elite, may get there first. But only when moral progress has reached the point where 'superior natures' make up not a narrow elite but rather a large segment of the population will shame be an efficacious way of acting on the rest. And by then, even the lower natures, who would not obey this morality without the extra motivation supplied by their sense of shame, will not be motivated by it alone.

Even if Mill has even larger aspirations for humanity's moral improvement than that of public-spirited citizenship, however, that does not diminish the importance that he attaches to instilling public spirit. As difficult as cultivating public spirit is, it is still an easier project than establishing the Religion of Humanity and one that could be accomplished more quickly (even if creating a society of truly public-spirited citizens would still be the work of many generations, whether starting from Mill's status quo or ours). We sympathize with people more easily when we see ourselves as having more in common with them, and the common ties of shared nationality therefore facilitate the growth of public spirit. (For this reason, Mill is not optimistic about the prospects for instilling public spirit in multinational states – nor, indeed, about the prospects for multinational states.[8]) Nor is there any practicable analogue to civic participation available for the training of 'world citizens'. So for now, and for some considerable time in the future, energy that is expended on cultivating public spirit will not be wasted. It will both bring us closer to Mill's grander ultimate goal and yield many benefits in its own right.

Mill holds that, as humanity improves, so too will its institutions and practices, in (to borrow Skorupski's phrase once more) a 'virtuous spiral'. His moral, social and political thought therefore has a utopian aspect. There is a danger in saying this, because to some people the label 'utopian' is necessarily a pejorative. They take calling someone a utopian to be a way of dismissing him or her as having a quixotic vision of social life, one that could never be realized. But 'utopian' does not have to be an insult, and it is not meant as one here. The *OED*'s second definition of 'utopia', following one that refers specifically to Sir Thomas More's island, is 'A place, state, or condition ideally perfect in respect of politics, laws, customs, and conditions.'[9] Admittedly, 'An impossibly ideal scheme, esp. for social improvement' is given as an alternate sense, one that developed somewhat later, but the question is not whether 'utopian' *can* be pejorative, only whether it *must* be.

Strictly speaking, Mill's vision of the future may not quite live up to this definition. He does not believe that politics, laws or customs will ever be literally the best that they could conceivably be, nor does he think that conditions will ever be such that everyone, without exception, can lead a genuinely happy – let alone perfect – life. Still, a society whose members all realize their developmental potential and virtually all manage to lead genuinely happy lives surely approaches near enough to absolute perfection that we should not be distracted by the difference.

One point that must be emphasized is just how far in the future Mill thinks this utopia lies. The improvement of mankind can only happen by very gradual steps. As should be clear from the foregoing chapters, Mill is enough of a realist to realize that to erect the institutions and practices now that he confidently expects will be most desirable many generations hence would court disaster. Humanity is highly perfectible, but it is and will remain very imperfect for a long, long time, and it would be the height of folly not to take that into account when making decisions about what is to be done.

As slow and gradual as he expects human progress to be, though, Mill would still be surprised and displeased by how little progress has been made from his day to ours. Collectively, we know much more than we did in the nineteenth century, due to the tremendous successes of the natural sciences. And, in the West, at least, the average person probably knows more, relative to the best educated people of the time, than in Mill's lifetime. This is because we have made a middling education available to virtually everyone, which is not a trifling accomplishment. However, it is questionable whether we have come any closer to turning a higher percentage of people into first-class thinkers. There is not much reason to believe that the average person's level of aesthetic development has risen nearly as much as Mill would have anticipated, if at all; witness the popularity of 'reality television', for instance. Nor is there much evidence that people today are in general more active or more energetic than they were in the Victorian era, either. Indeed, there is some evidence, such as the 'obesity epidemic', that might argue the contrary.

To our credit, there are certain respects in which we have taken enormous moral strides. Western societies have become more just, inasmuch as certain inequalities that were egregious in the nineteenth century have been, if not eliminated, at least greatly reduced in magnitude. During Mill's lifetime, after all, both the United States and the United Kingdom, along with other European nations, practised slavery. Racism and racial inequalities still exist, but no one can question the progress we have made. Misogyny and gender inequalities persist, too, but Western women today probably enjoy greater equality than many feminists of Mill's era could even imagine. The rights of animals have even become a topic of very serious discussion. We might see these changes as the result of an evolution in the rules that make up Western moral codes. Alternatively, we might view them as the result of a gradual appreciation of the full implications of rules that have long been accepted but that have been misapplied, as a result of arbitrary distinctions that were drawn between different groups of people (or of sentient beings). Despite this progress, though, it is questionable whether we are any closer to transcending selfishness or broadening our sympathies. What evidence is there that people are any more public spirited than in Mill's time, for instance?

There will be no agreement on why there has not been more of the progress in human development that Mill hopes for and expects. Some people will deny that human nature ever significantly changes – and they may question, perhaps with good reason, whether Mill was right to think that he could detect meaningful change in his own period. Those who agree with Mill about the possibility of progress will have answers for why it has not happened that reflect their ideologies, or vice versa. Some will point to capitalism, some to Christianity or organized religion generally, some perhaps to patriarchy and so on.

Whatever the reasons are, though, they do not seem to be among the factors that Mill himself is most worried about as potential impediments to improvement. The peril that apparently looms largest in his mind, or at least the one that he most explicitly identifies as a threat to the steady march of civilization in his published work, is society's failure to protect individual liberty. He identifies this as the reason that the Chinese culture (and not merely its economy) became 'stationary' and has remained so 'for thousands of years', and he warns that: 'The modern *régime* of public opinion is, in an unorganised form, what the Chinese educational and political systems are in an organised; and unless individuality shall be able successfully to assert itself against this yoke, Europe, notwithstanding its noble antecedents and its professed Christianity, will tend to become another China.'[10] On the whole, though, the freedoms of speech and action are today generally quite safe in the West against both legal and extra-legal coercion. Individuals freely carry out a wide range of experiments in living and the marketplace of ideas is teeming. Admittedly, we have in some ways moved in the direction of a 'mass culture' that has diminished some of the variety of situations that Mill contends is necessary, along with liberty, if people are to realize their individuality. Massive media corporations see to it that large numbers of people consume the same television programmes, music and films, for example. Still, it would be a mistake to overstate the extent to which this is true, and the internet has some ability to counteract our movement in this direction.

In the letter quoted in the epigraph for this chapter, Mill identifies the possible failure to adopt plural voting and proportional representation as threats to his 'bright hopes'. These 'perils' have mostly come to pass – especially in the English-speaking world, where proportional representation is used less than on the Continent. It would not be very plausible, though, to suggest that the fact that people have not become better than they are is in any significant way due to the principle of one person, one vote or the fact that voters are generally limited to electing someone from their own district (or, for that matter, to the secret ballot).

One way of explaining why people are not significantly better than they were in Mill's time that is not very substantive, but that is true as far as it goes, is that we do not know how to make them better. Mill's unfinished project, the construction of the great science of ethology, has yet to be carried out. And as a result, there is some uncertainty about what institutions and practices would in fact impart better habits to the next generation. It is important to appreciate that this uncertainty does not necessarily undermine any of Mill's positions. It does not weaken his arguments for the principle of utility and the existence of the higher pleasures. Nor does it weaken his argument for rule utilitarianism (and the further we are from a day in which people generally are sufficiently developed that it would no longer be necessary to rely on the conscience as a means of controlling their behaviour, the more it matters what rules people internalize). The cases he builds for individual liberty, for a qualified form of *laisser-faire* economy and for a qualified form of democratic form of government all turn in part upon ethological considerations, and these are the considerations that he emphasizes most. Even if we decide to attach less weight than Mill does to those considerations, though, on the grounds that we are not positive whether or how the measures for which he calls might affect people's characters, he always introduces further considerations alongside them. These are considerations that speak to the goal of effectiveness rather than that of education, and on many points they may be sufficient by themselves.

And if we cannot share Mill's confidence that his utopian vision of a world populated by highly developed individuals leading genuinely happy lives that are fully worthy of human beings is reachable, let alone that it will eventually be reached, then at least we can share his hope.

Notes

Chapter 1   A Singular Life

1   Michael St John Packe, *The Life of John Stuart Mill*, 9.
2   *Autobiography*, I, 9–15. All references to Mill's works will be to *The Collected Works of John Stuart Mill* and will include the title of the work (except when this is given in the text), the volume number, and the page number. Liberty Fund has purchased the rights to the *Collected Works* from the University of Toronto Press and generously made all 33 volumes available online in its Online Library of Liberty.
3   *Autobiography*, I, 17.
4   Richard D. Altick, *Victorian People and Ideas*, 17–50.
5   *Autobiography*, I, 67, 69.
6   Mill's career in India House is discussed in depth by Lynn Zastoupil in *John Stuart Mill and India*.
7   *Autobiography*, I, 137, 139. For more on this episode, see L. A. Paul, 'The Worm at the Root of the Passions'.
8   *Autobiography*, I, 151.
9   *Autobiography*, I, 143.
10   *Autobiography*, I, 147.
11   *Autobiography*, I, 147.
12   *Autobiography*, I, 145.
13   *Autobiography*, I, 156.
14   'Coleridge', X, 120.
15   X, 94.
16   See Mill's letter to Carlyle, XII, 207, and his letters to Gustave d'Eichtal, XII, 46–7, 71.
17   Bain, *John Stuart Mill*, 164n.
18   *Autobiography*, I, 193–9.

19 *Autobiography*, I, 193–9.
20 Packe, *The Life of John Stuart Mill*, 128–52.
21 *The Complete Works of Harriet Taylor Mill*, 360.
22 See Packe, *The Life of John Stuart Mill*, 348–57; Bain, *John Stuart Mill*, 93.
23 Letter to Harriet Taylor Mill, XIV, 141–2.
24 See Jo Ellen Jacobs, *The Voice of Harriet Taylor Mill*, 206–12, 245–51. For a fuller discussion of different views that have been advanced concerning Harriet's influence and claims to authorship, see Dale E. Miller, 'Harriet Taylor Mill.'
25 See Miller, 'Harriet Taylor Mill.'
26 On Mill's parliamentary career, see Bruce L. Kinzer, Ann P. Robson and John M. Robson, *A Moralist In and Out of Parliament*.
27 See Packe, *The Life of John Stuart Mill*, 466–72, and J. Joseph Miller, 'Chairing the Jamaica Committee: J. S. Mill and the Limits of Colonial Authority.'
28 X, 482, but cf. 450, where he says that 'the adaptations in Nature afford a large balance of probability in favour of creation by intelligence.'
29 'Theism', X, 450.
30 'Mill on Religion', 182.
31 Packe, *Life of John Stuart Mill*, 507. Packe's biography of Mill, cited several times in this chapter, has long been the scholarly standard. Several new biographies have very recently appeared, perhaps due to the bicentennial of Mill's birth. These include Nicholas Capaldi's *John Stuart Mill: A Biography*, Bruce L. Kinzer's *J. S. Mill Revisited*, and Richard Reeves's *John Stuart Mill: Victorian Firebrand*.

Chapter 2   Mill's Understanding of Human Nature

1 'Inaugural Address at St Andrews University', XXI, 217.
2 For a helpful discussion of the limitations of this standard approach, see Peter Markie, 'Rationalism versus Empiricism'.
3 *Treatise of Human Nature*, 1–7.
4 *An Essay Concerning Human Understanding*, 90.
5 *System of Logic*, VIII, 854.
6 See Philip Kitcher, 'Mill, Mathematics, and the Naturalist Tradition.'
7 *An Examination of Sir William Hamilton's Philosophy*, IX, 183. *Examination*, IX, 177–87. For more detailed discussion of this point, see Andy Hamilton, 'Mill, Phenomenalism, and the Self', and John Skorupski, *John Stuart Mill*, 229–35.
8 *Treatise of Human Nature*, 263–74.
9 See Skorupski, *John Stuart Mill*, 8, 192–7, and Quine's 'Epistemology Naturalized'.

10 'Natural Kinds', 126.
11 See *System of Logic*, VII, 307–11 (quoted phrases are from 307).
12 *Examination*, IX, 165n. Mill refers here to William George Ward.
13 This is a great oversimplification of the explanation given by Keith Lehrer, *Thomas Reid*, 35.
14 *Thomas Reid*, 31, 79.
15 Skorupski claims that this is an inconsistency in Mill's thought, because Mill's considered view is that the innateness of a belief is no guarantee of its reliability (*John Stuart Mill*, 29, 228–9). This is based on a passage in which Mill says that a conviction 'might be innate, i.e., prior to individual experience, and yet not be true' *if* it were possible for beliefs to be inherited, literally speaking – for us to be born with beliefs that our parents had formed, perhaps erroneously, from experience' (*System of Logic*, VII, 276.). But while Mill attributes the view that beliefs can be inherited to Herbert Spencer, he assuredly does not believe this himself.
16 Skorupski, 'Introduction', 6.
17 See Howard C. Warren, *A History of the Association Psychology*, 23–8.
18 *System of Logic*, VIII, 849.
19 *System of Logic*, VIII, 852.
20 'Bain's Psychology', XI, 347; a more detailed exposition of this point can be found in the *Examination*, IX, 210–40.
21 *Examination*, IX, 177–87.
22 *System of Logic*, CW, VIII, 856.
23 *Life of John Stuart Mill*, 14–15.
24 *System of Logic*, VIII, 857.
25 *System of Logic*, VIII, 857–8.
26 *System of Logic*, VIII, 859. On Mill's account of the animal element in human feelings, see 'James Mill's Analysis of the Phenomena of the Human Mind', XXXI, 220–1; see also 'Bain's Psychology', XI, 361–2.
27 See Letter to William George Ward, XIV, 26–7.
28 Some material in this section appeared previously in Dale E. Miller, 'Sympathy Versus Spontaneity: A Tension in Mill's Conception of Human Perfection' and is used with the permission of the *International Ethics and Politics Review*.
29 Barry Stroud, *Hume*, 197.
30 'Bain's Psychology', XI, 362.
31 'Sedgwick's Discourse', X, 60.
32 'Sedgwick's Discourse', X, 60f.
33 'Nature', X, 394.
34 *Utilitarianism*, X, 231–2.
35 For a more detailed discussion of this topic, see Dale E. Miller, 'Mill's Theory of Sanctions'.

36   See Laura J. Snyder, 'William Whewell'.
37   *Utilitarianism*, X, 229.
38   *Utilitarianism*, X, 228.
39   'Remarks on Bentham's Philosophy,'*CW*, X, 12.
40   *Utilitarianism*, X, 230.
41   *Examination*, IX, 463; Letter to William George Ward, XV, 649.
42   *Utilitarianism*, X, 230.
43   *Autobiography*, I, 141.
44   *Autobiography*, I, 143–7.
45   *Utilitarianism*, X, 230.
46   Letter to William George Ward, XV, 650. See also James Mill's *Analysis of the Phenomena of the Human Mind*, XXXI, 241–2, and the discussion of the 'sense of moral accountability', the belief that others would be justified in punishing us, in the *Examination of Sir William Hamilton's Philosophy*, IX, 454–65.
47   'Remarks on Bentham's Philosophy', X, 7. Cf. Janice Carlisle, *John Stuart Mill and the Writing of Character*, 1f.
48   'James Mill's Analysis', XXXI, 215. This does not contradict Mill's description of desire as a 'passive sensibility' (*Utilitarianism*, X, 238). When he gives this description, Mill is distinguishing between desire and the will itself and, while desire has a tendency to produce choice and action, not all desires are acted upon.
49   *Utilitarianism*, X, 238.
50   *Utilitarianism*, X, 239; *System of Logic*, VIII, 842–3.
51   *Examination*, IX, 466.
52   *System of Logic*, VIII, 840.
53   *System of Logic*, VIII, 869.
54   *System of Logic*, VIII, 869.
55   *The Liberal Self*, 133.
56   *System of Logic*, VIII, 872–3.
57   Letter to Alexander Bain, XV, 645.
58   Bain, *John Stuart Mill*, 78–9.
59   *Mill on Nationality*, 47.
60   An expanded version of this essay was published as a pamphlet in 1853, under the title 'Occasional Discourse on the Nigger Question'. This version is republished, under this title, in vol. XXIX of the Centenary Edition of *The Works of Thomas Carlyle*.
61   'Occasional Discourse', 379.
62   XXI, 93. Mill continues: 'But I again renounce all advantage from facts: were the whites born ever so superior in intelligence to the blacks . . . it would not be the less monstrous to assert that they had therefore a right either to subdue them by force, or circumvent them by superior skill. . . .'
63   See his 'Liberalism's Limits.'
64   One explored by Jennifer Pitts in *A Turn to Empire*, 133–62.

Chapter 3   The 'Proof' of the Principle of Utility

1   See Crisp, *Routledge Philosophy Guidebook to Mill on Utilitarianism*, 19.
2   *Nicomachean Ethics*, 14 (1099a7–20).
3   The desirability of distinguishing between versions of hedonism in this way was suggested to me by Dale Dorsey.
4   For more on the history of the term 'utility', as well as different perspectives on Mill's use of the term in particular, see John Broome, 'Utility', and Amartya Sen, 'Utility'. Passages in which Mill seems to equate utility with happiness can be found in *Utilitarianism* (X, 213, 240) and 'Bentham' (X, 110).
5   *Anarchy, State, and Utopia*, 42–5.
6   X, 210.
7   See for example David Brink, 'Mill's Deliberative Utilitarianism', and F. W. Garforth, *Educative Democracy*, 1–14.
8   Sumner, *Welfare, Happiness, and Ethics*, 88–91. This view goes by other names as well, including the 'motivational' or 'attitude' theory of pleasure.
9   Vol. 2, 184.
10   X, 213.
11   James Mill's *Analysis of the Phenomena of the Human Mind*, XXXI, 214.
12   Bentham, *Introduction to the Principles of Morals and Legislation*, 2.
13   *Utilitarianism*, X, 210.
14   Brown, 'What is Mill's Principle of Utility?'
15   'Sedgwick's Discourse', X, 52.
16   X, 207–8.
17   X, 208.
18   VII, 158.
19   X, 234.
20   X, 235.
21   Moore, 67.
22   Moore, *Principia Ethica*, 71–2.
23   *System of Logic*, VIII, 842.
24   X, 237.
25   See, for example, Moore, *Principia Ethica*, 212–14.
26   Skorupski, *John Stuart Mill*, 286. Skorupski actually compares this step of the proof with Mill's defence of induction, which he argues is grounded on reflective agreement in our 'spontaneous reasoning propensities'. The defence of induction, though, involves the 'circular' move of turning this method of inference back on itself, using that method to establish its own validity. The analogy with the defence of the memory may therefore be closer.
27   *System of Logic*, VII, 283.
28   *Utilitarianism*, X, 208.
29   See *Utilitarianism*, 237–8.

30 This treatment draws upon the approach of Geoffrey Sayre-McCord in his 'Mill's "Proof" of the Principle of Utility: A More than Half-Hearted Defense'.
31 *Utilitarianism*, X, 257–8n.
32 Letter to Henry Jones, XVI, 1414.
33 Sidgwick, *Methods of Ethics*, 127.
34 On the phenomenon of supertasters, see J. Prutkin, Fisher, E. M., Etter, L. et al., 'Genetic Variation and Inferences about Perceived Taste Intensity in Mice and Men'.
35 Butler, *Five Sermons*, 51.
36 Sidgwick, *Methods of Ethics*, 496–509.

Author's note: The reading of Mill on happiness defended in this section differs substantially from the one the author endorsed in the article 'Internal Sanctions in Mill's Moral Psychology', which was a reading first proposed by Fred Berger (*Happiness, Justice, and Freedom*, 30–63). Unfortunately, it is not possible to consider Berger's reading in detail here.

Chapter 4 The Higher Pleasures

1 *Utilitarianism*, X, 211.
2 Bentham, *Introduction to the Principles of Morals and Legislation*, 30–1.
3 Sidgwick, *Methods of Ethics*, 94.
4 Sigdwick, *Methods of Ethics*, 94.
5 *Utilitarianism*, X, 211.
6 VII, 73.
7 Cf. Crisp, *Mill on Utilitarianism*, 28–31; Jonathan Riley, 'Interpreting Mill's Qualitative Hedonism', 410–18; Brink, 'Mill's Deliberative Utilitarianism', 72.
8 Two interesting questions will have to remain unexplored here. The first is whether Mill recognizes only two qualitative grades of pleasure or many. The second is whether there are also qualitative differences between pains.
9 *Utilitarianism*, X, 211.
10 'Inaugural Address Delivered to the University of St Andrews', XXI, 217–57.
11 'Bentham', X, 96.
12 *Utilitarianism*, X, 245–6.
13 Note added to James Mill's *Analysis of the Phenomena of the Human Mind*, XXXI, 223–6. Note, by the way, that from the fact that the idea of infinity can be a source of aesthetic pleasure, it does not follow that aesthetic pleasure is of infinite value.
14 See *Utilitarianism*, X, 221.
15 *Inaugural Address*, XXI, 255.
16 *Utilitarianism*, X, 212.

17   Cf. Brink, 'Mill's Deliberative Utilitarianism', 81.
18   *Utilitarianism*, X, 213.
19   *Utilitarianism*, X, 213.
20   *Utilitarianism*, X, 213.
21   *Utilitarianism*, X, 212.
22   *Utilitarianism*, X, 213.
23   *Utilitarianism*, X, 215.
24   Elizabeth Anderson gives a similar example in 'John Stuart Mill and Experiments in Living', 9.
25   *John Stuart Mill*, 149.
26   See Josephine Kamm, *John Stuart Mill in Love*, 41; Jacobs, *The Voice of Harriet Taylor Mill*, 134–46.
27   *The Subjection of Women*, XXI, 285.
28   *The Complete Works of Harriet Taylor Mill*, 226.
29   *Utilitarianism*, X, 211, 213.
30   Portions of the preceding paragraphs first appeared in Dale E. Miller's explanatory notes appended to *Utilitarianism* in *The Basic Writings of John Stuart Mill* and are used here with the permission of Random House.
31   *System of Logic*, VIII, 952.
32   Briggs, *Making of Modern England 1783–1867*, 337.
33   'On Genius', I, 338.
34   See Nozick, *Anarchy, State, and Utopia*, 41.
35   *Utilitarianism*, X, 215–6.
36   'Chapters on Socialism', V, 740.
37   Skorupski, *John Stuart Mill*, 23.
38   *Utilitarianism*, X, 216.
39   *Utilitarianism*, X, 212.
40   *Autobiography*, I, p. 5.
41   *Principles of Political Economy*, III, 947–50; see also *On Liberty*, XVIII, 302–3.
42   'On Genius', I, 338.

Chapter 5   Utilitarianism: The 'Happiness Morality'

1   *Utilitarianism*, X, 232.
2   Crisp, *Routledge Philosophy Guidebook to Mill on Utilitarianism*, 67.
3   Shaw, *Contemporary Ethics: Taking Account of Utilitarianism*, 2.
4   Shaw, *Contemporary Ethics*, 10.
5   One alternative utilitarian view is that the action with the best outcome is the one that will maximize the average level of net happiness. Maximizing the average is not the same as maximizing the total if different actions would lead to different numbers of people existing in the future.
6   Bentham, *Fragment on Government*, 3.

7 See Smart, 'An Outline of a System of Utilitarian Ethics', 42–5; and Hare, *Moral Thinking*, 25–64; see also Shaw, *Contemporary Ethics*, 145–63.

8 For an attempt to answer this question, see Dale E. Miller, 'Actual-Consequence Act Utilitarianism and the Best Possible Humans'.

9 See Shaw, *Contemporary Ethics*, 30–1.

10 See Dworkin, *Taking Rights Seriously*, xi.

11 This version of the objection has been much discussed in the recent literature on utilitarianism. See, for example, Peter Singer, 'Famine, Affluence, and Morality'; Shelly Kagan, *The Limits of Morality*; and Tim Mulgan, *The Demands of Consequentialism*. Bernard Williams presents a similar objection, one that says that act utilitarianism undermines the 'integrity' of agents by allowing them insufficient scope to pursue their own life-projects; see 'A Critique of Utilitarianism', 108–18.

12 'An Outline of a System of Utilitarian Ethics', 58.

13 *Forms and Limits of Utilitarianism*, 62–118. See also J. J. C. Smart, 'An Outline of a System of Utilitarian Ethics', 10–12.

14 See Brad Hooker, *Ideal Code, Real World*, 80–5.

15 Smart, 'An Outline of a System of Utilitarian Ethics', 10.

Chapter 6   Mill's Theory of Right and Wrong

1 *System of Logic*, VIII, 949. Mill first draws the distinction between art and science in his 'On the Definition of Political Economy; and on the Method of Investigation Proper to It', IV, 309–39.

2 *System of Logic*, VIII, 951.

3 *System of Logic*, VIII, 952.

4 *System of Logic*, VIII, 949.

5 Earlier in the *Logic*, Mill defines 'prudence' as 'a correct foresight of consequences, a just estimation of their importance to the object in view, and repression of any unreflecting impulse at variance with the deliberate purpose' (VII, 107). This, though, does not tell us what the 'object in view' of the department of Prudence is – happiness, surely, but everyone's happiness or only the agent's?

6 *System of Logic*, VII, 107.

7 *System of Logic*, VIII, 684; *Utilitarianism*, X, 223. Cf. Mill's suggestion that prudence excludes the interests of others on *Utilitarianism*, X, 246; he seems to be using 'prudence' differently from 'expediency' in this paragraph.

8 'Whewell on Moral Philosophy', X, 172.

9 See 'Bentham', X, 112–13 and *Utilitarianism*, X, 221–2.

10 *System of Logic*, VIII, 945–6.

11 'Bentham', X, 111.

12 *Utilitarianism*, X, 258n.

13 *Utilitarianism*, X, 224.

14 XVII, 1881–2.

15 'Mill's Act-Utilitarianism', 67–8.

16 Lyons, 'Mill's Theory of Morality'; Gray, *Mill on Liberty: A Defence*, 19–48; Copp, 'The Iterated-Utilitarianism of J. S. Mill.' It would take us too far afield to delve into the different reasons that each of these commentators gives for declining to call Mill a rule utilitarian, although in brief Lyons has an especially narrow definition of 'rule utilitarianism'. Gray either does not recognize that Mill takes the operation of the conscience to be tied to rules in the manner that will be suggested here or defines 'rule utilitarianism' narrowly (in terms of a specific conception of 'social rules'); it is not entirely clear which is the case. According to Copp, Mill essentially combines a moral theory similar to the one that will be attributed to him here with act utilitarianism. On Copp's reading, Mill considers an action wrong if and only if the action itself is not optimific and punishing it via a 'psychological sanction' would be.

   J. O. Urmson was likely the first to argue for a rule-utilitarian reading of Mill, in 'The Interpretation of the Moral Philosophy of J. S. Mill'.

17 *Utilitarianism*, X, 246. One of the first interpreters to appreciate the significance of this passage was D. P. Dryer, in his essay 'Mill's Utilitarianism', xcv–cv.

18 Lyons, 'Mill's Theory of Morality', 106.

19 'Benevolence and Justice', 57. In the version of this paper republished in *Rights, Welfare, and Mill's Moral Theory* (Oxford: Oxford University Press, 1994), Lyons says that for Mill wrongness is only 'contingently and synthetically connected with external sanctions' (130).

20 'Mill's Theory of Morality', 110–11.

21 Norcross, 'The Scalar Approach to Utilitarianism', 224.

22 Letter to William George Ward, XV, 649.

23 See for example 'Whewell's Moral Philosophy', X, 178–9.

24 'Austin on Jurisprudence', XXI, 177.

25 See Bentham, *Introduction to the Principles of Morals and Legislation*, 170–203.

26 'Remarks on Bentham's Philosophy', X, p. 11. See Lyons, 'Mill's Theory of Morality', 106.

27 This bears some resemblance to what John Skorupski calls the 'Feeling/Disposition Principle'; see especially his 'Reasons and Reason', 358ff. While Skorupski has written extensively on Mill he has not, to my knowledge, suggested that Mill subscribes to this principle.

28 For Mill on the aesthetic emotions, see 'Bain's Psychology', XI, 363–4; 'Inaugural Address at St Andrews University', XXI, 255–6); see also a note Mill appends to an edition of his father's *Analysis of the Phenomena of the Human Mind*, XXXI, 223–6.

29 'Bentham', X, 112–13.
30 *Utilitarianism*, X, 220.
31 Letter to Henry S. Brandreth, XVI, 1234. This is a stronger statement than Mill's superficially similar account of the wrongness of lying in *Utilitarianism*, because in the latter he assumes that the lie benefits only the liar or some other particular person, whereas here the assumption seems to be that its consequences are good from an impartial point of view (see *Utilitarianism*, X, 223).
32 *Auguste Comte and Positivism*, X, 337–8. See also the letter to Henry S. Brandreth, XVI, 1234.
33 Here Mill anticipates Hare; see for example Hare's *Moral Thinking*, 52.
34 For further discussion of these points, see Eggleston and Miller, 'Mill's Misleading Moral Mathematics.'
35 Cf. David Brink, 'Mill's Ambivalence about Duty.'
36 'On the Definition of Political Economy', IV, 319–20.
37 See, for example, Mill's comparison between England and the Continent in this regard in his 'Inaugural Address at St Andrew's University', XXI, 253.
38 *Examination of Sir William Hamilton's Philosophy*, IX, 459–60n.
39 'On Marriage', XXI, 39.
40 See for example 'Civilization', XVIII, 120–4. See also 'On Liberty', XVIII, 224.
41 *Utilitarianism*, X, 214.
42 By Richard Brandt, *Ethical Theory*, 253, 380. Smart had previously used different terminology to draw the same distinction; see his 'Extreme and Restricted Utilitarianism'.
43 See Berkeley, 'Passive Obedience.'
44 On hearing an early formulation of some of the ideas in this chapter, Noah Lemos raised an objection along these lines.
45 See also Copp, 'The Iterated-Utilitarianism of J. S. Mill', 95. Even if Mill were somehow committed specifically to formulating his moral standard in terms of the appropriateness of guilt, he might still be able to meet this objection by saying that an action is wrong if it is appropriate for the agent to feel guilt for having decided to do it.
46 For more on this, see Dale E. Miller, 'Mill, Rule Utilitarianism, and the Incoherence Objection'.
47 Ten, *Mill on Liberty*, 48.
48 *Utilitarianism*, X, 207.
49 *Utilitarianism*, X, 224.
50 *On Liberty*, XVIII, 221.
51 *On Liberty*, XVIII, 221.
52 *Subjection of Women*, XXI, 328.
53 *Auguste Comte and Positivism*, X, 338.
54 *Utilitarianism*, X, 225.

55 'Whewell on Moral Philosophy', X, 183. On 182, Mill gives some examples of rather sweeping primary rules to which exceptions must sometimes be made. See also *Utilitarianism*, X, 223.

56 Cf. Henry West, who takes Mill to hold something like the hybrid view described in the preceding paragraph; see his excellent *An Introduction to Mill's Utilitarian Ethics*, 74–95, especially 87–8. In reply to West, Alan Fuchs adduces the same passages adduced here, and others, in which Mill asserts that exceptions to rules must still be rule-governed; see his 'Mill's Theory of Morally Correct Action', 152–3. See also Robert E. Hoag, 'Mill on Conflicting Moral Obligations'.

57 On this possibility, see Eggleston and Miller, 'India House Utilitarianism: A First Look'.

58 Amartya Sen and Bernard Williams, 'Introduction', 16.

59 *Utilitarianism*, X, 246–7.

60 Cf. Alan Ryan, *The Philosophy of John Stuart Mill*, 224–30; Lyons, 'Benevolence and Justice in Mill', 68–9.

61 *Utilitarianism*, X, 250.

62 Lyons is especially clear on the need to distinguish Mill's formal and substantive accounts of justice; see for example 'Mill's Theory of Justice', 11.

63 *Utilitarianism*, X, 255.

64 *Utilitarianism*, X, 242–3.

65 *Utilitarianism*, X, 252–3.

66 *Utilitarianism*, X, 255.

67 *Utilitarianism*, X, 255.

68 *Utilitarianism*, X, 251.

69 *Utilitarianism*, X, 259.

70 See Lyons, 'Mill's Theory of Justice', 14–15.

71 See Berger, *Happiness, Justice and Freedom*, 225.

72 *Utilitarianism*, X, 256. See also Lyons, 'Benevolence and Justice', 65.

73 *Principles of Political Economy*, II, 233. For a fuller exploration of Mill's views on slavery and the compensation of slave owners, see Dale E. Miller, 'Reparations for Emancipation: Mill's Vindication of the Rights of Slave Owners'.

74 *Utilitarianism*, X, 240–1.

75 *Utilitarianism*, X, 248.

76 *Utilitarianism*, X, 248–9.

77 *Utilitarianism*, X, 249.

78 'Sedgwick's Discourse', X, 73–4; see also 'Whewell on Moral Philosophy', X, 179.

79 See for example *On Liberty*, XVIII, 220–1 and *The Subjection of Women*, XXI, 262–3. The quoted phrase comes from 'Whewell on Moral Philosophy', X, 179.

80 'Bentham', X, 111.

81　See *Utilitarianism*, X, 207. Although W. D. Ross writes later than Mill, his 'ethic of prima facie duties' exemplifies the intuitionism to which Mill objects. See his *The Right and the Good*, 16–47.

82　*Utilitarianism*, X, 207, 249.

83　*Groundwork*, 31–3.

Chapter 7　Mill on Liberty and Individuality

1　Some material in this section is adapted from a set of explanatory notes written for *The Basic Writings of John Stuart Mill*, 302–13, and is reused with the permission of Random House.

2　Mill would have worked with Joseph Coulthard's 1854 translation of Humboldt. J. W. Burrow prepared a new translation, under the title *The Limits of State Action*, for Cambridge University Press in 1969.

3　Humboldt, *Limits of State Action*, 33.

4　*On Liberty*, XVIII, 220.

5　*On Liberty*, XVIII, 223–4.

6　*On Liberty*, XVIII, 292.

7　*On Liberty*, XVIII, 265.

8　*On Liberty*, XVIII, 271.

9　*On Liberty*, XVIII, 271.

10　*On Liberty*, XVIII. 271.

11　Mill, 'Tocqueville on Democracy in America [I]', XVIII, 80–83; 'Tocqueville on Democracy in America [II]', XVIII, 175–178. See also Tocqueville, *Democracy in America*, esp. vol. I, 264–97.

12　*On Liberty*, XVIII, 243. Cf. 'Utility of Religion', X, 407–8, where Mill's often-neglected remarks on the role that authority plays in determining most people's beliefs are in direct contradiction to the dead dogma argument.

13　'Bentham', X, 94.

14　*Autobiography*, I, 156 (from an early draft), 251, 253.

15　*On Liberty*, XVIII, 242.

16　*On Liberty*, XVIII, 292.

17　*On Liberty*, XVIII, 276.

18　Rees, *John Stuart Mill's* On Liberty, 137–55.

19　X, 218, 220.

20　XIX, 494. Mill is quoting himself here; this passage originally appeared in the slightly earlier essay 'Thoughts on Parliamentary Reform', XIX, 336.

21　Rees, *John Stuart Mill's* On Liberty, 143.

22　Wollheim, 'John Stuart Mill and the Limits of State Action', 6.

23　*On Liberty*, XVIII, 284–5.

24　*Principles of Political Economy*, III, 952.

25　Rawls, *Theory of Justice*, 54.

26 Barry, *Political Argument*, 174–86. Barry offers some further refinements of this definition, but they are not important in this context.
27 Locke, *A Letter Concerning Toleration*, 17; Talcott Parsons, *The Structure of Social Action*, 263.
28 Cf. John Gray, *Mill on Liberty: A Defence*, 53–7 (but see also Donner, *The Liberal Self*, 165–83).
29 *On Liberty*, XVIII, 292–3.
30 *On Liberty*, XVIII, 287.
31 *On Liberty*, XVIII, 224 (emphasis added).
32 *On Liberty*, XVIII, 224–5.
33 *On Liberty*, XVIII, 276.
34 'The Army Bill', XXIX, 413.
35 Despite the gender neutrality of 'whole people', Mill never explicitly recommends requiring military service from women, and indeed a few lines later in this speech he comments on the desirability of providing 'a few weeks training in the field in the first year of manhood'.
36 Lyons, 'Liberty and Harm to Others', 8.
37 Brown, 'Mill on Liberty and Morality', 135.
38 Lyons, 'Liberty and Harm to Others', 4–8.
39 There is another point of disagreement between Brown and Lyons as well, although it raises issues too complicated to deal with here. This is whether Mill's claim that people can be compelled to do 'any other joint work necessary to the interest of the society of which he enjoys the protection' would be inconsistent with the liberty principle even if Mill had presented it as a harm-prevention principle. See Brown, 'Mill on Liberty and Morality', 146, and Lyons, 'Liberty and Harm to Others', 8.
40 *On Liberty*, XVIII, 276.
41 *Utilitarianism*, X, 256 (V, 34).
42 Cf. Lyons, 'Benevolence and Justice', 65.
43 *On Liberty*, XVIII, 225.
44 Some of the material in this section originally appeared in Dale E. Miller, 'John Stuart Mill's Civic Liberalism' and is used with permission of *History of Political Thought*.
45 See *On Liberty*, XVIII, 225.
46 Ten, *Mill on Liberty*, 40–1.
47 Arneson, 'Democracy and Liberty in Mill's Theory of Government', 55–6.
48 *On Liberty*, XVIII, 305. See also *Considerations on Representative Government*, XIX, 410–12; 'De Tocqueville on Democracy in America [II]', XVIII, 169.
49 'The Army Bill', XXIX, 413.
50 'The Army Bill', XXIX, 414; 'Political Progress', XXVIII, 129; Letters to Edwin Chadwick and T. E. Cliffe Leslie, XVII, 1792 and 1805–6.
51 This represents a change of view from 'John Stuart Mill's Civic Liberalism', 111–12.

52 Letter to Carlyle, XII, 207.
53 *On Liberty*, XVIII, 270.
54 *On Liberty*, XVIII, 262–3. See David Brink, 'Mill's Deliberative Utilitarianism', 87–8.
55 *On Liberty*, XVIII, 261.
56 Gray, *Mill on Liberty: A Defence*, 45.
57 *On Liberty*, XVIII, 264.
58 'Nature', X, 393–6.
59 *On Liberty*, XVIII, 279.
60 *On Liberty*, XVIII, 266.
61 *On Liberty*, XVIII, 263.
62 X, 95; 'Inaugural Address Delivered to the University of St Andrews', XXI, 255.
63 *On Liberty*, XVIII, 263. See also *Representative Government*, XIX, 406–9.
64 *On Liberty*, XVIII, 264.
65 *On Liberty*, XVIII, 307–9.
66 *Representative Government*, XIX, 409.
67 See 'Centralisation', XIX, 605.
68 *On Liberty*, XVIII, 266.
69 *On Liberty*, XVIII, 261.
70 *On Liberty*, XVIII, 270.
71 *On Liberty*, XVIII, 262.
72 *On Liberty*, XVIII, 224.
73 Contrast this with the commentators who claim that Mill regards freedom, autonomy, and/or individuality themselves as parts of happiness, such as Garforth, *Educative Democracy*, 7–10.
74 Brown, 'Mill on Harm to Others' Interests', 397; Brown, 'Mill on Liberty and Morality', 137–8.
75 *On Liberty*, XVIII, p. 224.
76 'Civilization', XVIII, 122.
77 *On Liberty*, XVIII, 224. See also *Considerations on Representative Government*, XIX, 394.
78 'Civilization', XVIII, 122. See also *Considerations on Representative Government*, XIX, 395.
79 James Fitzjames Stephen, *Liberty, Equality, Fraternity*, 4–5.
80 Leslie Stephen, *Life of Sir James Fitzjames Stephen*, p. 308. In virtue of being Leslie Stephen's brother, J. F. Stephen is the uncle of Virginia Woolf.
81 *Liberty, Equality, Fraternity*, 89.
82 *Liberty, Equality, Fraternity*, 86.
83 *Liberty, Equality, Fraternity*, 23.
84 *Liberty, Equality, Fraternity*, 92–3.
85 *Liberty, Equality, Fraternity*, 82.
86 *Liberty, Equality, Fraternity*, 47.
87 *Liberty, Equality, Fraternity*, 82–3, 123.

88 Bain, *John Stuart Mill*, 111.
89 *On Liberty*, XVIII, 270.
90 *On Liberty*, XVIII, 282.
91 Roy Walmsley, 'World Prison Population List', 1.
92 Heather C. West and William J. Sabol, *Prisoners in 2007: Bureau of Justice Statistics Bulletin*, 21–2.
93 See for example Cassia Spohn and David Holleran, 'The Effect of Imprisonment on Recidivism Rates of Felony Offenders: A Focus on Drug Offenders'.
94 *Principles of Political Economy*, III, 936.
95 *On Liberty*, XVIII, 282.
96 See Rawls, *Political Liberalism*, 190–5; Dworkin, 'Liberalism.'
97 Skorupski, 'The Ethical Content of Liberal Law', 197–200.
98 Benn, *A Theory of Freedom*, 88.
99 Hart, *Law, Liberty, and Morality*, 32–3.
100 Graeme Paton, 'Wear Goggles When Using Blu-Tack: The Safety Rules Ruining Education'.
101 Sam Peltzman, 'The Effects of Automobile Safety Regulation'; Christopher Garbacz, 'Do Front-Seat Belts Put Rear-Seat Passengers at Risk?'; Garbacz, 'More Evidence on the Effectiveness of Seat Belt Laws'; Brendan Maguire, William R. Faulkner, and Richard A. Mathers, 'Seatbelt Laws and Traffic Fatalities: A Research Update'; cf. David L. Ryan and Guy A. Bridgeman, 'Judging the Roles of Legislation, Education, and Offsetting Behaviour in Seat Belt Use: A Survey and New Evidence from Alberta'.
102 See Jacob Sullum, 'Freedom Riders'.
103 Nock, 'On Doing the Right Thing', 172–3.
104 W. Kip Viscusi, 'The Lulling Effect: The Impact of Child-Resistant Packing on Aspirin and Analgesic Ingestions'.
105 *Principles of Political Economy*, III, 943.
106 Feinberg, *Harm to Self*, 12.
107 *On Liberty*, XVII, p. 294.
108 Humboldt, *Limits of State Action*, 88.

Chapter 8   Millian Normative Political Economy

1 Portions of this chapter first appeared in Dale E. Miller, 'Mill's "Socialism"' and are used with permission of *Politics, Philosophy and Economics*.
2 Blaug, *Economic Theory in Retrospect*, 179.
3 'On the Definition of Political Economy; and the Method of Investigation Proper to It', IV, 323.
4 For more on this aspect of Mill's thought, see Blaug, *Economic Theory in Retrospect*, 179–224.

5 *Principles*, II, 215.

6 Riley, 'Justice under Capitalism', 135.

7 For differing answers to the question of whether Mill was aware of Marx, see J. Salwyn Schapiro, 'John Stuart Mill, Pioneer of Democratic Liberalism in England'; Lewis S. Feuer, 'Discussion: John Stuart Mill and Marxian Socialism'; and Michael Evans, 'John Stuart Mill and Karl Marx: Some Problems and Perspectives', 273–98.

8 'Chapters on Socialism', V, 727.

9 *Principles*, II, 207.

10 *Principles*, II, 367.

11 *Principles*, III, 767.

12 *Principles*, III, 763; see also 'Chapters', V, 727–8.

13 See Mill's 'Inaugural Address Delivered to the University of St Andrews', XXI, 217–57. For a brief but informative overview of formal education in the Victorian period, see Richard D. Altick, *Victorian People and Ideas*, 246–55.

14 *Principles*, V, 869.

15 *Principles*, III, 767.

16 'Chapters', V, 715.

17 *Principles*, III, 794–5, although cf. 'Newman's Political Economy', V, 446–7.

18 *Principles*, III, 795; cf. 'Newman's Political Economy', V, 444.

19 'Thornton on Labour and its Claims', V, 656; 'Cooperation: Intended Speech', XXVI, 310–12; *Principles*, II, 215–6, 'Chapters on Socialism', V, 734–6.

20 'Primogeniture', XXVI, 336.

21 *Principles*, II, 207–8.

22 *Principles*, II, 218, 225; see also III, 887–9.

23 Alexander Bain, *John Stuart Mill*, 89.

24 *Principles*, II, 221.

25 *Principles*, II, 227, 230.

26 Abraham Hayward, 'John Stuart Mill.'

27 *Principles*, III, 819–21; see also *Principles*, II, 228–32.

28 *Principles*, III, 937–45. *Laisser-faire* is French for 'let do' or 'leave alone'. The more familiar *laissez-faire* is the imperative.

29 *Principles*, III, 947f.

30 *Principles*, III, 948.

31 *On Liberty*, XVIII, 302; see also *Principles*, III, 950.

32 *Principles*, II, 208.

33 *Principles*, II, 374–8, 765; see also 'Thornton on the Claims of Labour', IV, 376–80.

34 *Principles*, III, 765–6.

35 *Subjection*, XXI, 321.

36 *Subjection*, XXI, 326.

37 *Subjection*, XXI, 273–4, 280–1.

38 *Subjection*, CW, 297–8.
39 *Principles*, III, 897–906; 'Thornton on the Claims on Labour', IV, 385f; 'The Savings of the Working and Middle Class', V, 407–26; 'Letter to Karl D. Heinrich Rau', XIV, 94f.
40 *Principles*, III, 763–4.
41 'Chapters', V, 743.
42 *Principles*, III, 769–775.
43 I, I, 239.
44 *Principles*, II, 202f; 'Chapters', V, 738.
45 *Principles*, II, 203.
46 'Chapters', V, 737.
47 'Chapters', V, 749.
48 'Chapters', V, 739; see also *Principles*, II, 203, 210.
49 'Chapters', V, 738.
50 'Chapters', V, 750; *Principles*, II, 214; see also 'Vindication of the French Revolution of February 1848', XX, 354.
51 'Chapters', V, 748.
52 'Chapters', V, 737; *Principles*, II, 213f.
53 *Principles*, III, 775.
54 *Principles*, III, 777–90.
55 'Chapters', V, 793.
56 'Vindication', XX, 352.
57 *Principles*, III, 793f; see also 'Vindication', XX, 352f.
58 *Principles*, III, 791–3.
59 *Principles*, III, 793.
60 *Principles*, III, 792.
61 *Representative Government*, XIX, 405; see also *Principles*, II, 205.
62 *Autobiography*, I, 239–41; see also 'Vindication', XX, 354.
63 See his letters to her in XIV, 8–9, 11, and 19.
64 'Constraints of Communism', XXV, 1179–80; see also *Principles*, II, 209 and 'Chapters', V, 745–6.
65 'Chapters on Socialism', V, 745.
66 Arneson, 'Mill's Doubts about Freedom under Socialism', 234–5.
67 On the competition between socialistic enterprises, see Pedro Schwartz, *The New Political Economy of John Stuart Mill*, 225.
68 See Mill's letters to Leslie and Fawcett, XV, 857 and 859; see also Samuel Hollander, *Economics of John Stuart Mill*, 818.
69 *Principles*, III, 769.
70 Kurer, 'J. S. Mill and Utopian Socialism', 230.
71 For a discussion of some of these difficulties and of the experiences of worker-owned firms, see Carla Dickstein, 'The Promise and Problems of Worker Cooperatives'.
72 I owe this last point to Andrew Mason, in a discussion on socialism held at the University of Reading.
73 *Principles*, III, 962.
74 *Principles*, V, 961.

75 *Principles*, III, 962.
76 *Principles*, II, 360.
77 On the Poor Law Reform of 1834, see Samuel Mencher, *Poor Law to Poverty Program: Economic Security Policy in Britain and the United States*, especially 93–129.
78 See *Principles*, III, 733–46.
79 *Principles*, III, 754.
80 *Principles*, III, 756.

Chapter 9 Millian Democracy

1 Some of the material in this chapter initially appeared in Dale E. Miller, 'John Stuart Mill's Civic Liberalism' and is used with the permission of *History of Political Thought*.
2 *Representative Government*, XIX, 390–1.
3 Thompson, *John Stuart Mill and Representative Government*, 9; Pateman, *Participation and Democratic Theory*, 20.
4 *Principles*, III, 803.
5 *Representative Government*, XIX, 405.
6 On the republican conception of civic virtue see, for example, Shelley Burtt, 'The Good Citizen's Psyche'.
7 *Representative Government*, XIX, 405.
8 *Representative Government*, XIX, 390, 407.
9 'Tocqueville on Democracy in America [II]', XVIII, 169.
10 *Representative Government*, XIX, 411.
11 *Representative Government*, XIX, 412. The Athenian dicasteries were large public juries, like the one that convicted Socrates. The ecclesia was a popular assembly that voted on military and legislative issues.
12 *Representative Government*, XIX, 412.
13 *Representative Government*, XIX, 469. At this point in the text Mill is actually saying this is true of manual laborers in particular, for he is advocating the expansion of the franchise.
14 *Representative Government*, XIX, 468–9, 400–1.
15 *Representative Government*, XIX, 457–68 (the quoted passages appear on 468).
16 *Representative Government*, X, 535–6.
17 *Representative Government*, XIX, 412.
18 XXII, 244–5.
19 See Barthélemy Prosper Enfantin, *The Doctrine of Saint-Simon*, 4–6.
20 *Autobiography*, I, 181.
21 X, 325–6. See also 'Civilization', XVIII, 137–8.
22 *Representative Government*, XIX, 445.
23 *Representative Government*, XIX, 405; see also 'Chapters on Socialism', V, 739–40.

24 Willmoore and Carey, ' "The Roster Device": J. S. Mill and Contemporary Elitism', 34.
25 *Representative Government*, XIX, 450.
26 See 'Bentham', X, 109–10.
27 James Mill, 'Government', 41–2.
28 Ball, 'Introduction', xxi.
29 'Spirit of the Age', XXII, 241–2.
30 *Utilitarianism*, X, 216 (emphasis added).
31 Packe, *Life of John Stuart Mill*, 408.
32 *Representative Government*, 473.
33 Hamburger, *John Stuart Mill on Liberty and Control*.
34 *On Liberty*, XVIII, 282.
35 *On Liberty*, XVIII, 278.
36 See Maurice Cowling, *Mill and Liberalism*. Ten offers a rebuttal to Cowling in *Mill on Liberty*, 145–51.
37 *Auguste Comte and Positivism*, X, 314. See Thompson, *John Stuart Mill and Representative Government*, 85. For additional criticism of Hamburger, see Shigekazu Yamashita's review of *John Stuart Mill on Liberty and Control* and Ten's 'Was Mill a Liberal?'
38 See James B. Conacher, 'Introduction', *The Emergence of British Parliamentary Democracy in the Nineteenth Century*, 9–10; Altick, *Victorian People and Ideas*, 87–9.
39 *Considerations on Representative Government*, XIX, 442.
40 Thompson, *John Stuart Mill and Representative Government*, 9–10.
41 XIX, 324–5.
42 'Thoughts on Parliamentary Reform', XIX, 325.
43 'Thoughts on Parliamentary Reform', XIX, 330.
44 The plan was described in Hare's *Treatise on the Election of Representatives*.
45 The usual term is actually 'single transferable ballot' but in conjunction with plural voting it would be a multiple transferable ballot system.
46 See *Representative Government*, XIX, 454 and Letter to Thomas Hare, XV, 613.
47 On contemporary uses of the single transferable ballot, see FairVote, 'Choice Voting – The Optimal Proportional Representation Election Method.'
48 XIX, 456–7. See also 'Recent Writers on Reform', XIX, 362.
49 *Representative Government*, XIX, 459–60.
50 *Representative Government*, XIX, 477. See also his Letter to Max Kyllman, XVI, 998.
51 *Representative Government*, XIX, 477.
52 *Representative Government*, XIX, 478.
53 Letter to Earl Grey, XV, 941.
54 *Representative Government*, XIX, 447.
55 *Representative Government*, XIX, 176.

56 Arneson, 'Democracy and Liberty in Mill's Theory of Government', 46.
57 Duncan, *Marx and Mill*, 259, 263–4.
58 *Representative Government*, XIX, 430–2.
59 *Representative Government*, XIX, 430–2.
60 'Coleridge', X, 122–4.
61 Dennis Thompson makes the first of these claims: see *John Stuart Mill and Representative Government*, 100. Maria Morales and Bruce Baum both make the second; see Morales, *Perfect Equality*, 86, and Baum, *Rereading Power and Freedom in J. S. Mill*, 243–4.
62 Letter of William Rathbone, Jr., XV, 905.
63 *Representative Government*, XIX, 508.
64 *Representative Government*, XIX, 478.
65 'Representation of the People [5]', 85. Baum cites this speech in support of his reading. (See also *Autobiography*, I, 288–9.)
66 'Representation of the People [5]'.
67 This is of course an allusion to the anti-intellectual strand in American conservatism. For a recent pithy and trenchant discussion of conservative anti-intellectualism, see conservative writer David Brooks's column 'The Class War before Palin'.
68 *Representative Government*, XIX, 479.
69 'The Admission of Women to the Electoral Franchise', XXVIII, 152.
70 *Representative Government*, XIX, 481.
71 *Subjection of Women*, XXI, 302.
72 Letter to James Lorimer, XV, 748.
73 *Subjection of Women*, XXI, 329.
74 *Principles*, III, 955.
75 *Autobiography*, I, 285.
76 *Representative Government*, XIX, 470.
77 See for example Bernard Grofman, Lisa Handley, and Richard G. Niemi, *Minority Representation and the Quest for Voting Equality*, 8–9.
78 *Representative Government*, XIX, 471.
79 *Representative Government*, XIX, 472.
80 *Representative Government*, XIX, 469–70 (emphasis added).
81 'The Ballot', 243.
82 'The Ballot', 261.
83 'The Ballot', 263.
84 'The Ballot', 248–9.
85 *Representative Government*, XIX, 490.
86 'Thoughts on Parliamentary Reform', XIX, 336. The same passage appears in *Representative Government*, XIX, 494.
87 *Representative Government*, XIX, 488–9.
88 'Thoughts on Parliamentary Reform', XIX, 337.
89 'Thoughts on Parliamentary Reform', XIX, 338.
90 *Autobiography*, I, 274.
91 *Considerations on Representative Government*, XIX, 489–90.

92   'Thoughts on Parliamentary Reform', XIX, 333. The same passage appears in *Representative Government*, XIX, 491–2. On the composition of the pamphlet, see J. M. Robson, 'Textual Introduction', XIX, lxxxv.
93   'Thoughts on Parliamentary Reform', XIX, 333–7. The same passages appear in *Representative Government*, XIX, 492–5.
94   See, for example, Timothy Noah, 'Can Your Boss Fire You for Your Political Beliefs?' and 'Bumper Sticker Insubordination'. See also Dale E. Miller, 'Terminating Employees for Their Political Speech'.
95   'The Westminster Election of 1868 [3]', XIX, 340.
96   'Thoughts on Parliamentary Reform', XIX, 333. The same passage appears in *Representative Government*, XIX, 492.
97   *On Liberty and Liberalism*, 269. For Mill's letter see XV, 608.
98   See 'Grote's History of Greece [II]', XI, 3177–121.
99   XVIII, 305.
100   For more comprehensive criticisms of the two Mill theses, see Ten, *Mill on Liberty*, 151–66, and Rees, *John Stuart Mill's* On Liberty, 109–15.
101   Justman, *Hidden Text of Mill's* Liberty, 149.
102   Justman, *Hidden Text of Mill's* Liberty, 20.
103   Justman, *Hidden Text of Mill's* Liberty, 24.
104   Justman, *Hidden Text of Mill's* Liberty, 42.
105   Justman, *Hidden Text of Mill's* Liberty, 1.
106   Justman, 'The Abstract Citizen', 324.
107   *Representative Government*, XIX, 409.
108   For a fuller exploration of this point, see Dale E. Miller, 'Sympathy Versus Spontaneity'.

Chapter 10   Mill's Utopian Utilitarianism

1   Letter to Charles A. Cummings, XV, 843.
2   Halliday, *John Stuart Mill*, 1976.
3   On different readings of Hegel, see Paul Redding, 'Georg Wilhelm Friedrich Hegel'.
4   *Autobiography*, I, 145.
5   *Auguste Comte and Positivism*, X, 341–68.
6   'Utility of Religion', X, 419–20.
7   'Utility of Religion', X, 420–1. On the relation between the Mill's attraction to Manichaeism and the Religion of Humanity, see Colin Heydt, 'Narrative, Imagination, and the Religion of Humanity in Mill's Ethics'.
8   *Representative Government*, XIX, 547–9.
9   *Oxford English Dictionary*, 371.
10   *On Liberty*, XVIII, 273–4.

References

Altick, Richard D. (1973) *Victorian People and Ideas*. New York: Norton.

Anderson, Elizabeth (1991) 'John Stuart Mill and Experiments in Living'. *Ethics* 102 (Oct.): 4–26.

Aristotle (2000) *Nicomachean Ethics*. Trans. and ed. Roger Crisp. Cambridge: Cambridge University Press.

Arneson, Richard J. (1979) 'Mill's Doubts about Freedom under Socialism'. *New Essays on John Stuart Mill and Utilitarianism, Canadian Journal of Philosophy*, Supp. Vol. V: 231–49.

Arneson, Richard (1982) 'Democracy and Liberty in Mill's Theory of Government'. *Journal of the History of Philosophy* XX: 43–64.

Bain, Alexander (1967) *James Mill: A Biography*. Fairfield, NJ: Augustus M. Kelley.

Bain, Alexander (1969) *John Stuart Mill: A Criticism with Personal Recollections*. Bristol: Thoemmes.

Ball, Terence (1992) 'Introduction', in Terence Ball (Ed.), *James Mill: Political Writings*. Cambridge: Cambridge University Press, pp. x–xxviii.

Barry, Brian (1965) *Political Argument*. Berkeley: University of California Press.

Baum, Bruce (2000) *Rereading Power and Freedom in J. S. Mill*. Toronto: Toronto University Press.

Benn, Stanley (1988) *A Theory of Freedom*. Cambridge: Cambridge University Press.

Bentham, Jeremy (1948) *Introduction to the Principles of Morals and Legislation*. New York: Hafner.

Bentham, Jeremy (1988) *A Fragment on Government*. Ed. J. H. Burns and H. L. A. Hart. Cambridge: Cambridge University Press.

Berger, Fred (1984) *Happiness, Justice, and Freedom: The Moral and Political Philosophy of John Stuart Mill*. Berkeley: California University Press.

Berkeley, George (1953) 'Passive Obedience'. *The Works of George Berkeley, Bishop of Cloyne*. Vol. VI. Ed. A. A. Lue and E. E. Jessop. London: Thomas Nelson and Sons, pp. 17–46.

Blaug, Mark (1985) *Economic Theory in Retrospect* (4th edn). Cambridge: Cambridge University Press.

Brandt, Richard (1959) *Ethical Theory: The Problems of Normative and Critical Ethics*. Englewood Cliffs, NJ: Prentice-Hall.

Briggs, Asa. (1959) *Making of Modern England 1783–1867: The Age of Improvement*. New York: Harper.

Brink, David (1992) 'Mill's Deliberative Utilitarianism'. *Philosophy and Public Affairs* 21 (Winter): 67–103.

Brink, David O. (2007) 'Mill's Ambivalence about Duty'. San Diego Legal Studies Paper No. 07-97 (March 20). Accessed at SSRN: http://ssrn.com/abstract=978516; last visited February 2010.

Brooks, David (2008) 'The Class War before Palin'. *The New York Times* (10 October): A33. Accessed at www.nytimes.com/2008/10/10/opinion/10brooks.html?partner=permalink&exprod=permalink; last visited 1 November 2009.

Broome, John (1991) 'Utility'. *Economics and Philosophy* 7: 1–12.

Brown, D. G. (1972) 'Mill on Liberty and Morality'. *The Philosophical Review* 81 (Apr.): 133–58.

Brown, D. G. (1973) 'What is Mill's Principle of Utility?', *Canadian Journal of Philosophy* III (September): 1–12.

Brown, D. G. (1974) 'Mill's Act-Utilitarianism'. *Philosophical Quarterly* 24: 67–8.

Brown, D. G. (1978) 'Mill on Harm to Others' Interests'. *Political Studies* XXVI: 395–99.

Burtt, Shelley (1990) 'The Good Citizen's Psyche: On the Psychology of Civic Virtue'. *Polity* XXIII (Autumn): 23–38.

Butler, Joseph (1950) *Five Sermons Preached at the Rolls Chapel and a Dissertation upon the Nature of Virtue*. New York: Liberal Arts Press.

Capaldi, Nicholas (2004) *John Stuart Mill: A Biography*. Cambridge: Cambridge University Press.

Carlisle, Janice (1991) *John Stuart Mill and the Writing of Character*. Athens: University of Georgia Press.

Carlyle, Thomas (1899) 'Occasional Discourse on the Nigger Question'. Vol. XXIX of *The Works of Thomas Carlyle* (centenary edn). London: Chapman and Hall, pp. 348–83.

Cohen, Rachel (2004) 'Can You Forgive Him?' *The New Yorker* (8 November): 48–65.

Conacher, James B. (Ed.) (1971) *The Emergence of British Parliamentary Democracy in the Nineteenth Century: The Passing of the Reform Acts of 1832, 1867, and 1884–5*. New York: Wiley.

Copp, David (1979) 'The Iterated-Utilitarianism of J. S. Mill'. *New Essays on John Stuart Mill and Utilitarianism*, *Canadian Journal of Philosophy*, Supp. Vol. V: 75–98.

Cowling, Maurice (1963) *Mill and Liberalism*. Cambridge: Cambridge University Press.

Crisp, Roger (1997) *Routledge Philosophy Guidebook to Mill on Utilitarianism*. London: Routledge.

Dickstein, Carla (1991) 'The Promise and Problems of Worker Cooperatives'. *Journal of Planning Literature* 6: 16–33.

Donner, Wendy (1991) *The Liberal Self: John Stuart Mill's Moral and Political Philosophy*. Ithaca: Cornell University Press.

Dryer, D. P. (1969) 'Mill's Utilitarianism'. *Essays on Ethics, Religion and Society: Collected Works of John Stuart Mill*, Vol. X. Ed. J. M. Robson. Toronto: University of Toronto Press, pp. lxiii–cxiii.

Duncan, Graeme (1973) *Marx and Mill: Two Views of Social Conflict and Social Harmony*. Cambridge: Cambridge University Press.

Dworkin, Ronald (1977) *Taking Rights Seriously*. Cambridge, MA: Harvard University Press.

Dworkin, Ronald (1978) 'Liberalism'. *Public and Private Morality*. Ed. Stuart Hampshire. Cambridge: Cambridge University Press, pp. 113–43.

Eggleston, Ben and Miller, Dale E. (2007) 'India House Utilitarianism: A First Look'. *Southwest Philosophy Review* 23 (January): 39–47.

Eggleston, Ben and Miller, Dale E. (2008) 'Mill's Misleading Moral Mathematics'. *Southwest Philosophy Review* 24: 153–61.

Enfantin, Barthélemy Prosper (1972) *The Doctrine of Saint-Simon: An Exposition*. Trans. Georg. G. Iggers. New York: Schocken.

Evans, Michael (1989) 'John Stuart Mill and Karl Marx: Some Problems and Perspectives', *History of Political Economy* 21: 273–98.

FairVote. 'Choice Voting – The Optimal Proportional Representation Election Method'. www.fairvote.org/?page=225; last visited 23 September 2009.

Feinberg, Joel (1986) *Harm to Self*. Oxford: Oxford University Press.

Feuer, Lewis S. (1949) 'Discussion: John Stuart Mill and Marxian Socialism'. *Journal of the History of Ideas* X: 297–303.

Fuchs, Alan (2006) 'Mill's Theory of Morally Correct Action'. *The Blackwell Guide to Mill's Utilitarianism*. Ed. Henry R. West. Malden, MA: Blackwell, pp. 139–58.

Garbacz, Christopher (1992) 'Do Front-Seat belts Put Rear-Seat Passengers at Risk?' *Population Research and Policy Review* 11: 157–68.

Garbacz, Christopher (1992) 'More Evidence on the Effectiveness of Seat Belt Laws'. *Applied Economics* 24: 313–15.

Garforth, F. W. (1980) *Educative Democracy*. Oxford: Oxford University Press.

Goldberg, David Theo (2005) 'Liberalism's Limits: Carlyle and Mill on "The Negro Question."' *Utilitarianism and Empire*. Ed. Bart Schultz and Georgios Varouakis. Lanham, MA: Lexington, pp. 125–35.

Gray, John (1996) *Mill on Liberty: A Defence* (2nd edn). London: Routledge.

Grofman, Bernard, Handley, Lisa and Niemi, Richard G. (1992) *Minority Representation and the Quest for Voting Equality*. Cambridge: Cambridge University Press.

Halliday, R. J. (1976) *John Stuart Mill*. London: George Allen and Unwin.

Hamburger, Joseph (1999) *John Stuart Mill on Liberty and Control*. Princeton: Princeton University Press.

Hamilton, Andy (1998) 'Mill, Phenomenalism, and the Self'. *Cambridge Companion to Mill*. Cambridge: Cambridge University Press, pp. 139–75.

Hare, R. M. (1981) *Moral Thinking: Its Levels, Method and Point*. Oxford: Clarendon Press.

Hare, Thomas (1859) *Treatise on the Election of Representatives: Parliamentary and Municipal*. London: Longman.

Hart, H. L. A. (1963) *Law, Liberty and Morality*. London: Oxford University Press.

Hayward, Abraham (1873) 'John Stuart Mill'. [Obituary] *The Times* (10 May): 5.

Heydt, Colin (2006) 'Narrative, Imagination, and the Religion of Humanity in Mill's Ethics'. *Journal of the History of Philosophy* 44: 99–115.

Himmelfarb, Gertrude (1974) *On Liberty and Liberalism: The Case of John Stuart Mill*. New York: Knopf.

Hoag, Robert W. (1983) 'Mill on Conflicting Moral Obligations'. *Analysis* 43 (Jan.): 49–54.

Hollander, Samuel (1985) *Economics of John Stuart Mill*. 2 vols. Toronto: Toronto University Press.

Hooker, Brad (2000) *Ideal Code, Real World*. Oxford: Clarendon.

Humboldt, Wilhelm von (1993) *Limits of State Action*. Ed. J. W. Burrow. Cambridge: Cambridge University Press (reprinted 1969, Indianapolis: Liberty Fund.)

Hume, David (1978) *A Treatise of Human Nature*. Ed. L. A. Selby-Bigge. London: Clarendon.

Jacobs, Jo Ellen (2002) *The Voice of Harriet Taylor Mill*. Bloomington: Indiana University Press.

Justman, Stewart (1991) *The Hidden Text of Mill's Liberty*. Savage, MA: Rowman and Littlefield.

Justman, Stewart (1993) 'The Abstract Citizen'. *Philosophy and Social Criticism* 19: 317–32.

Kagan, Shelly (1989) *The Limits of Morality*. Oxford: Clarendon.

Kamm, Josephine (1977) *John Stuart Mill in Love*. London: Gordon & Cremonesi.

Kant, Immanuel (1997) *Groundwork of the Metaphysics of Morals*. Trans. and ed. Mary Gregor. Cambridge: Cambridge University Press.

Kendall, Willmoore and Carey, George W. (1968) ' "The Roster Device": J. S. Mill and Contemporary Elitism'. *Western Political Quarterly* XXI: 20–39.

Kinzer, Bruce L. (2007) *J. S. Mill Revisited: Biographical and Political Explorations*. New York: Palgrave Macmillan.

Kinzer, Bruce L., Robson, Ann P., and Robson, John M. (1992) *A Moralist In and Out of Parliament: John Stuart Mill at Westminster 1865–1868.* Toronto: Toronto University Press.

Kitcher, Philip (1998) 'Mill, Mathematics, and the Naturalist Tradition'. *The Cambridge Companion to Mill.* Ed. John Skorupski. Cambridge: Cambridge University Press, pp. 57–111.

Kurer, Oskar (1992) 'J. S. Mill and Utopian Socialism'. *The Economic Record* 68: 222–32.

Lehrer, Keith (1989) *Thomas Reid.* London: Routledge.

Locke, John (1955) *A Letter Concerning Toleration* (2nd edn). Indianapolis: Bobbs-Merrill.

Locke, John (1961) *An Essay Concerning Human Understanding.* Ed. John W. Yolton. London: Dent.

Lyons, David (1976) 'Mill's Theory of Morality'. *Noûs* 10: 101–20. (Reprinted 1994 in *Rights, Welfare, and Mill's Moral Theory*, New York: Oxford, pp. 47–65.)

Lyons, David (1978) 'Mill's Theory of Justice'. *Values and Morals: Essays in Honor of William Frankena, Charles Stevenson, and Richard Brandt.* Ed. Alvin L. Goldman and Jaegwon Kim. Dordrecht: D. Reidel, pp. 1–20. (Reprinted 1994 in *Rights, Welfare, and Mill's Moral Theory*, New York: Oxford, pp. 67–88.)

Lyons, David (1979) 'Liberty and Harm to Others'. *New Essays on John Stuart Mill and Utilitarianism, Canadian Journal of Philosophy*, Supp. Vol V: 1–19. (Reprinted 1994 in *Rights, Welfare, and Mill's Moral Theory*, New York: Oxford, pp. 89–108.)

Lyons, David (1982) 'Benevolence and Justice in Mill'. *The Limits of Utilitarianism.* Ed. Harlan Miller and W. H. Williams. Minneapolis: University of Minnesota Press, pp. 42–70. (Reprinted 1994 in *Rights, Welfare, and Mill's Moral Theory*, New York: Oxford, pp. 109–46.)

Maguire, Brendan, Faulkner, William R. and Mathers, Richard A. (1996) 'Seatbelt Laws and Traffic Fatalities: A Research Update'. *Social Science Journal* 33: 321–3.

Markie, Peter (2004) 'Rationalism versus Empiricism'. *The Stanford Encyclopedia of Philosophy* (Fall edn). Ed. Edward N. Zalta. Accessed at http://plato.stanford.edu/archives/fall2004/entries/rationalism-empiricism/; last visited February 2010.

Mencher, Samuel (1967) *Poor Law to Poverty Program: Economic Security Policy in Britain and the United States.* Pittsburgh: University of Pittsburgh Press.

Mill, Harriet Taylor (1988) *The Complete Works of Harriet Taylor Mill.* Ed. Jo Ellen Jacobs. Bloomington: Indiana University Press.

Mill, James (1826) *The History of British India* (3rd edn). 6 vols. London: Baldwin, Cradock, and Joy.

Mill, James (1878) *Analysis of the Phenomena of the Human Mind* (2nd edn). 2 vols. London: Longmans, Green, Reader, and Dyer.

Mill, James (1992) 'Government'. *James Mill: Political Writings*. Ed. Terence Ball. Cambridge: Cambridge University Press, pp. 3–42.

Mill, James (1992) 'The Ballot'. *James Mill: Political Writings*. Ed. Terence Ball. Cambridge: Cambridge University Press, pp. 225–67.

Mill, J. S. (1963–91) *The Collected Works of John Stuart Mill*. 33 vols. Gen. Ed. J. M. Robson. Toronto: Toronto University Press.

Millar, Alan (1998) 'Mill on Religion'. *Cambridge Companion to Mill*. Ed. John Skorupski. Cambridge: Cambridge University Press, pp. 176–202.

Miller, Dale E. (2000) 'John Stuart Mill's Civic Liberalism'. *History of Political Thought* XXI (Spring): 88–113.

Miller, Dale E. (2002) Endnotes and commentary for *The Basic Writings of John Stuart Mill: On Liberty, The Subjection of Women, and Utilitarianism*. New York: Random House, pp. 302–60.

Miller, Dale E. (2003) 'Actual-Consequence Act Utilitarianism and the Best Possible Humans'. *Ratio* XVI: 1 (March): 49–62.

Miller, Dale E. (2003) 'Mill's "Socialism"'. *Politics, Philosophy and Economics* 2(2) (June): 213–38.

Miller, Dale E. (2003) 'Sympathy Versus Spontaneity: A Tension in Mill's Conception of Human Perfection'. *The International Journal of Politics and Ethics* 3: 173–88.

Miller, Dale E. (2004) 'Terminating Employees for Their Political Speech'. *Business and Society Review* 109 (June): 225–43.

Miller, Dale E. (2005) 'Reparations for Emancipation: Mill's Vindication of the Rights of Slave Owners'. *Southern Journal of Philosophy* XLIII: 245–65.

Miller, Dale E. (2006) 'Mill's Theory of Sanctions'. *The Blackwell Guide to Mill's* Utilitarianism. Ed. Henry West. Malden MA: Blackwell, pp. 159–73.

Miller, Dale E. (2009) 'Harriet Taylor Mill', *The Stanford Encyclopedia of Philosophy* (Spring edn). Ed. Edward N. Zalta. Accessed at http://plato. stanford.edu/archives/spr2009/entries/harriet-mill/; last visited February 2010.

Miller, Dale E. (2010) 'Mill, Rule Utilitarianism, and the Incoherence Objection'. Forthcoming in *John Stuart Mill and the Art of Life*. Ed. Ben Eggleston, Dale E. Miller, and David Weinstein. New York: Oxford University Press.

Miller, J. Joseph (2005) 'Chairing the Jamaica Committee'. *Utilitarianism and Empire*. Ed. Bart Schultz and Georgios Varouakis. Lanham, MA: Lexington, pp. 155–78.

Moore, G. E. (1903) *Principia Ethica*. Cambridge: Cambridge University Press.

Morales, Maria (1996) *Perfect Equality: John Stuart Mill on Well-Constituted Communities*. Lanham, MA: Rowman and Littlefield.

Mulgan, Tim (2001) *The Demands of Consequentialism*. Oxford: Oxford University Press.

Noah, Timothy (2002) 'Can Your Boss Fire You for Your Political Beliefs? A Cautionary Independence Day Tale'. *Slate.* www.slate.com/id/ 2067578/. Posted 1 July 2002; last visited 16 November 2009.

Noah, Timothy (2004) 'Bumper Sticker Insubordination: A Kerry fan gets fired, and then hired, for her politics'. *Slate.* www.slate.com/id/2106714/. Posted 4 September 2004; last visited 16 November 2009.

Nock, Albert Jay (1928) 'On Doing the Right Thing'. *'On Doing the Right Thing' and Other Essays.* New York: Harper, pp. 161–78.

Norcross, Alastair (2006) 'The Scalar Approach to Utilitarianism'. *The Blackwell Guide to Mill's* Utilitarianism. Ed. Henry West. Malden, MA: Blackwell, pp. 217–32.

Nozick, Robert (1974) *Anarchy, State, and Utopia.* New York: Basic.

Oxford English Dictionary (1989) (2nd edn). Oxford: Oxford University Press.

Packe, Michael St John (1954) *The Life of John Stuart Mill.* New York: Macmillan.

Parfit, Derek (1984) *Reasons and Persons.* Oxford: Clarendon.

Parsons, Talcott (1949) *The Structure of Social Action.* Glencoe, IL: Free Press.

Pateman, Carole (1970) *Participation and Democratic Theory.* Cambridge: Cambridge University Press.

Paton, Graeme (2009) 'Wear Goggles When Using Blu-Tack: The Safety Rules Ruining Education'. *Telegraph.Co.Uk* (19 June). Accessed at www.telegraph.co.uk/education/educationnews/5569108/Wear-goggles-when-using-Blu-Tack-the-safety-rules-ruining-education.html; last visited 20 June 2009.

Paul, L. A. (1998) 'The Worm at the Root of the Passions: Poetry and Sympathy in Mill's Utilitarianism'. *Utilitas* 10: 83–104.

Peltzman, Sam (1975) 'The Effects of Automobile Safety Regulation'. *The Journal of Political Economy* 83 (August): 677–725.

Pitts, Jennifer (2005) *A Turn to Empire: The Rise of Imperial Liberalism in Britain and France.* Princeton: Princeton University Press.

Prutkin, J., Fisher, E. M., Etter, L. et al. (2000) 'Genetic Variation and Inferences about Perceived Taste Intensity in Mice and Men'. *Physiology and Behavior* 69: 161–73.

Quine, W. V. O. (19690 'Epistemology Naturalized'. *Ontological Relativity and Other Essays.* New York: Columbia University Press, pp. 69–90.

Quinton, Anthony (1993). 'Conservatism'. *A Companion to Contemporary Political Philosophy.* Ed. Robert E. Goodin and Philip Pettit. Oxford: Blackwell, pp. 244–68.

Rawls, John (1993) *Political Liberalism.* New York: Columbia University Press.

Rawls, John (1999) *Theory of Justice* (2nd edn). Cambridge, MA: Belknap.

Redding, Paul (2008) 'Georg Wilhelm Friedrich Hegel'. *The Stanford Encyclopedia of Philosophy* (Winter 2008 edn). Ed. Edward N. Zalta. Accessed at http://plato.stanford.edu/archives/win2008/entries/hegel/.

Rees, John (1985) *John Stuart Mill's* On Liberty. Oxford: Clarendon.

Reeves, Richard (2007) *John Stuart Mill: Victorian Firebrand*. London: Atlantic.

Reid, Thomas (1997) *An Inquiry Into the Human Mind on the Principles of Common Sense*. Ed. Derek R. Brookes. Edinburgh: Edinburgh University Press.

Riley, Jonathan (1989) 'Justice under Capitalism'. *Markets and Justice. Nomos* XXI. Ed. John W. Chapman and J. Roland Pennock. New York: New York University Press, pp. 122–62.

Riley, Jonathan (1998) 'Mill's Political Economy: Ricardian Science and Liberal Utilitarian Art', *The Cambridge Companion to Mill*. Ed. John Skorupski. Cambridge: Cambridge University Press, pp. 293–337.

Riley, Jonathan (2003) 'Interpreting Mill's Qualitative Hedonism'. *The Philosophical Quarterly* 53 (July): 410–18.

Robson, John M. (1977) 'Textual Introduction'. *Essays on Politics and Society: Collected Works of John Stuart Mill*. Vol. XVIII. Ed. J. M. Robson. Toronto: Toronto University Press, pp. lxxi–xcv.

Ross, W. D. (1930) *The Right and the Good*. Oxford: Clarendon.

Ryan, Alan (1987) *The Philosophy of John Stuart Mill* (2nd edn). Atlantic Highlands, NJ: Humanities Press International.

Ryan, David L. and Bridgeman, Guy A. (1992) 'Judging the Roles of Legislation, Education, and Offsetting Behaviour in Seat Belt Use: A Survey and New Evidence from Alberta'. *Canadian Public Policy* 18 (Mar.): 27–46.

Sayre-McCord, Geoffrey (2001) 'Mill's "Proof" of the Principle of Utility: A More than Half-Hearted Defense'. *Social Philosophy & Policy* 18 (Spring): 330–60.

Schapiro, J. Salwyn (1943) 'John Stuart Mill, Pioneer of Democratic Liberalism in England'. *Journal of the History of Ideas* IV: 127–60.

Schwartz, Pedro (1972) *The New Political Economy of John Stuart Mill*. (Spanish 1968 edn). London: Weidenfeld and Nicolson.

Sen, Amartya (1991) 'Utility: Ideas and Terminology', *Economics and Philosophy* 7: 277–83.

Sen, Amartya and Williams, Bernard (1982) 'Introduction'. *Utilitarianism and Beyond*. Cambridge: Cambridge University Press, pp. 1–21.

Shaw, William (1999) *Contemporary Ethics: Taking Account of Utilitarianism*. Malden, MA: Blackwell.

Sidgwick, Henry (1981) *The Methods of Ethics* (7th edn). Indianapolis: Hackett.

Singer, Peter (1972) 'Famine, Affluence, and Morality'. *Philosophy and Public Affairs* 1: 229–43.

Skorupski, John (1989) *John Stuart Mill*. London: Routledge.

Skorupski, John (1997) 'The Ethical Content of Liberal Law'. *Law, Values and Social Practice*. Ed. John Tasoulias. Aldershot: Dartmouth, pp. 191–

211. (Reprinted 1999 in *Ethical Explorations*, Oxford: Oxford University Press, pp. 213–33.)

Skorupski, John (1997) *'Reasons and Reason': Ethics and Practical Reason*. Ed. Garrett Cullity and Berys Gaut. Oxford: Oxford University Press, pp. 345–67. (Reprinted 1999 in *Ethical Explorations*, Oxford: Oxford University Press, pp. 26–48.)

Skorupski, John (1998) 'Introduction: The Fortunes of Liberal Naturalism'. *Cambridge Companion to Mill*. Ed. John Skorupski. Cambridge: Cambridge University Press, pp. 1–34.

Smart, J. J. C. (1956) 'Extreme and Restricted Utilitarianism'. *Philosophical Quarterly* 6: 344–54.

Smart, J. J. C. (1973) 'An Outline of a System of Utilitarian Ethics'. *Utilitarianism: For and Against*. Cambridge: Cambridge University Press, pp. 3–74.

Snyder, Laura J. (2008) 'William Whewell'. *The Stanford Encyclopedia of Philosophy* (Fall edn). Ed. Edward N. Zalta. Accessed at http:// plato.stanford.edu/archives/fall2008/entries/whewell/; last visited February 2010.

Spohn, Cassia and Holleran, David (2002) 'The Effect of Imprisonment on Recidivism Rates of Felony Offenders: A Focus on Drug Offenders'. *Criminology* 40: 329–58.

Stephen, James Fitzjames (1993) *Liberty, Equality, Fraternity*. Ed. Stuart D. Warner. Indianapolis: Liberty Fund.

Stephen, Leslie (1895) *The Life of Sir James Fitzjames Stephen*. London: Smith, Elder, & Co.

Stroud, Barry (1977) *Hume*. London: Routledge.

Sullum, Jacob (2005) 'Freedom Riders'. *Reason* 37 (November): 40–6. Accessed at www.reason.com/news/show/33169.html; last visited 19 June 2009.

Sumner, L. W. (1996) *Welfare, Happiness, and Ethics*. Oxford: Clarendon.

Ten, C. L. (1980) *Mill on Liberty*. Oxford: Clarendon Press.

Ten, C. L. (2002) *Politics, Philosophy & Economics* 1: 355–70.

Thompson, Dennis (1976) *John Stuart Mill and Representative Government*. Princeton: Princeton University Press.

Tocqueville, Alexis de (1945) *Democracy in America*. Trans. Phillips Bradley. 2 vols. New York: Vintage Books.

Urmson, J. O. (1953) 'The Interpretation of the Moral Philosophy of J. S. Mill'. *Philosophical Quarterly* 3: 33–9.

Varouxakis, Georgios (2002) *Mill on Nationality*. London: Routledge.

Viscusi, W. Kip (1984) 'The Lulling Effect: The Impact of Child-Resistant Packing on Aspirin and Analgesic Ingestions'. *The American Economic Review* 74: 324–7.

Walmsley, Roy (2009) 'World Prison Population List' (8th edn). London: King's College London International Centre for Prison Studies.

Accessed at www.kcl.ac.uk/depsta/law/research/icps/downloads/wppl-8th_41.pdf, last visited 6 June 2009.

Warren, Howard C. (1967) *A History of the Association Psychology*. New York: Scribner's.

West, Heather C. and Sabol, William J. (2008) *Prisoners in 2007: Bureau of Justice Statistics Bulletin*. Washington, DC: US Department of Justice. Accessed at www.ojp.usdoj.gov/bjs/pub/pdf/p07.pdf, last visited 14 June 2009.

West, Henry R. (2004) *An Introduction to Mill's Utilitarian Ethics*. Cambridge: Cambridge University Press.

Williams, Bernard (1973) 'A Critique of Utilitarianism'. *Utilitarianism: For and Against*. Cambridge: Cambridge University Press, pp. 77–150.

Wollheim, Richard (1973) 'John Stuart Mill and the Limits of State Action'. *Social Research* 40: 1–30.

Yamashita, Shigekazu (2001) Review of Joseph Hamburger, *John Stuart Mill on Liberty and Control*. *Utilitas* 13: 360–3.

Zastoupil, Lynn (1994) *John Stuart Mill and India*. Stanford: Stanford University Press.

Index

act utilitarianism, 71, 73–6, 77–85,
    90–3, 96, 102
  and considered moral
    judgements, 75–6
  decision procedure for, 74–5,
    102
  demandingness objection to, 75
  epistemic objection to, 73–5
  subjective, 74–5
actions, 20, 22, 26, 37, 71–7, 79,
    82–8, 90–1, 93–4, 97, 99–100,
    110, 114, 129, 199, 218n5
  morally wrong, 85–6
aesthetic emotions, 59–61, 67–9,
    80–1, 90, 220n28
altruism, 91–2, 157
America
  anti-intellectual conservatism in,
    231n67
  drug laws in, 147
  literacy tests in, 193
  moral character of people, 94–5
  political institutions in instill
    false sense of equality, 186
animals,
  animal element to human
    psychology, 21, 214n26
  animal instinct, 21–2, 108, 160
  animal pleasures, 64–5

suffering of, 120
  see also rights, animal
aristocracy, 4–5, 156, 185–6, 197
Aristotle, 18, 32, 116
army, 123, 128–9, 132
  citizen, 123, 131–2, 175
Arneson, R., 131, 166, 187
Art of Life, 79–83, 85, 89–90
associationism, 18–21, 22–5, 41–2,
    52–3, 108, 109
associations, mental, 18–21, 23–5,
    42, 49–51, 52–3, 61, 134
Austin, J., 88
authenticity, 52–3
axiology, 31, 37, 44, 62, 79–80

Bain, A., 21, 64, 145, 159
Ball, T., 178
Barry, B., 120
beauty, 60–1, 80–1, 90, 135, 137
  see also character, as a work of
    art
Benn, S., 149
Bentham, J., 4–5, 7–8, 9, 26, 37, 55,
    72, 89, 188
  see also felicific calculus; Mill,
    John Stuart, 'Bentham'
Berkeley, G., 96
Blanc, L., 155, 157, 163